ENGLISH AS A SECOND LANGUAGE

Secondary Cycle 2 – Year 1

THROUGH ENGLISH

Suzanne Gagné
Martine Picard
Elisa Shenkier

Project Supervisor
Judith Rohlf

Éditions Grand Duc
Groupe Éducalivres inc.
955, rue Bergar, Laval (Québec) H7L 4Z6
Téléphone: 514 334-8466 ▪ Télécopie: 514 334-8387
InfoService: 1 800 567-3671

ACKNOWLEDGEMENTS

The publisher wishes to thank the following people for their comments and suggestions during the development of this project:

Mr. Jacques Benca, retired teacher
Ms. Julie Boissé, École Jean-Rimbeau, C.S. des Chênes
Ms. Geneviève Boivin, École Horizon-Jeunesse, C.S. de Laval
Ms. Julie Bussière, Collège Jésus-Marie de Sillery, Sillery
Ms. Alexandra Coutlée, Académie Sainte-Thérèse, Sainte-Thérèse
Mr. Michel Fontaine, Collège Jésus-Marie de Sillery, Sillery
Ms. Many Hamphiboune, École Sophie-Barat, C.S. de Montréal
Ms. Mindy Handelman, École F.A.C.E, C.S. de Montréal
Ms. Isabelle Héroux, École Horizon-Jeunesse, C.S. de Laval
Ms. Annick Kerschbaumer, École secondaire de Rivière-du-Loup, C.S. de Kamouraska-Rivière-du-Loup
Ms. Kathleen Langlais, École secondaire de Neufchâtel, C.S. de la Capitale
Ms. Charline Lapointe, École Saint-Louis, C.S. de Montréal
Ms. Caroline Lavoie, École secondaire Mont Saint-Sacrement, Saint-Gabriel-de-Valcartier
Ms. Madelyn Lissade, École Sophie-Barat, C.S. de Montréal
Ms. Eve Marchand, École secondaire d'Oka, C.S. de la Seigneurie-des-Milles-Îles
Ms. Caroline Martin, École secondaire de la Ruche, C.S. des Sommets
Ms. Christine O'Gallagher, École secondaire du Triolet, C.S. de la Région-de-Sherbrooke
Ms. Marie-France Piley, École de l'Escabelle, C.S. des Chic-Chocs
Mr. James Sommerhalder, École Saint-Louis, C.S. de Montréal
Ms. Dany St-Pierre, École Natagan, C.S. Harricana
Ms. Dominique Tanguay, École de la Pointe-Lévy, C.S. des Navigateurs

ICT Consultant:
Mr. Ron Mastine

Scientific Revision:
Ms. Jane Davey, translator/reviser/writer
Ms. Christelle Not, environment sciences specialist

CONNECTING
THROUGH ENGLISH

We acknowledge the financial support of the Government of Canada through the Book Publishing Industry Development Program (BPIDP) for our publishing activities.
Government of Québec – Tax credit for book publishing – Administered by SODEC.

PRODUCT CODE 3581
ISBN 978-2-7655-0099-5

Legal deposit
Bibliothèque et Archives nationales du Québec, 2007
Library and Archives Canada, 2007

Printed in Canada

1 2 3 4 5 6 7 8 9 0 F 6 5 4 3 2 1 0 9 8 7

Contents

Guiding Questions

○ *How do passions and fame go hand in hand?*
○ *Is becoming famous important to you?*

Focus on...

- First, Second, Third... (ordinal numbers)

How to...

- Overcome Stress When Talking
- Link Your Passion to Fame

IN THIS UNIT...

You will learn about passions and fame and how the two are often intertwined. You will explore the temporary nature, as well as the glamour and price of fame. Throughout the tasks, you will reflect on the importance of fame for you personally. In the **final task**, you will share your own passion and explain how it might be linked to fame and whether or not fame is a goal for you.

Guiding Questions

○ *How superstitious are you?*
○ *How are superstitions and the little rituals we use helpful?*

Focus on...

- Verb Endings (simple present, simple past)
- Interrogative and Negative Forms (present, past)
- Asking Questions

How to...

- Participate in a Discussion (introduce, support, react, end)
- Read a Story

IN THIS UNIT...

You will first learn about superstitions that bring good luck or bad luck; you will then look at the rituals people often go through to help them succeed. As a **final task**, you will conduct a survey on the subject and learn how to create an effective poster to show your findings. You will then present your poster to the class.

Guiding Questions

- *What makes a room special?*
- *In what ways would you say that your special
  space is like a dream catcher?*

IN THIS UNIT...

You will explore your own room! Ideally, what would yours look like? You
will discover that how big a room is, what gadgets it contains and how
it is decorated are not the only things that matter. You will learn about
choices and the need to have a private space to be yourself, reflect and
find comfort. As a **final task**, you will write about your own special space.

Guiding Questions

- *What perceptions and stereotypes appear in
  fairy tales?*
- *Whose point of view is presented in fairy tales?*

IN THIS UNIT...

You will revisit the world of fairy tales. You will recall the fairy tales you loved
as a child and explore some new ones. You will become aware of stereotyping
and perceptions as you look at fairy tales from a different angle. As **a final
task**, you will write a letter which presents a new side – your side – of an
old story.

Guiding Questions

- *What do you know about Black history?*
- *How can learning about Black history help cultivate a culture of peace?*

Focus on...

- The Simple Past and Simple Present Tenses (regular, irregular verbs)
- Asking Questions Using Question Words

How to...

- Start an Information Log
- Search the Web

IN THIS UNIT...

You will explore Black history in a Canadian context and beyond. You will learn about some famous African Americans and the Underground Railroad. You will also learn how to organize an information log. As a **final task**, you will reinvest your newly acquired knowledge of Black history and challenge your classmates with the game "Freedom Bound."

Guiding Questions

- *What is the ultimate challenge?*
- *What can you, as an individual, do to help protect the environment and be a responsible resident of planet Earth?*

Focus on...

- Expressing Opinions (with modal auxiliaries)
- Transition Words

How to...

- Use a Dictionary
- Take Notes
- Recognize a Fact and an Opinion

IN THIS UNIT...

You will explore the messages and warnings sent by nature and learn how human activities affect the planet. You will come to understand the main issues of global warming. You will also take a serious look at the four Rs. As a **final task**, you will get involved by determining what you, as an individual, can do to help heal the planet.

Montreal, September 1

Dear Students,

Welcome to English and the start of a brand new year! We certainly hope that it will be one of new challenges and exciting adventures for you.

Our goal is to help you learn English through meaningful tasks and interesting topics. We've done our best to structure everything for your success in order to help you build your confidence in understanding and communicating effectively in English. Your job is to "give it your best shot."

We sincerely hope that you'll enjoy what we've put together and that you will learn more about yourself, others, and the world around you by *Connecting Through English*.

Have a great year!

Sincerely,
The Team

Elisa   Judith   Martine   Suzanne

P.S. To help you become familiar with your Student Book, we've prepared a special handout with a Scavenger Hunt. Your teacher will explain it to you. Enjoy!

E.   J.   M.   S.

Connecting Through English – An Overview

The Structure of the Book

This Student Book is organized to help you learn English and make you feel competent as a learner as you carry out various tasks. It contains **eight separate units** (learning and evaluation situations). The content of each unit has been carefully structured to help you develop your competencies in English as you gain knowledge and insights into yourself, others and the world. At the end of the book, there is a **Reference Toolkit** where you will find lots of helpful information. Have a look!

The Structure of Each Unit

THE OPENING PAGES

Each unit begins with a two-page spread. On these pages, in addition to the **title** of the unit, you will find a brief **summary** of what you will be doing in the unit and an illustration or series of **illustrations** to start off your discussions on what is to come. There are also two **Guiding Questions**. These questions will help you make sense of the topic presented in the unit and assist you to focus on its key issues. At the end of the unit, you should be able to answer both questions and explain why they are important.

TASKS AND ACTIVITIES

Each unit is divided into a series of tasks, which are then divided into activities. The tasks are a way of grouping activities together in a meaningful fashion. To introduce each task, there is a brief paragraph that explains what you will be doing. The activities that follow are the steps necessary to accomplish the task.

ICONS

Throughout the book, you will notice two icons:

A 🗎 indicates that there is a **handout** that goes with the activity.

A 📣 indicates that there is an **audio text**.

THE FINAL TASK

All of the tasks in each unit lead up to a Final Task. The Final Task is something that you will do or make *(a poster, a PowerPoint presentation, a written assignment...)* to show what you have learned in the unit. The Final Task is not necessarily long or complicated, but it allows you to use what you have learned in a logical and structured way.

EXTRA READING (OPTIONAL)

This section is not really part of the unit per se. That is, it is completely optional. It has been included to provide **additional texts** to read for students who work faster, who want more or who have more time in English. At the end of each text, there is a question to think about and discuss. Reading the question before reading the text will give you a purpose for reading.

OTHER THINGS TO DO (OPTIONAL)

This section is also completely optional. It provides suggestions for **fun projects** related to the topic of the unit.

WRAP-UP

The Wrap-Up is an important page. It allows you to reflect on what you have learned throughout the unit. It will help you **make connections** with what you have learned and assist you to transfer this knowledge.

The following special features are found throughout the book:

Focus on...

The explanation of a specific grammar point or notion needed to complete the task at hand.

For Fun and Practice

An exercise or activity to do in order to reinforce a specific grammar point or notion.

Proof that grammar doesn't have to be boring!

How to...

Step-by-step procedures and strategies to help you achieve success and develop expertise.

Talk About It!

Questions or prompts related to the subject to get you talking and discussing in English.

Think About It!

Thought-provoking questions or statements worth pondering over.

Food for thought!

Write About It!

Your chance to express yourself in writing on issues related to the task at hand.

Culture

A wealth of information.

Fun facts, great insights, interesting details about the lives of famous people and the world we live in.

Smile!

A short time out for an anecdote or a joke.

Something to make you laugh... or at least, smile!

⚠ WARNING

Something to avoid, watch out for or be aware of.

UNIT 1

15 Seconds of Fame

18947

IN THIS UNIT...

In this unit, you will learn about passions and fame and how the two are often intertwined. You will explore the temporary nature of fame, the glamour of fame and the price of fame. Throughout the tasks, you will reflect on the importance of fame for you personally. In the final task, you will share your passion and explain how it might be tied to fame and decide if that is your goal.

- How do passions and fame go hand in hand?
- Is becoming famous important to you?

n **TASK 1**, you will begin exploring the world of passions – those of others and your own.

Ah... Passions!

Get out your magnifying glass! You've got a little puzzle to solve.

Want a clue? Here you go: "To discover our passions is to discover our identity."

Good luck!

1. Look at the pictures. Each one is a close-up of a very small part of an object.

2. Examine them closely and make hypotheses as to what each one could be.

3. Write your guesses on the handout.

4. Share your answers with the group.

5. Use the *Conversation Cues* and the *How to Overcome Stress When Talking* boxes on the next page to help you.

CONVERSATION CUES		
Initiate	What's that?	
	Don't you see a...?	
	Do you think this could be a...?	
	Do you recognize this one?	
	What about this one?	
React and Maintain	I agree. I disagree.	
	No way!	
	I think so. I don't think so.	
	I don't have a clue. Do you?	
	Maybe it's a...	
	It looks more like a...	
	It's probably a...	
	I think this is a...	
	It must be...	
	I've got it! The bottom picture is a...	
	I think the one on the left (on the right, in the centre...) is a...	
End	Good job!	
	Let's do the next one.	
	We're finished! Now what?	

"Nothing great in the world has been accomplished without passion."

Georg Wilhelm
Friedrich Hegel

How to...

OVERCOME STRESS WHEN TALKING

1 Use the models, cues and examples given in class as a starting point.

2 Add a personal touch or comment.

3 Take a risk. Don't be afraid of errors.

4 Remember, the message doesn't have to be perfect to be understood.

5 Say something. Go for it!

ACTIVITY 2

Zoom In, Zoom Out!

Ah ha! It's not as easy as it looks, is it?

In this activity, you will listen to people talking about their passions. Each person's passion goes with one of the pictures on page 4. That should simplify things! As Sherlock Holmes would say, "Elementary, my dear Watson!" Or, put another way, "It's a piece of cake!"

Think About It!

- Who are the people in the texts?
  - Can you guess?
  - Can you make any "connections"?
- Did you notice that there is an extra object?
  - What is it? Why do you think it is there?
  - What are your passions?

1. Listen as five people each describe one of their passions.
   - Do the texts help you guess what the objects are?
2. Look at the guesses you made before listening to the texts.
3. Do you want to make any changes?
4. Listen again, this time paying particular attention to each person's name and to the mention of the person's passion.
5. Work with a partner to fill out the graphic organizer on the handout.
6. Take a few minutes to reflect on the questions in the **Think About It!** box.

---

piece of cake: very simple; easy.

Speaking of Passions…

By now you have surely figured out that the extra object in Activities 1 and 2 is a mirror. You've learned about some other people's passions. Now it's time to begin thinking about yours.

1. Have a good look at the words and expressions in the **Word Bank for Expressing Passions**.

2. Complete the handout about your passion. It will be useful in the Final Task.

WORD BANK FOR EXPRESSING PASSIONS

Verbs	Adverbs	Expressions	Adjectives
• to love	• very	• I can't live without…	• great
• to adore	• extremely	• I can't get enough of…	• super
• to really like	• really	… is/are to die for!	• tremendous
• to be crazy about	• completely		• fantastic
• to be hooked on	• absolutely		• incredible
• to be addicted to	• always		• unbelievable
• to be keen on	• often		• fabulous
• to be into	• sometimes		• awesome
	• seldom		• sweet
	• rarely		
	• never		

Are there words or expressions you want to add to the lists?

Example: I absolutely love collecting buttons! For me, it's more than a hobby; it's my passion! When I was nine years old, my grandmother showed me her fantastic button collection and I was hooked! I have buttons in all shapes and sizes, buttons from all over the world. In all, I have over 5,000! My collection is really awesome! Buttons are to die for!

n **TASK 2**, you will learn about how some people's passions have brought them fame. Will this fame last? Only time will tell.

From Passion to Fame!

Listen as three unusual stories about passions and fame are shared with you. Keep this question in mind as you listen: **How can a passion lead to fame**?

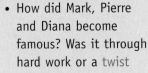

Talk About It!

- How did Mark, Pierre and Diana become famous? Was it through hard work or a twist of fate?

- Do you think it is more rewarding to become famous through hard work than by accident?

- How did each one react to fame?

- Whose story would you most like to be yours and why?

1. Listen to Mark's, Pierre's and Diana's stories to find out about their passions and fame.

2. Jot down three phrases describing each passion.

3. In your groups, discuss the questions in the **Talk About It!** box.

4. Use the *More Cues* box on the next page to help you.

to jot down: to write briefly; to write a short note.
twist of fate: by accident.

MORE CUES	
Initiate	Have you finished answering the questions? Can we start the discussion? So, what did you think of the 1st (2nd, 3rd) story? Which one did you like best? Which one did you like least?
React and Maintain	I think that... I agree. I disagree. Do you believe that all these stories are true? I think you're right (wrong)! Don't take it personally, but... Did you have any problems understanding them? We're right on! I know for a fact that... It's better to... I would rather... The same thing happened to a friend of mine... That reminds me of...
End	Let's work together on the next task. Thanks for the help. We did a good job!

"Fame is a four-letter word. And like tape, or zoom, or face, or pain, or love, or life, what ultimately matters is what we do with it."

Fred Rogers

Fleeting Fame

Some people become legends through hard work, talent, perseverance and timing; their fame lives on forever. More often, however, fame is short-lived and may even come unexpectedly. In this activity, you will explore some examples of fleeting fame.

1. In your groups, try to come up with examples of short-lived fame and unexpected fame.

2. Share your answers with the class and pool your examples.

3. As a class, brainstorm about where and how we often learn about fame that came to be unexpectedly.

4. Use these ideas to complete the handout.

"The poison chalice: fame."

Ray Davies

Culture

Have you ever heard of Andy Warhol?

Andy Warhol was a famous American pop-art artist who lived from 1928 to 1987. He is recognized for his paintings of commercial products, including Campbell soup cans.

Andy Warhol

He is also well known for his statement: **"In the future, everyone will be famous for 15 minutes."** Today, perhaps because of the fast pace of society, we often hear **15 seconds of fame**, instead of 15 minutes... Be it 15 minutes or 15 seconds, the idea is that everyone should have at least one special moment of glory in his or her lifetime.

Andy Warhol often confused people by interchanging words from his famous quote. Sometimes he would say, "In the future, 15 people will be famous," or "Every 15th person will be world-famous," or "In 15 minutes, everybody will be famous."

For Fun and Practice

Try creating a sentence and then give it different meanings by switching around the words *à la Warhol*.

---

fleeting: something that passes by quickly or lasts for only a brief moment.

short-lived: lasting only a short time.

Immortalizing Fame

"Here today, gone tomorrow." As we have seen, fame is very often short-lived. One generation's idols are soon replaced by those of the next generation. A quick search on the Internet will turn up numerous Halls of Fame. There's one for just about everything you can possibly imagine. It is a popular way of paying tribute to our present icons and immortalizing them for posterity.

Have you seen Canada's Walk of Fame in Toronto? Or maybe you have heard about the famous Hollywood Walk of Fame? How are the two different? How are they the same? This is what you will discover in this activity.

1. Work with a partner.

2. Each of you will be given a text to read. Text A is about Canada's Walk of Fame and Text B is about the Hollywood Walk of Fame.

3. Share the information in your text with your partner and together complete the Venn diagram on the handout.

Culture

Fun Facts

The Beatles by Andy Warhol, 1980

- What do Snow White, the Simpsons and Godzilla have in common? They all have their own star on the Hollywood Walk of Fame. So do Bugs Bunny, Kermit the Frog and many other cartoon characters.

- Did you know that every year, on the anniversary of his death, Beatles fans gather at John Lennon's star in Hollywood?

- There have been four stars stolen from the Hollywood Walk of Fame. Today, cameras are installed to discourage thieves.

- And the most "famous" Canadian family is... THE SUTHERLANDS! Donald Sutherland, Shirley Douglas and their son Kiefer Sutherland all have a star on Canada's Walk of Fame.

TASK 3

Fame! Glamour and glitz! Would you like to live the life of Hollywood fame? In **TASK 3**, you will look at fame, its attraction and its downsides.

Roll Out the Red Carpet!

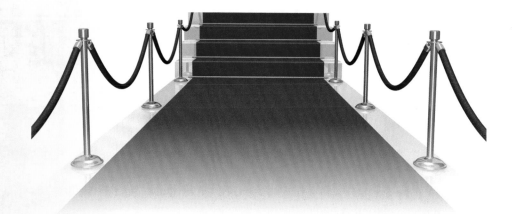

Talk About It!

- What does **celluloid** mean?
- What do you know about the stars mentioned in the song?
- Why do you think we celebrate some stars so much and then forget all about them?
- What does a celebrity have to do to have a long career and remain famous?

"Everybody's a dreamer and everybody's a star, and everybody's in movies, it doesn't matter who you are." – Ray Davies

Have you ever heard those words before? They are from the song *Celluloid Heroes*.

1. Before listening to the song *Celluloid Heroes*, try to predict what it's about from the illustration, the title of the activity and the quote.
   - What clues do they give you?
2. Listen to the song a first time. Focus on keywords and go for the global meaning.
3. Complete Part 1 of the handout.
4. Listen to the song again and complete Part 2 of the handout.
5. In your groups, try to answer the questions in the **Talk About It!** box. If necessary, use the cues at the beginning of the unit to help you.

Drum Rolls!

Celebrities: luxury, fast cars, villas, the easy life... In this activity, you will read about three famous people and how each of them dealt with fame.

1. Look at the pictures and try to guess the subject of each text.

2. Read the title of each text on the next pages.
   ○ Do you have anything to add to your initial ideas?

3. Share your answers with the class.

4. Read the texts.
   ○ Why did these people become famous? Did their fame last?
   ○ How did they handle fame?

5. Complete the handout.

6. Share your answers in your groups.

Cues

- I think that...
- I'm sure that...
- I'm not certain about the second one.
- Maybe it's about...
- The first text will talk about...

Focus on...

FIRST, SECOND, THIRD...

These are called **ordinal numbers** because they show the specific position or **order** of something (*the first/second/third one; the first/second/third answer*).

To show order, you can also use words like:

- **the next** one: *I know the next answer.*
- **the** one **after that**: *The answer after that is...*
- **the** one **before that**: *The answer before that is...*
- **the next to the last** one: *The next to the last answer is...*
- **the last** one: *The last answer is...*

The Winning Numbers

Jean-Guy Lavigueur didn't know how to read, write or count. He was a widower with four kids. He had been on welfare for a year and a half.

One day, he lost his wallet, and in the wallet was... a lottery ticket. Fortunately for him, William Murphy, an anglophone, came to his home with some wonderful news: he had found Jean-Guy's wallet! Unfortunately, Yves, the eldest son, couldn't understand English and promptly turned him away.

The story could have ended there, but Murphy came back with a translator. It took all of 15 seconds to change Lavigueur's destiny. Murphy had brought him back the lost wallet and, in it, a winning lottery ticket worth $7,650,267, the biggest prize won up to that time.

Celebrity was immediate for the family. Although they had become rich and famous, their problems multiplied. The family was soon divided. Louise sued her father for part of the winnings. In addition, the family seemed to waste the money, and there were soon rumours of bankruptcy. The father purchased a 22-room mansion, but he died of emphysema before he could really enjoy it. Before his death, he often spoke of his unhappiness. Winning the lottery had isolated him from his friends. It had also made him the laughingstock of many people. For him, fame and money were definitely not synonymous with happiness.

Culture

The lottery ticket was for the 6/49 draw. The drawing was held on March 29, 1986, just in time to make headlines on April Fool's Day!

A New Sport

James A. Naismith was born in 1861 near Almonte, Ontario. He was an excellent student and a great athlete. While studying psychology in Springfield, Massachusetts, he was asked to invent an indoor sport. He hung two old peach baskets on opposite walls of the gym and set the rules of a new game called "basketball." Within a month, by December 1891, the sport had become a hit and a new star was born: James A. Naismith. The game was so successful that it got great reviews in many magazines.

James A. Naismith

widower: man whose wife has died.

welfare: government program to help people who do not have jobs.

to sue: to take legal action in order to obtain justice.

laughingstock: the object of jokes or ridicule.

to hang: to suspend.

Naismith was asked to have the sport named Naismith ball, but he refused to do so. He eventually became a doctor and a teacher. Naismith published many books in his attempts to help society. He led a remarkable and rewarding life, away from fame.

Rebel Without a Cause

James Dean couldn't be more famous. In fact, he has received more fan mail posthumously than any other person. Although he died in 1955, according to *Forbes* magazine, his estate still earns about $5,000,000 per year.

James Dean began his acting career by doing a soda commercial, but soon afterwards, he turned to movies. With his performance in the lead role of *Rebel Without a Cause* in 1955, he became an instant star with teenagers, who identified with him. He spoke to them, moved them and challenged their indifference. It is said that within a week, red jackets like the one he wore in the film were sold out all over the US.

Unfortunately, Dean's passion for automobiles got the best of him. At age 24, he collided with another car on Highway 46, near Cholame, California, and was killed.

After his death, his Porsche Spyder 550 became infamous for being the vehicle that not only killed him, but also the one that injured and killed several other persons. Over the years, many people came to believe that the car was jinxed. In 1960, it was stolen and it has never been seen since.

Although Dean made only three films in his short life, he became – and has remained – an icon, a classic example of lasting fame, in spite of himself.

---

posthumously: after death.

estate: the property of a person after his death.

infamous: bad reputation.

to jinx: to cause misfortune or bad luck.

to sport: to wear or display in an ostentatious or proud manner.

Culture

Did you know that...?
Blue jeans became fashionable only after James Dean, Elvis Presley and Marlon Brando sported them. Before that, they were just work clothes.

When looking at magazines or watching reality shows, many teens often marvel at how lucky teen idols are! But is teen fame really all that it's cracked up to be? That's what you will explore in **TASK 4**.

Young and Famous

"I want to be famous." "I will be famous!" "I absolutely must be famous!"

For some people, the wish for fame is an obsession. Do you know of anyone who has this desire? It's time to examine the pros and cons of such a life.

"Fame is the thirst of youth."

Lord Byron

1. Look at the illustration and brainstorm in class.
   ○ What teen celebrities do you know?
   ○ How are the lives of famous teens different from yours?

2. Read the article on the next page.

3. Complete the handout.

4. Share your answers in your groups and together answer the question in the **Talk About It!** box.

---

cracked up to be: claimed to be.
Here it means: *Does teen fame live up to its reputation of glamour and fun?*

The Fame Game

Think about the latest sports heroes. Lots of them are young; indeed, many of them are still in high school. Look at the covers of entertainment magazines. They are filled with young faces. Many teens are eager to play the fame game. And, what a game it is: a game with no set rules and lots of losers.

It's easy to be enticed by the glamour, popularity and money that fame brings, but what about the downside? Separation from friends and family, paparazzi, temptations such as drugs and alcohol... Living in the fast lane is not always easy. And, how many of the idols of today will go on to make full careers of their passions? How many others will quickly fade into oblivion? "Here today, gone tomorrow," or so the saying goes...

It is "normal" to want to be famous and it's okay to become a teen celebrity, as long as you understand the risks involved and the price you may have to pay.

---

indeed: in fact; in truth; in reality.

to be enticed: to be attracted to; to be tempted.

downside: negative aspect of something that is generally considered positive; disadvantage.

paparazzi: photographers who follow celebrities in the hope of taking candid pictures of them.

ACTIVITY 2

The Price of Fame

If presented with the opportunity, teens may find it hard to resist a chance at fame. What would you do?

1. Look at the title of the activity and the illustrations. That will help you form an idea of the subject of the texts.

2. Read along as you listen to the texts.

3. Try to put yourself in the shoes of these teens.
   ○ Would you have made the same choices?

4. Reflect on the questions in the **Think About It!** box.

5. Complete the handout.

6. In your groups, answer the question in the **Talk About It!** box.

Think About It!

- Would you like to be young and famous?

- What if your "15 seconds of fame" never comes?

- How important is your passion to you?

Cues

- *I would rather (be..., have...) than...*
- *I would like to...*
- *I am willing to sacrifice...*
- *I'm not willing to pay the price.*
- *I would not mind (having..., leaving..., paying...)*
- *I would give up... for...*

Talk About It!

- Is fame worth the price and the sacrifice?

Stella

Her parents called her Stella, meaning star, a name destined for fame. When she was six months old, she appeared in her first TV commercial, an ad for diapers. At three, she was one of the little kids we saw eating cereal. At seven, she began acting in movies. By the time that Stella was 11, she had tasted fame. She had made a fortune. She had appeared on the covers of dozens of magazines all over the country. Stella had

---

diaper: folded cloth or paper worn by babies.

truly become a star and for many, a teen idol, but her fame came with a price. Stella became anorexic. At age 13, her weight dropped to 35 kg and she almost died. The wake-up call was brutal. She quit the fast lane and slowly got back her health. "I can never get back all the moments I missed as a kid: going bike-riding and trick-or-treating, playing with dolls and having birthday parties, but I can become a normal teen. I want to attend a regular high school, go to football games and the mall, watch movies — not act in them — and hang out with my friends. For me, all the glory, glamour and money are no longer worth the sacrifice."

Christopher

When Christopher was 15, he was approached by a scout. He was offered fancy clothes and gadgets and even promised a new car, although he was, at the time, still too young to drive! In return, he would have the chance to "play with the pros." The offer was more than tempting, and at first, it seemed like an easy decision to make, a dream come true. In his head, his bags were already packed. Then it hit him. He would have to leave everything he knew and loved: the place where he grew up, his family and friends, his girlfriend... He would miss out on his last year of high school and graduating with his class. Here at home, he already was a star. Would that still be true? What if he couldn't cut it? He began to feel the pressure and the pain of possible disappointment. He knew that fame often came with a price. He wasn't sure it was a price he was ready to pay just yet. For the moment, he was comfortable living his passion. Maybe in a year or two...

"Fame is a bee.
It has a song
It has a sting
Ah, too, it has a wing."

Emily Dickinson

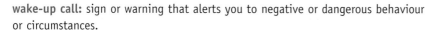

wake-up call: sign or warning that alerts you to negative or dangerous behaviour or circumstances.

to hang out with: to spend time with.

scout: someone employed to discover and recruit talented persons, especially in the fields of entertainment and sports.

to cut it: to perform up to expectations (informal).

fter exploring passions and the consequences and the price of fame, it's time to go back and have another look at your own passion. In the **FINAL TASK**, you will present your passion and decide if it is one that is likely to bring you fame.

And Back to Passions Again!

"I dream for a living."

Steven Spielberg

It's your turn to reveal your passion to the class. Do you think your passion could lead you to fame? Would you like that to happen?

1. Think about your passion and how you will present it.
   ○ What object could you use to represent this passion?
   ○ How could you illustrate this object without giving away what it is?
   ○ What medium would you like to use? A drawing, a photo, something else?

2. Look at the pictures in Task 1, Activity 1 as a model. Let your imagination run wild.

3. Use the *How to Link Your Passion to Fame* box on the next page and follow the steps on the handout.

4. Add your passion to the *Class Wall of Fame*.

5. Take five minutes to reflect on the connections between fame and passion. Use the **Think About It!** box.

Think About It!

Choose one of the following:
- Have you ever experienced fame firsthand? *(Example: Have you ever won a tournament or sung in a show?)* How did you feel?
- What are the most exciting 15 seconds of fame that you could wish for?
- Do you have any dreams for the future? Are they linked to your passion?

LINK YOUR PASSION TO FAME

Cues
- *I would like... /I wouldn't like...*
- *I really hope that...*
- *It's my dream to...*
- *It's my life goal to...*
- *It's not important to me that...*
- *I don't care if...*
- *I have no desire to...*

1 Say what your passion is:
- *My passion is singing. I absolutely love singing!*

2 Say if you would like this passion to lead you to fame and elaborate a little:
- *I would like to be famous for my singing and record an album.*
- *I have no desire to become famous for my singing because it's too difficult and my real ambition is to become a lawyer.*

3 Say if it is realistic:
- *For me, I think it's realistic because I know I have talent and I will work hard.*
- *It's not possible. I'm good, but not that good. I'm not ready to make the sacrifices.*

Culture

Wannabes and Has-beens

A **wannabe** is an ambitious and aspiring young person. It comes from the expression: *to want to be.*

A **has-been** is a person who is no longer popular.

It comes from the present perfect form of the verb **to be**: *has been.*

In show business, there are a lot of both!

"I might not be famous one day. But I'd still be happy."

Salma Hayek

A Second Chance

Parker grabbed the ball on the rebound, swivelled and dribbled down the court to the Huskies' basket. Seven... Six... Five... Four... There was no time for a pass. Skilfully, he skirted Blair and leaped high into the air to give it his best shot. There was the screech of a whistle as he came crashing down to the floor: a whistle few paid attention to, for all eyes were glued to the ball. It slammed into the backboard, bounced onto the hoop, against the backboard again and spun around on the top of the hoop several times, as if debating which way to fall. Then, just as the final buzzer blasted, it fell – outside the hoop.

Disbelief. Discouragement. Disappointment. Someone in the crowd booed. Disgust. The cheerleaders, hyped for the wave of victory, dropped their pompoms. Parker closed his eyes. They had lost the championship game, and it was his fault. What was to be the chance of a lifetime, the dream every aspiring athlete hopes for, his 15 seconds of fame as it's called, had turned into his worst nightmare. He'd blown it. And he felt terrible. "Park-er, Park-er, Park-er..." The chanting would not go away.

to swivel: to turn on one foot; to change directions fast.

to skirt: to go around; to pass by very closely.

whistle: a shrill sound.

hoop: basket.

hyped: prepared for; expecting.

blown it: failed.

"Come on, Parker." Randall, the team captain, tapped him on the shoulder. "Come on, man, we need this point. You can do it, man. Let's go!"

Parker snapped to his senses. "Hey, that's right!" There had been a whistle. He had been fouled! Two shots were his! How often did you get a second chance at fame?

Beads of sweat formed on his brow as he took his place at the foul line. He wiped his wet palms on his shorts and caught the ball from the ref. Deliberately, he bounced it several times, trying to calm down, forcing his heart to adopt a slower rhythm. Absolute silence came over the gym. You could have heard a pin drop. Parker blinked, wiggled his shoulders, concentrated on his movements, bounced the ball a last time and released it. A clear, clean shot. The ball soared through the air and sunk into the basket. Swoosh! The crowd went wild.

The ref threw him the ball for his second shot, but no one really cared that he sunk that one as well. They had already won the game, and victory was his. His team picked him up and carried him off the court as the fans roared and the cheerleaders screamed his name. Better than anyone, Parker understood the fragility of victory. He knew he would have to come back down to Earth and deal with the real world soon. But for now, at least, he wanted to savour the sweet taste of glory and his second chance at fame.

 ○ What is meant by "the fragility of victory"?

_____

fouled: there has been a violation of the rules.

sweat: perspiration.

brow: forehead.

to blink: to open and close your eyes rapidly.

to soar: to fly; to rise with little apparent effort.

to sink the ball: to get the ball into the basket.

A Fortunate Meeting

Most people couldn't remember anything about Rosie Barton except that she enjoyed phys. ed. class and seemed a very ordinary girl. And nobody knows where she went after the dramatic event. Have you seen her?

My buddy and I had taken my parents' quads out. We had been having fun, sliding and skidding on the ice near a snowmobile trail. Bent on mischief, we switched around the signs on the trail, laughing our heads off at the thought of watching the confused and disoriented snowmobilers.

We were heading back home when suddenly I saw a black shadow over off to my left. I heard a sickening crash just as I lost control of my quad. I ended up lying on the trail with a very funny-looking, badly twisted leg. My friend Christopher was unconscious and I could make out a strange dark shadow farther down the path.

---

bent on mischief: intending to annoy, to make trouble.
laughing our heads off: laughing very loudly.

At this moment, like an angel, Rosie Barton flew over to the scene. She had been cross-country skiing on that beautiful day. Cross-country skiing was her true passion and it gave her the physical strength and endurance that she was about to need. She looked at us and jumped on her skis for the marathon of her life.

I don't know how fast she travelled or how long she had to ski, but when I saw her flushed face in the newspaper a couple of days later, I could tell that she was indeed a real heroine.

If you see her, please tell me. I wish I could thank her for saving our lives...

○ Did fame change Rosie's life?

Culture

Magic Fingers, Magic Feet: Two Teen Celebrities

Wolfgang Amadeus Mozart: We all know that Mozart could play and compose music when he was very young. Did you know that Mozart wasn't really appreciated for his compositions during his own lifetime? The famous man died poor, aged 35, and was buried in a common grave.

Edson Arantes do Nascimento: Perhaps you have never heard that name before, but this man is the best soccer player ever. Who is he? Does the nickname "Pelé" ring a bell? Pelé, a Brazilian, started his professional career at 14 and broke every record. He once said, "I was born for soccer, just as Beethoven was born for music." He could have said Mozart!

Fleating Fame

Actually, my family's only brush with fame comes from my great-uncle Benny who became Davy Crocket's hat...

OTHER THINGS TO DO

1

Who are your Top 10 stars? Imagine an award ceremony. What award would you give each one?

3

Prepare a word puzzle based on the passions students presented.

2

Go on the Internet and visit the *Hockey Hall of Fame* or another hall of fame. Choose three members and make a collectible card for each. Explain how they became an icon and use one thing they said as a quotation for your card.

4

Do research about a celebrity whose fame has stood the test of time and present your results in an original way.

WRAP-UP

Look Back

○ You should be able to tell what the pictures on pages 2-3 represent and why they are there.

○ You should be able to explain what is meant by "the price of fame."

○ You should be able to answer the Guiding Questions on page 3 and explain the title.

Think About It

○ Think about all the passions we've read and heard about. You should be able to talk about some of them.

○ Think about your own passions and how they fill your life.

○ Think about your dreams for the future.

Now What?

At this moment of your life, what is more important to you: passion or fame?

3-2-1... Take a Bow!

Name three famous persons you didn't know before doing this unit.	List two new vocabulary words or expressions you have learned.	Find an idea for a new passion you could develop.

Don't forget to select some of your work for your portfolio!

UNIT 2

JINXES and Jitters

IN THIS UNIT...

In this unit, you will learn all about superstitions and the rituals people go through for good luck and to help them perform better. You will conduct a survey on the subject and learn how to create an effective poster in order to present the results.

Rearview mirror

Charles Li

○ How superstitious are you?

○ How are superstitions and the little rituals we use helpful?

dandelion

Black cats, four-leaf clovers, walking under a ladder...
In **TASK 1**, you will explore the world of superstitions and share your opinions about some of them. What do you and others think? Are superstitions for real?

Just in Case

Curious to find out the meaning of the word **jinx**? Tune in to Matt and Meagan on FM 930. You are sure to discover a great deal of interesting information.

> **⚠ WARNING**
>
> This text is a bit long! Remember, it's okay not to understand everything... Take a risk!

Talk About It!

- Which superstitions did you already know?
- Which superstitions are new to you?
- Do you know someone who is very superstitious? Explain.

1. Before listening, look at the title and the illustration.
   ○ What do they tell you about the text?

2. Complete Part 1 of the handout.

3. As you listen to the radio show, pay attention to the superstitions mentioned.
   ○ How many can you list?
   ○ Were you able to find all 13 of them?

4. Listen again! Complete Part 2 of the handout.

5. Now it's time to share what you've learned. Use the questions in the **Talk About It!** box to help you.

VERB ENDINGS

Choose the **present** tense or the **past** tense and pronounce it clearly.

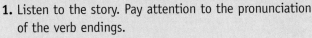

Simple Present Tense	Simple Past Tense
Remember to emphasize the "S" at the end of the verb in the third person singular: *Example:* She **believes** it is an old wives' tale.	Regular verbs end in "ED." *Examples:* I **finished** [t] the story. I **imagined** [d] the situation.
	Irregular verbs have a completely different form from the infinitive. *Example:* to go → I went

Remember, there is a list of irregular verbs in the Toolkit at the end of your Student Book pp. 326-327.

For Fun and Practice

Pronouncing Clearly

1. Listen to the story. Pay attention to the pronunciation of the verb endings.

2. With a partner, take turns reading the text out loud. Let's hear those verb endings!

3. Help each other get it right.

My old Aunt Agatha became very superstitious after a chain of events that occurred on Friday, April 13th. She opened the door to go out and a big black cat dashed into the house in front of her. Dear old Aunt Agatha began to chase it. Of course, the cat was much faster! In despair, she grabbed a heavy dictionary and threw it at the poor animal. She missed. Crash! She smashed the mirror instead. Great! Seven years of bad luck and a wild beast on the loose! The scared cat retreated behind the sofa. Aunt Agatha didn't give up. She got down on her hands and knees and followed it. Imagine the scene!

Fortunately (for both of them), Agatha found a shiny penny while down on all fours. "Find a penny, pick it up. All day long you'll have good luck!" She remembered the saying from her youth. She picked up the penny and put it in her pocket and... her luck changed!

Aunt Agatha swears that all this is true. She shows the penny to everyone, keeps her dictionary under control and never ever leaves the house without first checking for black cats!

---

old wives' tales: traditional beliefs passed down over generations that often contain a mixture of truth and superstition.

How to...

PARTICIPATE IN A DISCUSSION

When it's your turn, think of a sentence to **introduce** your point of view. Then **support** your opinion with an explanation, a fact or an example from your own experience or that of someone you know. Remember, you can also **react** to what someone else has said during the discussion. Finally, make sure you say something to **end the conversation**.

> • *In my opinion...*
> • *I think that...*
> • *I really believe that...*
> • *Etc.*

1 ▌ **Introduce** your opinion or point of view.

> • *I know that...*
> • *I learned that...*
> • *It happened to me.*
> • *... because...*
> • *Etc.*

2 ▌ **Support** it with a fact, an example or a reason.

3 ▌ **React** to the opinions of others.

> • *I agree completely.*
> • *I disagree.*
> • *That's amazing (unbelievable, strange, incredible, crazy, ridiculous...).*
> • *What you just said is...*
> • *Wow! Fantastic!...*
> • *Etc.*

4 ▌ **End** the conversation.

> • *Well, that's what I think.*
> • *That's all I have to say.*
> • *I want to hear what Eric has to say.*
> • *It's Carolyn's turn to give her opinion.*
> • *Etc.*

> Keep a list of different ways to say "super." Can you find at least 10?

Example:

Read the following conversation.
Can you identify the four steps in the discussion?

ANNA: What do you guys think about people keeping old stuff for good luck?

TYLER: I think it's silly. They should get rid of it. Don't you agree, Nick?

NICK: You bet! How can your old sneakers bring you good luck anyway? What do you think, Anna?

ANNA: Well... I don't know about smelly, old sneakers, but I always wear this chain I inherited from my aunt. It's old and not very valuable, but I will never throw it out. I think it brings me good luck.

NICK: Really?

ANNA: Absolutely!

NICK: Hey, Tyler, maybe that's why she always gets such good marks!

TYLER: Awesome! Maybe we can borrow it!

Culture

Triskaidekaphobia

Now, there's a word to impress your friends! So, what does it mean?

Someone who has triskaidekaphobia is afraid of the number 13. And this fear is really quite common! Did you know that because of this superstition, many public buildings and hotels do not have a 13th floor? Also, some airports have no Gate 13. The number 13 is also often avoided in addresses and room numbers. This superstition also affects Formula 1 racing. Car 13 was removed after two drivers were killed in cars with that number. The Italians even omit this number from their national lottery.

Many people have a special relationship with the number 13. For you, is the number 13 lucky or unlucky? Are you triskaidekaphobic?

4, Not 13
Did you know that in many countries in Asia it's the number 4 that is considered unlucky? This is because it is pronounced almost like their word for **death**.

Good Luck, Bad Luck

What's your opinion?

What people won't do for good luck or to avoid bad luck! It's unbelievable!

- Are these superstitions for real? Do they work for you?

- Or do you simply consider them to be old wives' tales?

Discuss them in your groups and try to see if you all share similar points of view about superstitions.

This activity presents a great number of superstitions that you and your friends may or may not believe in. Are you superstitious? Are your friends superstitious? Let's hear from you!

1. Look at the illustration.
   ○ How many superstitions can you identify?
   ○ Do they represent good luck or bad luck?

2. Share your answers with your partner. Use the **Talk About It!** box.

3. Complete the handout.

Focus on...

INTERROGATIVE AND NEGATIVE FORMS

		QUESTIONS	NEGATIVE STATEMENTS
		Yes/No Questions	*Wh- questions*	
Present Tense		• **Do** you believe in good luck charms? • **Does** she agree with you? • **Doesn't** he have a black cat?	• **Which** superstitions do you believe in? • **Why** doesn't he like Friday the 13th?	• I **don't** believe in superstitions. • It **doesn't** bring me luck.
Past Tense		• **Did** you think it was true? • **Didn't** she pick up the penny?	• **When** did she walk under a ladder?	• They **didn't** break the mirror.

For extra help,
see the Toolkit at the end
of your Student Book.

TASK 2

In **TASK 2**, you will learn to distinguish between superstitions and rituals. You will see that superstitions are about luck. Rituals, on the other hand, are generally carried out to help performance.

ACTIVITY 1

Calm Those Jitters!

To overcome stress or as a morale booster, many people have their own rituals or habits to help them perform better. Here are three examples.

1. Read each account.
2. Try to extract the elements of the rituals each person adopted.
   o How are the teens' rituals alike?
   o What's different?
3. Complete the handout.

Culture

Did you know...?

The Finance Minister always buys and wears a brand new pair of shoes for the presentation of a new budget.

Jeremy

"On the day of a game, I get up at 6:30 a.m. I have my usual breakfast of orange juice, oatmeal, toast and a tall glass of milk. Then I head off to team training. When I get back, I always eat hamburger steak, watch some TV and take a long nap. Then, four hours before warm-up, I eat pasta. And in the two and a half hours before practice, I always chew gum and drink tons of water. I arrive at the locker room around 5 p.m. I tape up three or four sticks, jump in the spa for three or four minutes and suit up. I used to have trouble playing every game with the same intensity. Having this routine really helps me stay focused. I play better and have more self-confidence."

---

to suit up: to put on a uniform or equipment.

Kyle

"I play the trumpet in a stage band. I'm the youngest member in the group and I felt pretty nervous at first. I needed to find a way to calm my jitters and gain self-confidence, so I started my own little ritual. On the day of a show, I drink lots and lots of water. It helps keep my energy level up and my head clear. I eat only certain foods and never anything new or rich, just in case... On show days, I practise for only 30 minutes instead of the usual two hours, but then I lie on my bed and rehearse the difficult parts in my head. I watch a bit of TV or listen to music and take a short nap. I always arrive very early before a show and take my time setting up. I want everything just so. Then I go over the program and pieces we'll be playing, using my trumpet, but not actually playing it. By then, I'm ready. The other members begin to arrive and set up, and, as a group, we have our own little ritual. Having this routine really helps my playing, so I follow it religiously."

Vanessa a.k.a. Power

"My goal is to become a pro video gamer and I'm working very hard on it. Following a strict routine helps me stay grounded and shows my parents that I'm serious about this. That's important! I practise for at least five hours every single day. Sitting in front of a screen for so long is tiring and hard on the eyes, so after two or three hours, I always go for a long run — rain or shine. I shower and eat, and then it's back to my computer again for a few more hours of play and practice. I stop periodically to stretch and do a few exercises to loosen my wrists. I drink lots of water and stay away from sugar. I also keep a positive attitude. On my wall, I have a picture of Fatality that I look at for inspiration. My mantra is: 'Don't give up. You can do it!' I find that repeating it often gives me a boost. I like following this ritual because of the benefits it brings me."

---

to rehearse: to practise.

just so: exactly right; a certain way.

a.k.a.: **a**lso **k**nown **as**; alias.

What the Experts Have to Say

Rituals may be nothing more than pure superstitions. But whether they are funny or totally unrealistic, or require strict discipline, rituals do exist and are proven to be beneficial as long as they help you be at your best.

1. Look at the illustration above. What is different from the illustration on page 30?

2. Listen to what the experts have to say on ways to calm those jitters before an important event.

3. Complete the handout.

Culture

Up and Over!

The hockey goalie Patrick Roy was known for his game rituals. For example, he never skated on the lines, but always jumped over them.

Smile!

READ A STORY

Does reading a story in English seem like a big job?

When you see a whole bunch of text and lots and lots of words, do you tend to panic?

Here are some strategies to help you. With a little patience and practice, you'll find reading easier and maybe even fun! Give it a try. You can do it!

▶ Before you begin reading

1. Look at the **title** and **illustrations**.
   - What information do they give you about the story?
   - Can you make any predictions?
     Example: I think this story is about...

▶ While reading the story

2. If there is a word you don't know, **keep on reading**. You may get the meaning from the context, or you may be able to understand the text anyway. Read for the **general idea**.

3. Let yourself become part of the action. Imagine you are there. **Visualize** the story, like a film in your mind.

4. Don't try to read the whole thing at once. **Read a section and stop**.
   Think about what you do understand. Do you have any questions?

5. Stop and try to **predict** what might happen next.
   Example: I think that (Parker will miss the shot because in the title it says "**second** chance").

6. Make **connections** to the story:
   Example: (Parker) is like me. We both (play basketball and want to be great players).

   Example: (The game) reminds me of (a football game I attended).

▶ After reading the story

7. Try to make sense of the story: Identify **the beginning**, **the problem**, **the solution** and **the ending**.

8. Think about why the author wrote this story:
   Example: The message the author wished to convey is...

   Example: I think the author wanted to show that...

9. **Share** your opinions about the story:
   Example: I think this story is... because...

WARNING

The following story contains vocabulary, key verbs and lots of sentences. Enjoy at your own risk!

Sometimes It Doesn't Take Much to Totally Lose It…

1. Look at the title and the illustrations. Can you guess what the story is about?

2. Read the story to find out why Christina panicked and what she did next.
   ○ Would you have handled the situation in the same way?

When you see a (STOP), stop reading and complete a section of the handout.

The Road to Freedom

Monday morning, October 19th. Christina had been waiting for this moment for 16 years and two days. Well, not really quite that long, but she had been waiting for this special day for a very long time. She had turned "sweet 16" on Saturday, and today was the day she would take her written test for her learner's permit. For the past month she had been getting ready. She'd studied the *Driver's Handbook* backwards and forwards from cover to cover and taken the on-line practice test over a dozen times. She knew when to yield and when to slow down. She knew all about construction zones and how far to park from a fire hydrant. Her older brother had questioned her over and over. She knew it all; this girl was ready. (STOP)

---

to yield: to allow someone/something to pass first.

As images of road signs paraded through her mind, Christina donned her favourite sweater and jeans and for luck, she put on the gold bracelet she had inherited from her grandmother. Yes, she was definitely ready and on her way to freedom on wheels.

"Come on, Brian! Let's go! I don't want to be late!"

Eagerly, Christina began to fill in the usual general information — name, address and so forth — and then proceeded on to Question 1. (STOP)

"Oh no, what was the answer? Was it five metres or eight?" For the life of her, she couldn't remember. She went on to Question 2. To Question 3... Her palms began to sweat and her face became flushed. She could not remember a single answer. Not one. What was wrong with her? She couldn't keep her legs still and her heart sounded like a tom-tom on the warpath. Everything was one big jumbled mess in her head. Christina had panicked. (STOP)

"Breathe in; breathe out. Sl-ow-l-y... Breathe in; breathe out..." She let the words sink in: "Breathe in; breathe out..."

Gradually, she calmed down. "Okay... Now what?" Another pang of terror swept through her. "Breathe in; breathe out... Again. G-o-o-d... Now... What was it that psychologist on the radio had said to do? Yeah, that's it — VIS-U-AL-IZE."

Christina calmed her jitters and the butterflies in her stomach and closed her eyes. She conjured up an image of herself studying the *Driver's Handbook* and saw how well she was able to answer even Brian's trickiest questions. She saw herself acing the test and, she saw herself... sitting behind the wheel! As she got hold of her senses, the fog in her mind cleared and the answers began jumping off the pages. She touched the bracelet on her wrist. "Thank you, grandma. Thank you, doctor, whatever your name is." (STOP)

With renewed confidence, Christina whizzed through the test and proudly took her first step to freedom on wheels.

---

to don: to put on (clothing).

flushed: red in the face.

pang: a sudden, sharp sensation.

to conjure up: to imagine.

to ace: to succeed easily; to pass with flying colours.

ou now know that superstitions do exist. It's time to find out if people your age are as superstitious as the people you heard and read about. In **TASK 3**, you will be conducting a survey that will help shed some light on the subject.

Finding Out What Others Think

It's important to know how to go about conducting a good survey. This activity will help you.

1. Work in your groups.

2. Together read and follow the steps for producing a good survey.

3. Complete the handout.

The Production of a Good Survey

PREPARE THE SURVEY

Select the superstitions and rituals you want to investigate.

Target your audience.

Write your focus sentence stating the hypothesis you want to prove.

Prepare your questionnaire.

> It is okay if the initial hypothesis is proven to be false. Hey, that's why people conduct surveys in the first place!

CONDUCT THE SURVEY

Interview people from your targeted audience.

Initiate the conversation properly.

Explain the purpose of your survey.

Ask your questions.

Conclude properly.

COMPILE THE RESULTS

Organize your data.

Calculate the percentages.

Select the best kind of graph to use to present your data.

Produce the graph accurately.

DRAW ACCURATE CONCLUSIONS

Connect your conclusions to your initial hypothesis.

to shed light: to make clear; to find an answer.

accurately: correctly; with precision.

Let's Do Some Editing!

You want to make sure that the questions in your survey are correctly formulated. This activity will help you do so.

1. Examine the table below.
2. Check if the questions on your survey are formulated correctly.
3. Make any necessary changes.
4. Complete the handout.

> For more help on asking questions, see the Toolkit at the end of your Student Book pp. 310-313.

Focus on...

ASKING QUESTIONS

Here's how to ask and answer a question in the present tense:

1. Yes/No Questions without a question word:

AUXILIARY	SUBJECT	VERB	REST OF THE QUESTION	ANSWER	
Do	you (I/we/they)	walk	under ladders?	Yes, No,	I **do**. we **don't**. (do not)
Does	he (she/it)	play	soccer?	Yes, No,	he **does**. he **doesn't**. (does not)

2. Questions with a question word:

Q. WORD	AUXILIARY	SUBJECT	VERB	REST OF THE QUESTION	ANSWER
What	do	you	play	on the computer?	I play video games.
When	does	he	arrive	in the locker room?	He arrives at around 6 o'clock.
Where	do	Linda and Ty	meet	their friends?	They meet them at the park.
Who	–	–	meets	Ty after school?	Mindy meets him. (She does.)

3. Exception! The verb *to be*

For the verb ***to be***, <u>do not use</u> ***does*** or ***do***; simply inverse the subject and the verb:

STATEMENT	QUESTION	ANSWER
She **is** an athlete.	**Is** she an athlete?	Yes, she **is**./No, she **isn't**. (is not).
You **are** ready.	**Are** you ready?	Yes, you **are**./No, you **aren't**. (are not).
Joe and I **are** superstitious.	**Are** we superstitious?	Yes, we **are**./No we **aren't**. (are not).
I'm afraid of cats.	**Am** I afraid of cats?	Yes, I **am**./No, I'm **not**. (am not).

*M*aking a poster is easy. Making a GREAT poster is a definite challenge. But it can be fun if you know how. You will learn what it takes to make a poster that people want to read. In the **FINAL TASK**, you will make a poster showing the results of your surveys and present it to the class. Good luck!

*P*oster with Pizzazz

It's time to present the results of your survey on a poster. Your poster is a kind of advertisement of your results. If you want your poster to be read, it must have certain qualities.

1. Read the information given.

2. Take good notes on what it takes to make a poster great, because your poster must have it all. Complete the handout.

ATTRACTIVE

- Make sure that your fonts and background colours go well together. Your text must be easy to see.
- Don't use too many colours; you don't want to make your audience dizzy!
- In addition, strive for visual unity or harmony. Borders, lines and repeated geometric shapes can work well.
- Decide on the look you want your poster to have and go for it. Keep it clean and fresh!

READABLE

- Make sure your poster is readable. A text that has spelling or grammatical errors and complicated sentence structure is difficult to read.
- Use action verbs, short sentences and punchy phrases. And remember to proofread!
- Decide as a group what the general message will be. Keep t his message short and simple.
- Find a keyword or phrase for your title and – go from there!

K.I.S.S.

Keep
It
Short and
Simple

---

pizzazz: a lot of style, sparkle, liveliness.

to proofread: to look for errors in a text.

SHORT

- Make the punchline visible and brief. People will remember a catchy title.
- Your illustrations should support the title.
- Skip details and unnecessary information. And once again, K.I.S.S.!

CLEAR

- Stand back and look at your poster. If you cannot easily read it, your audience will certainly not be able to either.
- Don't use too many different fonts. It can be distracting.

R.A.S.C.O

READABLE
Check it.

ATTRACTIVE
Choose a simple concept.

SHORT
Keep it to the point.

CLEAR
Choose the fonts wisely.

ORGANIZED
Make it easy to follow.

For a Poster with Pizzazz!

Keep your hands and all work surfaces clean!

On your poster, you need a **title**, the **results** and the **conclusions** drawn from your survey.

ORGANIZED

- Consider this:
People approach new information in a defined spatial sequence. First they look at the top centre, then they track vertically from top to bottom, and horizontally from left to right.
- Put the most important piece of information at the top in the centre and make sure the other ideas flow on the page.
- Before you do the final version of your poster, plan ahead! Allow ample time to assemble and place everything on the page, including the title, graphics and text. This is referred to as the **layout**. Don't rush this step. If your poster is messy, no one will read it.

ample: enough, sufficient.

Poster Know-how

It's now time to produce your poster.

1. Follow the steps in the **Production of a Poster** box closely.
   Use the handout.

2. Don't be afraid to consult others as you go along.

The Production of a Poster

PRE-PRODUCTION

❶
Brainstorm about different ways to present the results on a poster.
❷
Determine the elements you want to include.
❸
Choose fonts and colours.
❹
Plan the layout: position the title,
graphs and any other pertinent elements on the board.
❺
Validate your choices with classmates and the teacher.

PRODUCTION

❶
Mount the poster according to the layout.
❷
Validate the preliminary version by presenting your poster
to a sample audience.
❸
Edit and add the final touches, taking feedback into account.
❹
Plan the presentation of the results.

POST-PRODUCTION

❶
Review the whole process.
❷
Objectively evaluate your work and participation
as an individual and as a team.

Grab Their Attention!

In this activity you will learn how to communicate effectively when presenting the results to your classmates.

Does presenting something in front of others give you the jitters? Here are some strategies to help you get ready. With a little practice, you may discover that you were born to perform in front of an audience. Relax and give it a try!

"3-2-1... On the Air"
Maybe you can find a little ritual that works for you!

Tips and Hints
for Effective Communication

1. Become familiar with the information. **Practice** giving it.

2. Prepare a short **introduction** and **closing**. This will contextualize your presentation and get your audience's attention.

   > *A connection with current events, sharing a personal experience or even asking a question can help guarantee success.*

3. Watch the **tone of your voice**. You want to create a pleasant and relaxed atmosphere. This should also help you relax.

4. Practise **handling your support material**.

   > *This part could get tricky if you haven't taken the time to synchronize everything!*

5. Also, whenever possible, **keep eye contact** with the audience and take pride in presenting your information. Your audience will certainly appreciate that.

The Origins of Some Popular Superstitions

Ever wonder what's behind Friday the 13th, breaking a mirror and other superstitions? Whether you are a believer or not, superstitions have been around for ages. Find out for yourself!

Friday the 13th

In most Western cultures, Friday the 13th is considered an unlucky day. Why? The idea that this day brings bad luck has its roots in Christianity. Christ is said to have been crucified on a Friday and the number of people at the Last Supper was 13. Judas, the Apostle who betrayed Jesus, was the 13th guest. Adam and Eve were expelled from the Garden of Eden on a Friday and Noah left on his ark on a Friday.

The number 13 also has connections to ancient Rome, where witches were said to gather in groups of 12. If ever there was a 13th among them, it was thought to be the devil.

Sneezing

Has anyone ever said "Bless you" or "God bless you" when you sneezed? Well, this is another good example of how old superstitions lose their original meaning, but still stick with us. A long, long time ago, in about the 6th century, people used to congratulate those who sneezed because it was believed that they were expelling evil from their bodies. Later on, the plague ravaged Europe and people began sneezing violently. Sneezing was a sign that these people were extremely sick and might die. Therefore, the Pope passed a law requiring people to bless them. At the same time, it was required that anybody sneezing cover their mouth with a cloth or their hand. This was obviously to stop the spread of the disease. Those who sneezed were blessed and congratulated, as it was believed that a violent sneeze would drive evil from their bodies.

Spilling Salt

During the Middle Ages, salt was a very expensive commodity used mainly for medicinal purposes. For this reason, spillage was to be avoided at all costs. And if you did spill salt, you had to take a pinch of it and throw it over your left shoulder. The idea of throwing spilled salt over the left shoulder is linked to its medicinal use. If it could not be administered, the next best thing was to throw a pinch of spilled salt into the eyes of the evil spirits that brought sickness upon us. These spirits were thought to lurk behind your shoulder, waiting for an opportunity to strike.

To bring good luck or to ward off bad luck, throw a pinch of salt over your shoulder and all will be well.

Breaking a Mirror

Breaking a mirror brings seven years of bad luck, or so the superstition says. That's an awfully long time to believe that you have bad luck, so let's find out the truth behind it. Long before mirrors were invented, people used to see their reflections in pools of water. They believed this reflection to be their soul or their Other Self. And they believed that any interference with the Other Self would injure it. Hence, when mirrors were invented and they were broken, it was thought that the Other Self was harmed.

So, where did this seven-year thing come in? Well, the Romans believed that life renewed itself every seven years, and since a mirror meant "broken" health, it was believed that the person who broke one would need seven years to recover.

Knocking on Wood

Trees were once thought to be the homes of magical creatures. If a person wished to be granted a favour, he would go up to a tree, lightly touch the bark of the tree once and ask that the request be granted. He would then knock again as a way of saying "Thank you."

to lurk: to wait out of sight.
to ward off: to get rid of.
to injure: to hurt.
to harm: to hurt; to injure, to harm and to hurt are synonyms.
bark: outer covering of a tree.

The Shoes of Champions

Nick couldn't wait any longer. The special delivery had to arrive.

The UPS truck hadn't had time to back out of the driveway before Nick had the wrapping paper ripped off the package. At last, they had arrived. He set the box on the kitchen table, opened the lid and peeled back the shiny tissue paper. Carefully, he took them out and set them on the table, his fingers trembling ever so slightly. Wow! He had been saving up for them forever. Now they were his. He couldn't believe his eyes. And so he just sat there, staring at them.

"Nick! Get those off the table! You know it's bad luck to put shoes on the table."

"Not these ones, Mom. They're the shoes of champions. Aren't they the most beautiful shoes you've ever seen?" And without quite realizing what he was doing, Nick picked up his new left soccer shoe and gently kissed the toes. "The shoes of champions," he kept repeating. Little did he know, it was the start of a new ritual.

Eventually, the odor of sweat replaced the smell of something brand new, and the soft white leather bore the brutal scuffs of victory.

They were still the shoes of champions. After each game, Nick would wipe off the cleats, return the shoes to their original box and cover them with the tissue paper, now crumpled and torn. The right foot always went in first so that the left one would be ready to put on first. Then, before each and every game, he would get fully dressed and ready to go, except for his shoes. At the last moment, he would carefully open the box, push back the paper and remove the left shoe. He would touch it gently to his lips as he mumbled three times, "The shoes of champions..." Then he would put it on and repeat the procedure with the right shoe.

Although this may seem a bit strange to us outsiders, no one in the locker room looked twice. In fact, most of the guys had something they did for luck, or as they put it, "just in case." For example, Big John always banged his forehead on his locker door nine times ("Ouch!"), Frank always listened to the same song (*Born to Be Wild*) and Taylor took the soccer ball to be used in the game and spun himself around on it 14 times while the other guys counted. Yes, the pre-game good-luck rituals were numerous and varied. Jack

---

lid: cover; top.

to stare at: to look at something for a long time.

scuff: mark on a smooth surface.

applied ruby red nail polish to his big toes before every game (he promptly removed it afterwards!), Kyle wore his shorts backwards and Sam got down on his knees in the locker room, bowed his head and recited the Lord's Prayer. I've also been told that the guys had a special mantra they would chant all together over and over just before game time, followed by 30 seconds of absolute silence. While anywhere else in school these acts would surely have been pointed out as geeky and the individuals made into objects of ridicule, here in the locker room, they were "normal." Even Coach Watkins, known for his no-nonsense approach and gruff ways, didn't seem to mind a bit. "Keeps 'em focused and builds their confidence," he said.

And so it was – and is, that locker room antics go beyond mere horsing around and playful camaraderie. Partly because of rituals, it is there that respect is born and trust is established. And, it is there, of course, that we find the shoes of champions.

○ Would you consider Nick any different from other athletes?

---

geeky: strange; not "cool."

gruff: rough; unfriendly.

antics: strange, silly, ridiculous behaviour.

The Power of Simple Words

You don't know what to do when the pressure gets high? Why not use a mantra to help you cope in difficult moments?

Recent studies at the University of California show that repeating a word or a series of keywords can either reduce your heart rate and calm you down, or increase your level of adrenalin and push you to perform.

These meaningful words or phrases are called mantras. The word *mantra* means *advice* or *suggestion*. In our daily life, we use words to get things done and obtain everything we need because the mind seems to respond to them. In a sense then, every word is a mantra.

Historically, mantras were used in worship. But with time, people realized that they could be used in other areas of their lives. Sports psychologists believe in their use to help athletes enhance performance. Also, the use of mantras has been used in various treatments, such as for weight loss. In fact, every one of us can benefit from using a mantra as a way of getting in touch with ourselves, to adopt new behaviour or to reduce stress before an important event, such as a competition or an exam. A mantra helps us focus on what it is we want; it influences our state of mind to raise our energy level and keep us positive.

The proper technique to make a mantra work is to first practise repeating it during calm moments. After that, the brain will automatically call upon it when necessary. The words can be anything from "Take it easy" to "Go for it."

---

to enhance: to increase; to make bigger or better.

Here are a few popular English mantras some people use in day-to-day activities. You may be surprised to see that you have already heard of some of them before; maybe you have even used one of them.

1. "Life is not a dress rehearsal."

2. "In this life we cannot do great things. We can only do small things with great love." (Mother Teresa)

3. "Don't do the right things for the wrong reasons."

4. "Live all you can."

5. "You must be the change you wish to see in the world." (Ghandi)

6. "If you don't ask, they can't say no."

7. "Eyes on the prize."

8. "You can make a difference."

9. "Give it your best shot."

Not every mantra listed above will speak to you. The idea is to find a word or phrase that is meaningful to you and make it part of your life. Use it when you need comfort and courage to keep on going.

 ○ Is talking to yourself helpful or totally ridiculous?

Smile!

Early Morning Rituals

An elderly captain of a battleship had a ritual each morning while at sea. His lieutenant commander noticed that his boss would go to the wall safe, take out a piece of paper, open it, bow his head and murmur a few words that seemed very pious. This went on every day for many months. Finally, the commander retired and his lieutenant commander was promoted to take his place. The very first thing the lieutenant commander did was open the safe and take out the wrinkled piece of paper. Very carefully, he unfolded it and read these words: "Port = Left, Starboard = Right."

OTHER THINGS TO DO

1

Find out about the origin of other superstitions. Research the superstitions that intrigue you most.

2

Use the Internet to find out more about the rituals of famous athletes. Alternatively, choose a musician or an artist.

3

Read the short story "The Hockey Sweater" by Roch Carrier.

4

Make up a word puzzle based on vocabulary and expressions in the unit.

Look Back

- Look back at the pictures on pages 28-29.

- You should now be able to explain why each of them is there.

Think About...

- Think about all the superstitions and rituals we've discussed.

- You should be able to name a few and talk briefly about those that you find most interesting, the weirdest, etc.

- You should be able to make the distinction between a superstition and a ritual.

- Think about your own superstitions and rituals.

Now What?

- Can you answer the questions on page 29?

- Are you able to draw any conclusions as to how superstitions and rituals are helpful or why they are not?

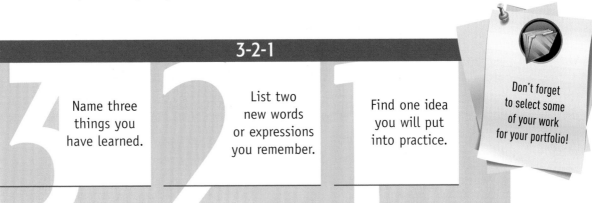

3-2-1

Name three things you have learned.

List two new words or expressions you remember.

Find one idea you will put into practice.

Don't forget to select some of your work for your portfolio!

UNIT 3

Dream Catchers

IN THIS UNIT...

In this unit, you will talk about a typical teen's room and think about your own room. You will imagine the ideal room and how you would like yours to look. You will read about the importance of having your own private space and reflect on priorities. You may discover that the size of a room and the gadgets it contains is not what really matters. As a final task, you will write a description of your own special space, and share how it reflects who you are.

○ What makes a room special?

○ In what ways would you say that your special space is like a dream catcher?

Please!
Do NOT
DISTURB!

*I*n **TASK 1**, you will share with others what you think a typical teenager's room looks like and you will compare that to your own room.

A Typical Room

By definition, a bedroom is a place used primarily for sleeping. For most teens, however, a bedroom is much more than that. It is their living quarters, a place to call their own and a place to hang out.

1. Brainstorm on what you will probably find in a teenager's bedroom. Look at the illustration for ideas.

2. Work with a partner to describe the room in the illustration. Use the **Bedroom Vocabulary** and the **Focus on...** boxes to help you.

3. Complete the handout.

Focus on...

THERE IS/THERE ARE

There is/there are is a common structure used to indicate that something is present:

	THERE IS	THERE ARE
Affirmative	**There is** a desk in the room.	**There are** posters on the walls.
Negative	**There is** not a single table in the room.	**There are** not any books* on the shelf.

Use **there is** with a singular noun:

Examples:
There is a TV in my room.
There isn't a stereo in my room.

Use **there are** with a plural noun:

Examples:
There are two blue chairs.
There aren't any bookcases.

* Note: In English, we use the negative plural form with **no**, **zero** and **not any** for things we can **count**:

Examples:
There are no curtains.
There are zero magazines.
There are not any posters on the walls.

BEDROOM VOCABULARY

BEDS	FURNITURE	ACCENTS	ACCESSORIES	OTHER
• twin bed	• dresser	• wallpaper	• clock radio	• closet
• double bed	• chest of drawers	• curtains	• telephone	• folding doors
• bunk beds	• wardrobe	• blinds	• lamp	• floor
• canopy bed	• nightstand	• rug	• desk lamp	• walls
• futon	• table	• carpet	• shelf (shelves)	• ceiling
• sofa bed	• chair	• bedspread	• mirror	
• murphy bed	• desk	• pillow	• knick-knacks	
	• bookcase	• cushion		

Focus on...

COMMON PREPOSITIONS OF LOCATION

- on (on top of)
- in (inside)
- under (underneath)
- above (over)
- between (in between)
- in front of
- in back of (behind)

- across from (facing)
- against
- next to
- near
- far from
- to the left of
- to the right of

murphy bed: a bed that pulls down from the wall.

My Room

In this activity, you will reflect on where you sleep. You may have your own room or share a room with a sibling or other family member. Or, you may sleep in another room, on the couch, for example. You will take a short survey about where you sleep. It's sure to tell you something about your tastes and your personality.

1. Take a moment to think about your room.
   - Do you have your own room or do you share a room?
   - What do we find in it?
   - What gadgets do you have? What souvenirs?
   - What do you like most about your room?

2. Take the survey on the next page. Write your answers on the handout.

3. Compare and talk about your answers with a partner. Use the **Cues** to help you.

For Fun and Practice

Choose one word to describe your room. That's right, only one!

Share your answer with the class.

Cues

- I found **question** _____ the most difficult to answer.
- How about you?
- Which answer did you select for **number** _____ ?
- My room is usually pretty neat, but my mother thinks (says)...
- My parents think that I should...
- I think (don't think) my room is (big, neat, wild...) enough.
- I wish I could have...

Notice that there is no **"the"** before **question** and **number**.

---

sibling: brother or sister.

couch: sofa.

A Look at My Room

Take a few minutes to answer these questions. Remember, there are no right or wrong answers!

1
a) I have my own room.
b) I share a room.
c) I sleep in another room.

2 I think my room is:
a) too small
b) too big
c) just right

3 How do you feel about your room?
a) I love my room.
b) I hate my room.
c) I don't care one way or the other.

4 Do you make your bed?
a) yes, always
b) sometimes
c) only when there is company coming
d) Someone else makes it for me.

5 Where do you usually do your homework?
a) on my bed
b) on the floor
c) at a desk
d) not in my room

6 If you could put up a poster of anything you wanted, what would it be?
a) an actor, actress or a music poster
b) an animal or nature poster
c) a sports poster
d) other

7 Why is having your own room most important to you?
a) It's a place to be alone.
b) It's a place to keep my special stuff.
c) It's not really important to me.

8 How do you think your room compares to your friends' rooms?
a) Mine is better.
b) Some of my friends have nicer rooms; my room is nicer than some.
c) I like my friends' rooms better.

9 How much time do you spend in your room when you are at home and not sleeping?
a) I spend most of my time there.
b) I spend some time there.
c) I'm almost never in my room.

10 How clean is your room?
a) It's very clean.
b) It's clean enough for me, although...
c) I have to admit, it's a mess!

11 Where do you usually hang out with friends at your house?
a) in my room
b) in the living room
c) in another room

12 If you had a theme for your room, what theme would you choose?
a) a beach or ocean theme
b) a sports theme
c) a music or film theme
d) other or none

Consider compiling your classmates' answers to the survey and making a graph to show the results.

What colour is your room?
What colour would you like it to be?

ACTIVITY 3

My Dream Room

Who hasn't dreamed of the perfect room? A room designed exactly for you, a room to fit your personality and your needs. What would this dream room look like? Would it be quite similar to or very different from your present room?

1. Think of your room as it is now and consider the changes you would like to make.
    - What would you change?
    - What would you get rid of? What would you keep?
    - What would you add?

2. Use the **Think About It!** box to help you.

3. Complete the handout.

4. Compare your dream room with that of your partner.

"I don't care what it looks like or how big it is.

I'd just like to have a real room all to myself, a room of my own."

Think About It!

Things to Consider...

- Would your dream room be fairly big or small and cozy?
- Would you like your room to have a special atmosphere or theme?
- Would you like a high-tech room with all kinds of gadgets and electronic gizmos?
- Would you have a place to do your schoolwork? A place to hang out?

cozy: comfortable, snug and warm.

gizmo: gadget.

THE CONDITIONAL TENSE

How to form the conditional tense:

Affirmative	Negative
subject + would + verb + rest of the sentence	subject + would not (wouldn't) + verb + rest of the sentence
Example: They **would buy** new furniture.	*Example:* He **wouldn't change** a thing!

When to use the conditional tense:

Use the conditional tense to talk about **hypothetical choices** or for actions that could be done under certain conditions.

Example: I would redecorate if I had the money.

Note: After **if**, use the **past tense**, not the conditional.

Example:
If I **repainted** my room, I would choose bright blue.

For Fun and Practice

I Would if I Could

If the decision were yours, what would you do? What wouldn't you do? Why or why not?

- I would change my old twin bed for a queen-size waterbed.
- I'd find room for a mini-fridge and a snack bar.
- I'd swap my brother for a wide screen TV.
- I would definitely get rid of the ugly, purple, flowery wallpaper.
- I'd add tons of shelves on the walls.
- I'd have a real bed instead of a sofa bed.
- I'd transfer my bedroom to the attic.

Talk About It!

Choices

If you couldn't leave your room for an entire week-end, what two things, other than food and water, would you like to have with you?

---

to swap: to exchange one thing for another; to trade.

to get rid of: to dispose of; to do away with; to give away or to throw away.

attic: open space at the top of a house, just below the roof, often used for storage.

Worn out teddy bears, old videos, a picture collection… These are all objects that might seem insignificant if they aren't attached to fond memories or past aspirations. In **TASK 2**, you will explore the reasons why some objects are priceless to their owners.

My Favorite Things

In *The Sound of Music*, F7rauleir Maria, the new governess, sings *My Favorite Things* to reassure the children in her care during a thunderstorm. Much like Maria, most of us have objects that bring us comfort and reassurance. What are a few of your favorite things?

1. Read the lyrics of *My Favorite Things* on the next page.

2. With your partner, make a list of all of the favourite things in the song.

3. Complete the first part of the handout together.

4. Think about your favourite things.
   ○ What are they?
   ○ Where do you keep them?
   ○ How do they make you feel?

5. Share your answers with your partner. Use the **Cues** to help you.

6. Complete the rest of the handout.

Cues

My favorite things…
- comfort me
- reassure me when I'm feeling sad, lonely, depressed, upset, scared…
- make me nostalgic
- bring me happiness

I keep my favorite things…
- in a safe place
- tucked away in my closet or hidden from view
- out for me to look at
- in my memory

Culture

FYI
Favorite vs. Favourite

British spelling favours the ending **–our**, while American spelling uses **–or**.

In Canada, we often see both spellings, but the British form is preferred.

Some other **–our** words are: *colour*, *flavour*, *humour* and *honour*.

---

governess: woman employed to educate and train the children in a private home.
lyrics: words of a song.

My Favorite Things

Raindrops on roses and whiskers on kittens,
Bright copper kettles and warm woolen mittens,
Brown paper packages tied up with strings –
These are a few of my favorite things.

Cream-colored ponies and crisp apple strudels,
Doorbells and sleigh bells and schnitzel with noodles,
Wild geese that fly with the moon on their wings,
These are a few of my favorite things.

Girls in white dresses with blue satin sashes,
Snowflakes that stay on my nose and eyelashes,
Silver white winters that melt into springs –
These are a few of my favorite things.

When the dog bites,
When the bee stings,
When I'm feeling sad,
I simply remember my favorite things.
And then I don't feel so bad!

Culture

The Sound of Music

Rodgers and Hammerstein's 1965 film *The Sound of Music* is one of the most beloved musicals of all times. It stars Julie Andrews as Maria, a postulant who becomes the governess of seven children and introduces them to music. It is based on the Broadway musical of the same name and the book, the *Story of the Trapp Family Singers*.

The film won five Academy Awards, including Best Picture, and is the most successful movie musical of all time.

Julie Andrews as Maria

kettle: a metal pot for cooking.

strudel: a thin pastry with fruit filling.

schnitzel: a thin veal cutlet dipped in batter and fried.

ACTIVITY 2

My Treasure Chest

In this activity, you will listen to a few teens talk. They will use lots of adjectives to describe their dream rooms and their favourite things.

Talk About It!

• Which of the teens' rooms do you identify with most? Why?

• Did you find any of the descriptions of the dream rooms totally off-the-wall? Explain.

1. Listen as some teens describe their dream rooms and their favourite things in those rooms.

2. Pay close attention to the adjectives they use in their descriptions.

3. Read the **Focus on The Order of Adjectives** box on the next page.

4. Complete the handout.

5. If necessary, listen to the texts a second time and check your work.

6. Discuss in your groups using the **Talk About It!** box.

off-the-wall: very unconventional or unusual (*informal*).

THE ORDER OF ADJECTIVES

- In English, adjectives almost always go **before** the nouns they describe:

Examples: a **big** bed, a **messy** room, a **private** place, a **yellow** desk...

- Sometimes, we want to describe a noun with more than one adjective. The general order is:

Opinion	Before	Fact
An opinion is what you THINK about the noun.		A fact is what is DEFINITELY TRUE about the noun.
Example: A **nice**, blue bedspread.		*Example:* An old, **brown** desk.

- You can also use the word **with** in your descriptions:

Examples:
A beautiful new chair **with** large, red, vertical stripes.
A fantastic poster **with** two wild white horses in a vast field.

For a long string of adjectives, here is the usual order:

Determiner	Opinion	Appearance	Age	Colour	Origin	Material	Noun
a, an, the, ten... *two*	*beautiful*	(size, shape, condition) *big*	*old*	*red*	*Chinese*	*brass*	*lamps*
an	*itsy-bitsy*	*teeny-weeny*		*yellow*		*polka dot*	*bikini*

(Note, however, that sometimes this order is changed to show emphasis.)

WARNING

Adjectives **NEVER** take the plural:
17 funn**y**, blac**k** bags

For Fun and Practice

- Work with a partner
- Orally describe each of the following items using a string of adjectives. Use your imagination!
  – *A radio*
  – *Your little sister's bedspread*
  – *The little bear's chair*
  – *A picture painted by your Aunt Gertrude for your room*

ACTIVITY 3

A Question of Values

In Task 1, you imagined your dream room. In this activity, you will read a story about someone else's perfect room. You may find it alters your perceptions of the ideal room.

1. Look at the title of the activity, the title of the story on the next page and the illustration. What do they tell you about the story?

2. Read the story.
   ○ What do you think the teen was trying to express? Why?

3. Complete the first part of the handout.

4. Share your answers with a partner.

5. In your groups, answer the discussion questions in the **Talk About It!** box on page 70.

6. Finish completing the handout.

> If you find the story difficult, refer to the strategies you learned in Unit 2 or see **How to Read a Story** in the Toolkit on p. 278.
> Remember, it's not necessary to understand every single word!

A Room to Die For

Juliana looked again at the magazine spread in front of her. "A Room to Die For" was the title the editor had chosen. The pictures were stunning, the look incredible, the colours... wow! "A room where beauty meets function, a room where dreams come true," she read.

She glanced around her room. It really and truly was a work of art. And down to every single detail, from the colours in the paintings on the wall to the small picture frame on her desk... every single thing matched perfectly. The room also contained everything hi-tech a teen could possibly want. A computer, TV, stereo, phone, mini-refrigerator... Her room had it all. It was the envy of her friends and now, also of thousands of other teens around the country. "You're so-ooo lucky!" she was told over and over.

Juliana opened the door to her walk-in closet and went inside. She picked up Tony, her most precious possession in the whole world. It saddened her to think that ever since they had moved into the new

Juliana had the perfect room, or at least that's what she thought...

---

to die for: remarkable; highly desirable (*informal*).

stunning: extremely attractive, splendid.

to glance: to give a brief look at.

house and redone her room, the teddy bear that had sat on her bed since she was four years old was now relegated to a corner of the closet because "it was old and worn and didn't match." Cradling Tony to her chest, she lay on her perfect bed with its perfect pillows and cried.

She thought about the way things used to be. She thought about Miguel, her best friend... She let her mind wander back to last week when he had finally invited her over for supper. She thought about how ashamed Miguel said he was about where he lived and how he said that he envied Juliana.

Juliana played the film of that visit to the small, two-room apartment over in her mind. She remembered the crowded combination kitchen-living room, which also doubled as a bedroom for Miguel, but especially she remembered the smell of roast chicken, the light atmosphere at the kitchen table as Miguel and his mother shared the stories of the day, the smiles and the laughter. She thought about how after supper, they had sat on the old sofa and shared secrets... Juliana could still see the walls papered with Miguel's drawings and photos of memories past. She saw his football trophy proudly displayed on a shelf. She thought about the handmade quilt neatly draped over the back of an armchair and listened again and again in her mind as Miguel's mother explained how each patch had been made from clothes he had outgrown and told of the tales each one held. She remembered the dream catcher hanging in the window and how comfortable and safe she had felt there... And then, she remembered how she had felt when she noticed the article about her perfect room, which had been carefully clipped from the magazine and left on the coffee table. It was her turn to feel ashamed. No fancy decorating or expensive design or electronic equipment could ever really bring happiness. It was her turn to be envious. Miguel was the lucky one; he was the one who had the room to die for.

Juliana decided it was time to bring Tony out of hiding and back on her bed where he belonged. It was a first small step in the right direction.

"She remembered the dream catcher hanging in the window."

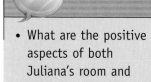

Talk About It!

- What are the positive aspects of both Juliana's room and Miguel's "room"?

- What do you think is really important or essential in a bedroom?

---

to relegate: to send to a place of exile; to banish.

to cradle: to hold gently and carefully.

ashamed: embarrassed.

draped: casually placed.

to outgrow: to become too small.

where he belonged: where he should be.

Culture

The Tradition of the Dream Catcher

A dream catcher is usually placed in a bedroom. It is most often hung above the bed as protection from nightmares.

Positive dreams are said to slip through the hole in the centre of the dream catcher and glide down the feathers to the person asleep. Negative dreams, on the other hand, will get caught in the web and disappear with the first rays of the sun.

The legend of the dream catcher varies from one Indian tribe to another.

Focus on...

THERE, THEIR AND THEY'RE

What's the Difference?

There: a place; in contrast to "here."

> *Example*: Put the bed **there**.

Their: the possessive form of "they."

> *Example*: **Their** room is blue.

They're: the contraction of "they are."

> *Example*: **They're** at home.

---

nightmare: bad dream.

*I*n **TASK 3**, you will discover why nothing should be taken for granted. Disasters, like hurricanes, floods and fires sometimes force people to give up their most prized possessions. In such times, people have little choice but to keep their chins up. Coping with such tragedies takes strength and courage. It forces us to establish our priorities.

A Day to Forget

December 12, 2004, will always be a special day for Brianna. It's not her birthday; it's not a holiday. It's Day One of the most life-changing event in her short 18 years of existence.

1. Read the blog below to find out what happened to Brianna.
   - Would you have reacted the same way?
   - Do you know anyone who has experienced the same type of disaster?

2. Answer the question in the **Write About It!** box on page 74.

3. Complete the handout.

4. Share your answers with your partner.

My Thoughts.com
A place to share... A space to care

Post 1712   previous   next   Search this site: [   ]

First posted by Brianna Newberry on December 12, 2007
Okay, here's my story. It happened two years ago today, but it's still very fresh and vivid in my mind and I've gotta admit, I'm still upset...

---

to take for granted: to underestimate the value of something.

to keep your chin up: to remain positive in a difficult situation.

gotta: got to (*informal*).

upset: in a state of emotional distress; perturbed.

I was sitting in fourth period math, not really listening to Mr. Norton drone on and on about algorithms or whatever. I was thinking instead about my older sister. Ever since she went away to school in the fall, I kinda miss her. Don't get me wrong! I love having my own room now and not having to fight over the phone and the bathroom, but… Anyway, there I was thinking about Lili and how I couldn't wait until tomorrow when she came home for the holidays and how much fun we were going to have when I got a message to report to the office at once. I gathered my stuff and walked down the hall, thinking about how lucky I was to get out of class early until… until I saw my father and the look on his face. I swear I'll never ever forget that look as long as I live. He'd come to get me and tell me in person that there had been a bad fire at our house. No one had been hurt, and the walls were still standing, but there was a lot of damage. I remember collapsing on the floor as I heard words I didn't really understand and certainly didn't want to hear. And, I remember screaming right there in the middle of the office. One minute I was a happy teen daydreaming in math class, the next I was almost homeless. You can't begin to imagine what it's like to learn that everything you take for granted as a part of who you are – clothes, makeup, the comfortable disorder in your room, even the unfinished homework on your desk – everything has gone up in smoke. Like I said, it's been two years, but I'm still bitter.

I remember how very different Christmas was that year and how mixed up I felt: grateful for life and family and yet, extremely angry at fate. I remember spending Christmas Eve crowded around a table that was much too small to share an order-in Christmas dinner… The small artificial tree my mom purchased from the dollar store and set proudly on top of the TV in the corner… The forced, but sometimes genuine laughter we shared…

Eventually we were able to move back into our revamped house and pick up the pieces. Generally speaking, things are now back on track. Like I said, it has been two years. I've got a new bed, new clothes, and so on, but there are things you can never replace. I'm learning to deal with that. I have learned, though, how very, very important it is to have a place to call home.

Thanks for letting me share this. Brianna

End of post. Comments to date: 24.   *To add your comment, <u>click here</u>*

Comment posted by Lester, on June 9, 2007, at 7:07 a.m.

I just wanted to say that I, too, understand how you feel. My family was a victim of Katrina. We lived in a tent for a while. Now we share a small mobile home with another family while they are rebuilding our house. It's tough not having all your stuff and everything, but we were lucky. Some people lost their lives. I can't wait to have my own room again. It's very cramped here!

---

to drone on and on: to speak in a monotonous manner.

kinda: kind of (*informal*).

bitter: marked by resentment or disappointment.

cramped: very tight quarters; having very little room or space.

Comment posted by Daniella on January 28, 2007, at 10:01 a.m.

I don't know how you managed. I couldn't live without all my stuff. Fire sucks.
Girl, you are an inspiration to us all! Keep the spirits! Luv ya!

Comment posted by John D. on December 14, 2006, at 11:22 p.m.

My dad's a firefighter, and he often brings home stories like yours. You're right
about the importance of having a place to call home. You made me realize that.
Thanks! And, Merry Christmas to you and your family.

Comment posted by Cody on December 14, 2006, at 10:27 p.m.

Hey, Brianna, it happened to me too. We lost everything, including my dog. :-(
It's tough, but we gotta hang in there. Cody

Comment posted by Kristin on December 13, 2006, at 9:45 p.m.

Dear Brianna, I know how you feel. Our house burned down almost 10 years ago
when I was only seven. All I saved was a doll and some funny pink shoes.
They have become my most prized possessions! Don't despair. The hurt and anger
eases with time. I know. I've been there. Love, Kristin

Write About It!

How would you respond to this article? Write a personal comment to Brianna.

Culture

Did You Know...?

A **blog** is a Web site or Web page presented like a journal with entries made
in reverse chronological order (i.e., the most recent entry is the one presented
first). There are blogs on just about any subject you can imagine, from
pastimes and hobbies to serious discussions on politics and social issues.

Blogs are interactive in the sense that readers are invited to post their
comments. Some blogs also contain photos and videos, as well as text.

The word **blog** comes from the words **web** + **log** (web logs refer to logging
done on the Web). It was coined by Peter Merholtz in 1999 when for fun,
he used the expression *we blog*. It stuck, both as a verb and a noun.
And, as the saying goes, the rest is history!

There are over 60 million blogs on the Web, enough to satisfy
even the most avid blogger!

---

to manage: to get by; to survive; to deal with successfully.

to hang in there: to not give up; to hold on (*informal*).

to despair: to abandon hope; to lose heart.

logging: the action of keeping a log or a journal.

to stick: to last; to remain in existence; to become permanent.

Priorities

If you had to leave your space very abruptly and could take along only three personal possessions, what would they be?

1. Take a moment to brainstorm about all the possible items you might select. Consider the reasons why you would select them.

2. Decide upon the three you value the most.

3. Complete the handout.

A BASEBALL

Dirty, old, leather
A baseball like so many others
Proudly displayed in my room
A souvenir from the Expos game
I attended with grandpa
A ball hit into the stands
And caught by me
It's my favourite possession.

MY PINK SHOES

Scuffed and worn, outgrown
Little pink shoes with tiny
satin bows
Sit on my shelf
In memory of days gone by
My most precious possession
The shoes I was wearing the day
our house burned to the ground.

For Fun and Practice

- Choose one of your three items.

- Write a similar poem about your item using the model on the handout. In your poem, you will be asked to:
  - Say what your favourite possession is.
  - Describe it using adjectives.
  - Explain why you selected this particular item and where you keep it.

- Share your text with your partner first to get feedback. Then share it with others.

---

scuffed: with marks from having been worn.

A dream catcher is usually hung by a window or above a bed. It sifts through our dreams, letting in the good ones and keeping out the bad. Your special space should do just that – give you a place to find comfort and peace, a place to take off the masks and be yourself. In the **FINAL TASK**, you will describe your special space – present or future.

ACTIVITY 1

*M*y Room, Another Look

As a final task, it's now your turn to describe your own special space. It may be the room you have now or the room you would like to have one day. Furniture and gadgets, or even the decoration, may or may not be relevant. The choice is yours!

*"My room...
All I really need is
an empty hook to
hang my troubles
on, an empty box
to store my
memories in and
an empty space on
a wall to display
my aspirations
and imagination.
For me, the rest
is immaterial."*

1. Read the quotation.
   ○ How could it apply to your space?

2. Write a descriptive paragraph about your room – the room you have now or the room you would like to have. Use the **How to Write a Paragraph** box on the next page.

3. Your paragraph should answer this question:
   ○ If someone enters your room, how would they know that it is yours, and no one else's? In other words, what makes your space unique?

4. Use the graphic organizer on the handout to structure your ideas and help you organize your text. Use the tools presented in this unit to help you compose your text.

5. Follow the steps in **The Writing Process** box on page 78.

6. Read the **How to Proofread** box on page 79.

7. Work with a partner and proofread your texts before writing your final copy.

8. Illustrate your text with drawings, photos, a collage, etc...

---

immaterial: unimportant; irrelevant.

WRITE A PARAGRAPH

1 | **Choose the <u>subject</u>.**

My Bedroom

2 | **Determine what you want to say about the subject <u>in general</u>.**

Choose a fact	or	Give your opinion
My bedroom is very small.		I think that my bedroom is too small.

3 | **Choose a fact or an opinion and write <u>one sentence</u> about the subject. This is the topic sentence.**

Examples:
Fact: My bedroom is small.
Opinion: I think I need a bigger room.

4 | **Determine at least <u>three ideas, arguments</u> <u>or examples</u> to support the sentence.**

Examples:
- I have to do my homework on my bed; there is no room for a desk.
- I can't have more than one or two friends over; there is no room to sit.
- I can't open the closet door very wide; my bed is in the way.
- There is no room to put anything else.

5 | **Write a <u>one-sentence conclusion</u>.**

Try this:
- If your first sentence is a **fact**, end with an **opinion**.
- If it is an **opinion**, end with a **fact**.

My room is very small. There is no room to do anything! I can't have many friends over, because there is nowhere to sit, and I can't bring in chairs, because there is no room. I can't even open the closet door all the way! My room is so small that there is no room for a desk, so I have to do my homework in the kitchen or lying on my bed. I would like to have a TV in my room, but you guessed it – there is no room! I like my room, but it really is too small. Maybe I should move into the garage!

***

I think that my bedroom is way too small! There is no room for a desk or a TV. I can't have my friends over because there is no room to hang out in my room. I can't even open my closet door all the way because of my bed. I need more space. My room is not big enough for me and my stuff, and I'm seriously thinking about moving into the garage.

The Writing Process

PREPARING TO WRITE

- Be clear about the message you want to send (the purpose) and for whom you are writing.
- Brainstorm for additional ideas with others.
- Use examples provided in magazines.
- Organize your information using the graphic organizer on the handout.

WRITING THE DRAFT(S)

- Concentrate on getting your ideas on paper; don't worry about mistakes at this time.
- Find and add information to support your main idea.

REVISING

- Ask someone to give you feedback on:
  - The structure of your paragraph
  - The logical sequence of your information
  - Synonyms and your choice of words
  - The variety of sentence structures used
- Make changes, taking the feedback into account. If in doubt, ask for a second opinion.

EDITING

- Ask someone to give you feedback on:
  - Punctuation
  - Spelling
  - Choice of verb tenses
  - Use of prepositions of location
  - Use and placement of adjectives
  - Use of adverbs.
  - Etc.
- Make proper corrections to your text.

PUBLISHING

- Write or type your polished copy.
- Add an illustration.

Revising vs. Editing

We **revise** a text for clarity, organization and ideas.

We **edit** a text for spelling and grammar.

PROOFREAD

It's okay to have your own personal proofreading strategies as long as they do the job.

If you have trouble staying on topic or your texts often fall short, the following tips may help you stay on top of things.

Tips of the Trade:

1 | **Read your text for the content.**

> *Make sure all the required elements are present. Double-check everything!*

2 | **Read your text out loud.**

> *Reading and hearing every single word will help you notice awkward phrasing or incorrect use of words.*
> *If it doesn't sound right, then it must be wrong.*

3 | **Try proofreading your text from the bottom up.**

> *It will force you to pay attention to individual sentences.*

4 | **Take a break!**

> *In a rut? Even a five-minute break can help you get some distance and allow you to see your text in a new way.*

5 | **Develop a buddy system.**

> *Ask a partner to read your text. Having another person may help you locate the awkward or missing elements.*
> *Ask your partner to read for a specific task.*

6 | **Stay focused.**

> *Once you are satisfied with the content, check for spelling and grammar errors.*
> *Scan for one element at a time. Otherwise, it's easy to lose track of your intention.*

Fly Away Home

by Eve Bunting

My dad and I live in an airport. That's because we don't have a home and the airport is better than the streets. We are careful not to get caught.

Mr. Slocum and Mr. Vail were caught last night.

"Ten green bottles, hanging on the wall," they sang. They were as loud as two moose bellowing.

Dad says they broke the first rule of living here. Don't get noticed.

Dad and I try not to get noticed. We stay among the crowds. We change airlines.

"Delta, TWA, Northwest, we love them all," Dad says. He and I wear blue jeans and blue T-shirts and blue jackets. We each have a blue zippered bag with a change of blue clothes. Not to be noticed is to look like nobody at all.

Once we saw a woman pushing a metal cart full of stuff. She wore a long, dirty coat and she lay down across a row of seats in front of Continental Gate 6. The cart, the dirty coat, the lying down were all noticeable. Security moved her out real fast.

Dad and I sleep sitting up. We use different airport areas.

"Where are we tonight?" I ask.

Dad checks his notebook. "Alaska Air," he says. "Over in the other terminal."

That's OK. We like to walk.

We know some of the airport regulars by name and by sight. There's Idaho Joe and Annie Frannie and Mars Man. But we don't sit together.

---

to bellow: to shout.

to notice: to attract attention.

cart: two-wheeled or four-wheeled vehicle used to transport luggage.

regulars: people who come to a place frequently.

"Sitting together will get you noticed faster than anything," Dad says.

Everything in the airport is on the move — passengers, pilots, flight attendants, cleaners with their brooms. Jets roar in, close to the windows.

Other jets roar out. Luggage bounces down in chutes, escalators glide up and down, disappearing under floors. Everyone's going somewhere except Dad and me. We stay.

Once a little brown bird got into the main terminal and couldn't get out. It fluttered in the high, hollow spaces. It threw itself at the glass, fell panting on the floor, flew to a tall, metal girder, and perched there, exhausted.

"Don't stop trying," I told it silently. "Don't! You can get out!"

For days the bird flew around, dragging one wing. And then it found the instant when a sliding door was open and slipped through. I watched it rise. Its wing seemed OK.

"Fly, bird," I whispered. "Fly away home!"

Though I couldn't hear it, I knew it was singing. Nothing made me as happy as that bird.

The airport's busy and noisy even at night. Dad and I sleep anyway. When it gets quiet, between two and four a.m., we wake up.

"Dead time," Dad says. "Almost no flights coming in or going out."

At dead time there aren't many people around, so we're extra careful.

In the mornings Dad and I wash up in one of the bathrooms, and he shaves. The bathrooms are crowded, no matter how early. And that's the way we like it.

Strangers talk to strangers.

"Where did you get in from?"

"Three hours our flight was delayed. Man! Am I bushed!"

---

luggage: suitcases; baggage.
to flutter: to flap wings without flying or on short flights.
girder: a beam to support a roof.
exhausted: very tired.

---

bushed: very tired.

Dad and I, we don't talk to anyone.

We buy doughnuts and milk for breakfast at one of the cafeterias, standing in line with our red trays. Sometimes Dad gets me a carton of juice.

On the weekends Dad takes the bus to work. He's a janitor in an office in the city. The bus fare's a dollar each way.

On those days Mrs. Medina looks out for me. The Medinas live in the airport, too – Grandma, Mrs. Medina, and Denny, who's my friend.

He and I collect rented luggage carts that people have left outside and return them for fifty cents each. If the crowds are big and safe, we offer to carry bags.

"Get this one for you, lady? It looks heavy."

Or, "Can I call you a cab?" Denny's real good at calling cabs. That's because he's seven already.

Sometimes passengers don't tip. Then Denny whispers, "Stingy!" But he doesn't whisper too loud. The Medinas understand that it's dangerous to be noticed.

When Dad comes home from work, he buys hamburgers for us and the Medinas. That's to pay them for watching out for me. If Denny

and I've had a good day, we treat for pie. But I've stopped doing that. I save my money in my shoe.

"Will we ever have our own apartment again?" I ask Dad. I'd like it to be the way it was, before Mom died.

"Maybe we will," he says. "If I can find more work. If we can save some money." He rubs my head. "It's nice right here, though, isn't it, Andrew? It's warm. It's safe. And the price is right."

But I know he's trying all the time to find us a place. He takes newspapers from the trash baskets and makes pencil circles around letters and numbers. Then he goes to the phones. When he comes back he looks sad. Sad and angry. I know he's been calling about an apartment. I know the rents are too high for us.

"I'm saving money, too," I tell him, and I lift one foot and point to my shoe.

Dad smiles. "Atta boy!"

---

to look out for: to watch out for; to take care of.

cab: taxi (short for taxi cab).

stingy: tight with money; ungenerous.

"If we get a place, you and your dad can come live with us," Denny says. "And if *we* get a place, you and your mom and your grandma can come live with *us*," I say.

"Yeah!"

We shake on it. That's going to be so great!

After next summer, Dad says, I have to start school. "How?" I ask. "I don't know. But it's important. We'll work it out." Denny's mom says he can wait for a while. But Dad says I can't wait.

Sometimes I watch people meeting people. "We missed you."

"It's so good to be home."

Sometimes I get mad, and I want to run at them and push them and shout, "Why

do *you* have homes when we don't? What makes *you* so special?" That would get us noticed, all right.

Sometimes I just want to cry. I think Dad and I will be here forever.

Then I remember the bird. It took a while, but a door opened. And when the bird left, when it flew free, I know it was singing.

Culture

Eve Bunting was born in Northern Ireland. She moved to the United States as a young mother. Bunting has written over 200 books for children and teens. She has a definite talent for storytelling and a way with words.

Eve Bunting

○ What does the bird represent in the story?

to shake on it: to shake hands to show commitment.

Private. Do Not Enter.

Michael went in his room and slammed the door. He kicked off his shoes, sending one onto a heap of yesterday's clothes. The other knocked over the half-empty can of soda on his nightstand. He pushed aside a pile of sports magazines and lay on his unmade bed watching the cola dribble out of the can and onto an empty pizza box on the floor.

He looked around. Okay, so his room was a little untidy. So what? It was supposed to be his room, his own private space. Maybe he liked the "lived-in" look... He pulled off his socks and aimed for the plastic basketball hoop that hung on his closet door. The second one got stuck on the rim. Whatever.

Michael had waited for a very long time to have his own room. And, now that he had finally gotten it, he couldn't believe that his parents expected him to keep it like the rest of the house – "spick and span." Was it his

---

to slam: to shut hard with a bang.

heap: pile.

untidy: messy; not neat.

---

spick and span: very, very clean.

fault that his mother was a clean freak while he preferred "casual disorder"? Anyway, what right did she have going into his room without asking for permission? Didn't the "Keep Out!" and "No Trespassing!" signs taped to his closed door mean anything to her?

Michael had another look around... A few clothes here and there, the towel from his morning shower draped over the chair, a bunch of crumpled papers near (but not in) the wastepaper basket, a knocked over pile of CDs, the contents of his hockey bag dumped over in one corner... It was no big deal, and surely nothing to go ballistic over.

He'd keep his promise and clean his room – tomorrow. For now, he had other plans. He slipped his earphones over his ears, flipped off the light and let the music rip, transporting him to a different corner of his perfect, private space.

My Old Room
by Sonya Sones

Does the sun still stream
through the window every morning
in what used to be my bedroom,

stream through the leaves
on the maple tree outside
and shimmer the carpet alive,

even though I'm not there to see it,
not there to feel its warmth
slipping across my face?

Who sleeps
in my bedroom now?
Whose face does the sun slip across?

o How is the situation described here typical for many teens?

---

clean freak: person who is a maniac about cleaning (*informal*).

no trespassing: a zone or place that is off limits, that you must not enter.

crumpled: rolled up in a ball.

dumped over: overturned.

to let the music rip: to turn up the volume and let the music play.

to stream: to flow freely and abundantly.

to shimmer: to shine with a diffused light.

"We'd better go clean our rooms -
Mom's getting serious."

OTHER THINGS TO DO

1
Make a collage
of what your ideal
room would look like
and describe it.

3
Make your own dream
catcher and find
a special place
to hang it.

2
Watch the movie
The Terminal and use
a graphic organizer to
show the links you can
make with this unit.

4
Write a poem
or a song about
your special place.

Look Back

Look back at the illustration on pages 56-57. You should now be able to explain why this title was chosen for this particular unit and why it is appropriate.

Think About It…

○ Think about all the items you dream of having in your personal space.

○ You should be able to make choices about which things are really important to you and which you could bear to part with.

○ Think about how and why certain things take on a whole new meaning with time and experience.

Now What?

○ Answer the questions on page 57.

○ At this point, are you able to distinguish between things that are part of your cosmetic world and things that are part of your soul world?

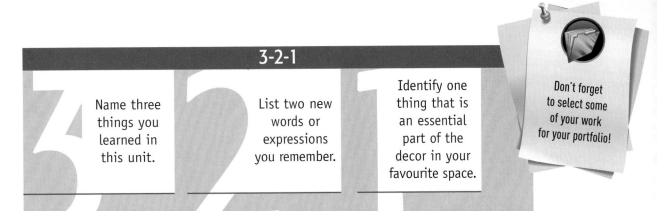

3-2-1

Name three things you learned in this unit.

List two new words or expressions you remember.

Identify one thing that is an essential part of the decor in your favourite space.

Don't forget to select some of your work for your portfolio!

UNIT 4

ONCE UPON ANOTHER TIME

IN THIS UNIT...

In this unit, you will explore the world of fairy tales and become aware of stereotyping and perceptions. You will be asked to write a letter to present the point of view of an antagonist, a minor character or even an object. In this short letter, you will present a new side – their side – of an old story.

The Regal Café

n **TASK 1**, you will revisit the magical world of fairy tales. Which ones do you still remember? Which ones inspired you the most? How have they influenced your perceptions?

Timeless Tales Trivia

Do Snow White, Cinderella and the Big Bad Wolf ring any bells? Hopefully they do, because you're about to be the next contestants on "Timeless Tales Trivia," the quiz show that's rocking the nation. See how well you can remember the original versions of these timeless tales.

WARNING

You don't have much time! So, you must concentrate as much as possible. Remember... don't let little details distract you. Your team is counting on you!

1. Before listening, look at the title and the illustration.
   ○ What do they tell you about the text that you will listen to?

2. As you listen to the quiz show, pay careful attention to each question as it is asked. Use the full 15 seconds to think about your answer.

3. Write it down on the handout. Then consult your team.

4. Listen again!

5. After listening, add up your points.

6. Share what you know about fairy tales.

7. Answer the questions in the Talk About It! box.

8. Finish completing the handout.

Focus on...

STRUCTURING A QUESTION

Here are two quick ways to consult with others:

1. Use the basic question structure with the verb *to be*.

Verb *to be*	Subject	Object
Is	it	Cinderella?

2. Use question tags.

Question tags are used in conversation to solicit a reaction from the person you are talking to. Most often, but not always, this reaction will be in the affirmative form.

Compare the following. What answer do you think the person is expecting to hear?

Subject	Verb	Object	Tag
It	is	Cinderella,	isn't it?
It	isn't	Snow White,	is it?
That	could be	Goldilocks,	couldn't it?

> **Notice that...**
>
> if the verb is in the *affirmative*, the tag will be in the negative form.
>
> But...
>
> if the verb is in the *negative*, the tag will be in the affirmative form.

Smile!

Just for Laughs

Q: What did the three bears buy after Goldilocks' visit?

A: New *fur*niture!

Talk About It!

- Which fairy tales did/do you like the most? Why?
- Which fairy tales did you not know?
- What were your perceptions of fairy tales when you were younger? How have these perceptions changed?
- Did your parents read you fairy tales when you were younger?

ACTIVITY 2

*O*nce Upon a Time

This activity presents a number of well-known fairy tales. They will help you understand the common structure used when writing a fairy tale.

1. Select and read some original fairy tales.

2. Compare these stories in order to extract the main characteristics of fairy tales:
   ○ The setting, including the scenery and the landscape depicted through both the words and illustrations:
     – What's common and what's different?
   ○ The features of the characters:
     – How do the main characters look?
     – How do they act?
     – How do the other characters in the stories react to the main characters?
   ○ The conflict and the resolution:
     – How do the characters try to solve the problem?
     – What is the sequence of actions?

3. Complete the handout.

4. Share your answers with your partner.

Smile!

To All the Princesses Out There...

A frog and a toad share similarities, of course, but to the eye of an expert, they are two very different creatures. A clear distinction is given below for all the princesses out there who really need to know the difference.

• A frog tends to be moist and slimy, and it jumps.

• A toad tends to be dry and warty, and it walks.

• A group of frogs is called an **army** and a group of toads is called a **knot**.

So princesses everywhere, beware! Watch who – or rather what – you kiss!

The Characteristics of a Fairy Tale

THE SETTING

Stories are part of oral tradition and, as such, most fairy tales happened a long time ago in a fantastic and magical world – wherever that is – in the presence of royalty, with a beautiful princess and a handsome prince.

The setting situates the readers as to **when** and **where** the story takes place. It gives indications about **time** and **place**.

> A fairy tale usually begins with "*Once upon a time...*" or "*Long ago and far away...*"
>
> Therefore, most fairy tales are written in the past tense.

THE CHARACTERS

In every fairy tale, the characters are always either **good** or **evil**. There is a **hero** and a **villain**. They have magical powers or get help from magical creatures like elves, witches or fairies.

Honesty is rewarded and foolishness or evil is punished.

> And, of course, the good character always wins.
>
> That's a must!

THE CONFLICT AND THE RESOLUTION

Fairy tales have a problem that needs to be solved. It often takes three attempts to solve it.

Just think of the story *The Three Little Pigs*...

> And, the villain always loses.

THE ENDING

All fairy tales teach a lesson and they all end in the same way.

> "*... and they lived happily ever after.*"
>
> That's another must!

*I*n **TASK 2**, you will have the chance to speak your mind. As children, many of us were often enchanted by the magical world of princesses and sometimes traumatized by the evil queens, wicked old witches, horrible ogres, mean giants and nasty stepmothers. But do teenagers still carry the dreams of handsome princes and living happily ever after into their adult worlds? Does the dream of a magical world still hold true today?

a Point of View

At one time or another, most girls dream of becoming a fairy princess. What about boys? Do they want to become princes?

1. Read the opinion text on the next page.
   - Do you think it was written by a man or a woman? Why?

2. Consider the author's point of view.
   - What is the author's opinion? Do you agree with it?
   - Whose point of view is expressed in the story?
   - What indicates this point of view?

3. Complete the first part of the handout.

4. Share your answers with your partner.

5. Finish completing the handout.

Ribbit

We hear a lot about the Cinderella complex and the Cinderella syndrome. What about the prince? Do people really believe that the prince has an easy time of it?

Okay, I'll admit it's cool to have all the chicks falling madly in love with you and all... But look at the price Prince Charming had to pay to hook up with Cinderella. Think of how many smelly feet and catfights he had to deal with first!

And, from a guy's point of view, do you sincerely believe a man, even a prince, wears fancy white clothes by choice? All the guys I know prefer jeans or sportswear. It's hard to imagine Prince Charming shooting baskets or hanging out or checking the oil in his car.

And, as for gallantry – opening doors, holding hands – I'm learning that girls are into that kind of stuff. "It's soooo romantic," they say. But, believe me, it's not always that easy. The last time I offered to carry a girl's books, I was so nervous I dropped them — in a mud puddle. And, when I offered my hand to help my date up a high step, my palm was so sweaty it felt like a slimy fish. Talk about romantic...

I think that at one time or another, all girls probably dream of being a princess swept off her feet by a handsome prince. I also think that, like me, a lot of guys do, of course, want the beautiful princess. But somehow, at the same time, they wish that they could remain a frog a little while longer.

chicks: girls, women (*informal speech*).

to hook up with: to connect with; to get together with.

gallantry: acting with courtesy.

What a Perspective!

A Question of Opinion

- According to you, boys, is it true that girls still dream of living the life of a princess? Do you want them to?

- And what about you, girls? Do you expect boys to behave like princes? Or are those days gone forever?

Great! Finally someone has had the guts to share an honest opinion on this delicate question of relationships between boys and girls. What's your opinion on the subject?

1. Use the text and the elements of discussion from Activity 1.
   - How do you perceive the gender roles presented in fairy tales?
   - Have they influenced men and women's roles today in any way?
   - Have the gender roles presented in fairy tales had any influence at all on you?

2. Discuss the questions in the Talk About It! box.

3. Complete the first part of the handout.

4. Share your answers with your partner.

5. Finish completing the handout.

Not quite sure how to discuss this?
Have a look at *How to Participate in a Discussion* in the Toolkit, p. 268.

Smile!

The Frog and the Princess

Once upon a time, in a land far away, a beautiful, independent, self-assured princess happened upon a frog as she sat contemplating ecological issues on the banks of an unpolluted pond in a verdant meadow near her castle.

The frog hopped into the princess' lap and said, "Elegant lady, I was once a handsome prince, until an evil witch cast a spell upon me. One kiss from you, however, and I will turn back into the dapper, young prince that I am. And then, my sweet, we can marry and set up housekeeping in my castle with my mother, where you can prepare my meals, clean my clothes, bear my children and forever feel grateful and happy doing so."

That night, the princess dined sumptuously on a feast of lightly sautéed frog legs seasoned in a white wine and shallot cream sauce.

> Whose point of view is presented here?

Culture

BTW...

What's the meaning of *protagonist* and *antagonist*?

Protagonist refers to the main character or the central figure of a story. The protagonist is not always the hero of the story, but the story is always about the protagonist. Usually, there is only one protagonist in a story, but in some cases, there can be more than one.

Protagonist comes from the Greek *protos* (meaning first), not from the Latin prefix *pro-*, as many people think.

Antagonist refers to a character or characters against whom the protagonist must contend. Antagonists are major characters whose values and behaviours are in conflict with the main character. Antagonists are not necessarily human.

For Fun and Practice

- Make a class list of popular fairy tales.
- Find the protagonists and antagonists in each one.
- Post the list in the classroom.

BTW: widely used acronym for **b**y **t**he **w**ay.

*Y*ou may think you know a story but, in fact, you often only know one side. **TASK 3** presents another side. You will see that perceptions are, in fact, everything. Perceptions can twist a story around in no time at all. See for yourself!

*W*hat If…

Wait a minute here! Why are stepmothers, wolves and dragons always portrayed as mean, evil, lazy characters while princes and princesses, cats and little people are portrayed as nice, intelligent, lovable characters? Let's change the course of action of some well-known stories. Let's play with the parts a little and show how changing a few elements could, in fact, turn the whole story around.

1. Read the proposed changes below.

2. Select one.

3. Imagine a different ending for the story keeping in mind the proposed changes.

4. Complete the handout.

What if, in the story…

Goldilocks and the Three Bears, the main character, Goldilocks, was actually a spoiled brat?

What if, in the story…

Snow White and the Seven Dwarfs, the Queen just happened to be the nicest person in the whole world?

What if, in the story…

Peter Pan, Peter fell in love with Wendy and wanted to spend the rest of his life with her?

What if, in the story…

Cinderella, the glass slipper fit one of the stepsisters?

What if, in the story…

Hansel and Gretel, the children had found their way home very quickly?

What if, in the story…

The Beauty and the Beast, the Beauty was in fact ugly?

---

spoiled brat: ill-natured child who gets everything he or she wants.

𝒶 Twist of Fate

A wolf has been accused of killing – or I should say eating – three pigs. This activity presents the other side of the traditional fairy tale we know. This time you will get the wolf's version. Let's hear it from Alexander the Wolf himself.

1. Read the story below.

2. Focus on how this version differs from the traditional one.
   ○ What stereotypes and perceptions are portrayed in this story?
   ○ How do they compare with those in the original version?
   ○ What's the same? What's different?

3. Complete the handout.

The True Story of the Three Little Pigs!

By A. Wolf

As told to Jon Scieszka

"Everybody knows the story of the Three Little Pigs. Or at least they think they do. But I'll let you in on a little secret. Nobody knows the real story, because nobody has ever heard *my* side of the story. I'm the wolf. Alexander T. Wolf. You can call me Al. I don't know how this whole Big Bad Wolf thing got started, but it's all wrong. Maybe it's because of our diet. Hey, it's not my fault wolves eat cute little animals like bunnies and sheep and pigs. That's just the way we are. If cheeseburgers were cute, folks would probably think you were Big and Bad, too.

THIS IS THE REAL STORY.

Way back in Once Upon a Time time, I was making a birthday cake for my dear old granny. I had a terrible sneezing cold. I ran out of sugar. So I walked down the street to ask my neighbor for a cup of sugar. Now this neighbor was a pig. And he wasn't too bright, either. He had built his whole house out of straw. Can you believe it? I mean who in his

—————

to run out of: to be missing something.

right mind would build a house of straw? So of course the minute I knocked on the door, it fell right in. I didn't want to just walk into someone else's house. So I called, "Little Pig, Little Pig, are you in?" No answer. I was just about to go home without the cup of sugar for my dear old granny's birthday cake.

That's when my nose started to itch. I felt a sneeze coming on. Well I huffed. And I snuffed.

And you know what? The whole darn straw house fell down. And right in the middle of the pile of straw was the First Little Pig — dead as a doornail. He had been home the whole time. It seemed like a shame to leave a perfectly good ham dinner lying there in the straw. So I ate it up. Think of it as a big cheeseburger just lying there. I was feeling a little better. But I still didn't have my cup of sugar. So I went to the next neighbor's house. This neighbor was the First Little Pig's brother. He was a little smarter, but not much. He had built his house of sticks. I rang the bell on the stick house. Nobody answered. I called, "Mr. Pig, Mr. Pig, are you in?" He yelled back, "Go away Wolf. You can't come in. I'm shaving the hairs on my chinny chin chin."

I had just grabbed the doorknob when I felt another sneeze coming on. I huffed. And I snuffed. And I tried to cover my mouth, but I sneezed a great sneeze.

to huff: to blow.

to snuff: to inhale through the nose (like sniff).

And you're not going to believe it, but this guy's house fell down just like his brother's. When the dust cleared, there was the Second Little Pig – dead as a doornail. Wolf's honor. Now you know food will spoil if you just leave it out in the open. So I did the only thing there was to do. I had dinner again. Think of it as a second helping. I was getting awfully full. But my cold was feeling a little better. And I still didn't have that cup of sugar for my dear old granny's birthday cake. So I went to the next house. This guy was the First and Second Little Pig's brother. He must have been the brains of the family. He had built his house of bricks. I knocked on the brick house. No answer. I called, "Mr. Pig, Mr. Pig, are you in?" And do you know what that rude little porker answered? "Get out of here, Wolf. Don't bother me again."

Talk about impolite! He probably had a whole sackful of sugar. And he wouldn't give me even one little cup for my dear sweet old granny's birthday cake. What a pig!

I was just about to go home and maybe make a nice birthday card instead of a cake, when I felt my cold coming on. I huffed. And I snuffed. And I sneezed once again.

Then the Third Little Pig yelled, "And your old granny can sit on a pin!" Now I'm usually a pretty calm fellow. But when somebody talks about my granny like that, I go a little crazy. When the cops drove up, of course I was trying to break down this Pig's door. And the whole time I was huffing and puffing and sneezing and making a real scene. The rest, as they say, is history.

The news reporters found out about the two pigs I had for dinner. They figured a sick guy going to borrow a cup of sugar didn't sound very exciting.

So they jazzed up the story with all of that "Huff and puff and blow your house down."

And they made me the Big Bad Wolf. That's it. The real story. I was framed.

But maybe you could loan me a cup of sugar.

---

second helping: second portion.

to sit on a pin: to go to hell.

to jazz up: to embellish.

to frame someone: to make up evidence or to incriminate falsely.

Culture

Jon Scieszka (pronounced Sheh-ska; it rhymes with fresca) was born in Michigan in 1954. He attended military school and began studying medicine before becoming a teacher. Then he became an author. Most of his books are fractured fairy tales that present a different point of view. He says that he writes because he "love[s] to make kids laugh."

August 26, 2006

Éditions Grand Duc
955 Bergar Street
Laval, QC H7L 4Z6

Dear Authors,

As soon as I learned that you were preparing a unit on fairy tales for your English book *Connecting Through English*, I knew that I had to write to you. The object of my letter is very clear: to make sure that you give wolves fair treatment in your unit.

Throughout fairy-tale history, wolves have been given a bum rap. They are always portrayed as evil; however, things are not always as they seem. Here are two classic examples.

First of all, *Little Red Riding Hood*... She was supposedly tricked by a mean old wolf, but what was a child her age doing in the woods alone? What responsible parents would send their young daughter on such a dangerous errand? And, what was she doing talking to strangers anyway? Wasn't she taught anything? You can't blame the wolf for being hungry; that's not a crime...

Then, there's the case of the wolf in the *Three Little Pigs*. The Big Bad Wolf, he's called. In this story, he was definitely framed. Just ask his lawyer; all the proof is there.

Please promise me that in your unit you will give wolves a fighting chance and that, if possible, you will publish this letter.

Thank you for your attention.

Yours truly,
Douglas D. Fender

P.S.: Giants are often mistreated as well, but that's another story! Good day!
D.D.F.

bum rap: unfairly given a bad reputation.

errand: short trip taken to perform a specified task, usually for another person.

WRITE A LETTER

> • Write the complete date, including the **month**, **day** and **year**.
> • Write **the address**.
>   – Put a comma after the city.
>   – Use the official two-letter abbreviation for the province.

1 | Heading

2 | Greeting

> • Skip a few lines before writing the GREETING.
>
> *Examples:* Dear _____,
>   Mr. + a man's name
>   Ms. + a woman's name
>   Dear Sir, Dear Madam:
>
> *(for someone you don't know)*

3 | Body

- In the introduction, state the purpose of your letter.
- In the next paragraphs, give explanations and arguments.
- In the last paragraph, summarize what you wish to accomplish by writing the letter.

> *BODY*
> This is the main part of the letter. It is the message.

4 | Closing

> *CLOSING*
> Depending on to whom you are writing, the closing will vary.
>
> *Examples:* Sincerely,
>   Your friend,
>   With love,
>   (or something creative)
>
> Capitalize only the first word and put a comma at the end.

5 | Signature

> Remember to sign your name under the CLOSING.

> *Did you forget to write something? If so, add a postscript by writing P.S. followed by your final message. Sign your initials to show that it comes from you.*

---

purpose: reason; intention.

Now it's your turn to write a letter in which you will present the point of view of an antagonist, a minor character or even an object. In the **FINAL TASK**, you will express a new side of a well-known story.

Twist and Turns

At the time the authors wrote their tales, they couldn't have had a clue as to how our society would evolve. They couldn't know, for example, how the roles of men and women would change. As a final task, you will write a letter to the person or character of your choice to express a different point of view – your point of view – on one aspect presented in one of the fairy tales read during this unit.

1. Reread the letter on page 102.

2. Determine whose point of view you wish to present in your letter.

3. Decide to whom you will write your letter.

4. Follow the guidelines on the handout to help you structure your ideas and organize your letter.

5. Use the various tools presented in this unit to help you compose your letter.

6. Don't be afraid to consult others as you go along.

Culture

The First Little Pig Wasn't So Dumb After All!

Guess what? An architect has recently turned to building houses using... straw! That's right, the same material used by the first little pig in the famous fairy tale. Straw has actually been proven to be environmentally friendly and very energy efficient, and it is now considered a great material to use as insulation. It took us over 100 years to reach the conclusion the first little pig had all along. I guess we could say that this first little pig, who is generally considered the least intelligent brother of the three, was definitely a visionary.

SAY AND TELL

"Say" and "tell" have similar meanings. They are both used to report speech.

Here is a simple way to use them correctly:

- *You **say** something **to** someone.*
- *You **tell** someone something.*

SAY
To say something
Say is followed immediately by a noun clause or a direct quote.
Examples: The third pig **said** that he saw the wolf. The third pig **said**, "I saw the wolf."
To say something to someone
Say is followed by "to" and a person. This is known as reported speech.
Example: He **says to his brother** that he has seen the wolf.

TELL
To tell someone something
It can also be used for a direct quote, but you must mention the person who is being addressed.
Example: The third pig **told his brother**, "I saw the wolf."
To tell someone something
Tell is also used for reported speech, but there is no "to."
Example: He **tells his brother** that he has seen the wolf.
"Tell" is also used to give instructions.
Example: He **told** him how to build his house.

For Fun and Practice

Hear the Voices

1. Work with a partner.
2. Take turns reading the quotations out loud. Tell each other who said these quotes and, if possible, to whom they were addressed by using "say" and "tell" properly.

   - "Let me in. Let me in or I'll huff and I'll puff and I'll blow your house in!"
   - "Grandmother, what big eyes you have!"
   - "Oh dear! Oh dear! I shall be late!"
   - "Someone's been eating my porridge and he ate it all up!"

The Writing Process

PREPARING TO WRITE

●

Be clear about the message in the letter you want to send (the purpose)
and to whom you are sending it (the targeted audience).

●

Brainstorm with others for additional ideas.

●

Do more research and take notes.

●

Organize the information into an outline on the handout.

WRITING THE DRAFT(S)

●

Concentrate on getting your ideas on paper;
don't worry about mistakes yet.

●

Find and add information to support your opinion.

REVISING

●

Ask someone to give you feedback on:
- The format of the text
- The task requirements
- The logical presentation of the information
- Other words you could use
- The variety of sentences used

●

Make changes taking the feedback into account.
In case of doubt, ask for a second opinion.

Revising vs. Editing

We **revise** a text for clarity, organization and ideas.

We **edit** a text for spelling and grammar.

EDITING

●

Ask someone to give you feedback on:
- Punctuation
- Spelling
- Choice of verb tenses
- Use of prepositions
- Etc.

●

Make proper corrections to your text.

PUBLISHING

●

Make a polished copy.

How to...

PEER EDIT

One good reason for using peer editing or small group editing is to get feedback – helpful feedback! Here's how to go about it.

TO GIVE FEEDBACK:

Listen *carefully:*
- *Don't interrupt*
- *If necessary, take notes*

Give feedback:
- *Use a checklist*
- *Mention strong points*
- *Offer suggestions*

Avoid:
- *Negative comments*
- *Automatic stamp of approval*
- *Getting off track*

TO RECEIVE FEEDBACK:

Read *your text to your partner.*

Listen *carefully:*
- *Don't interrupt*
- *Take notes*

Ask for help:
- *Ask for clarification if necessary*
- *Ask for help with specific things*
- *Don't make excuses*
- *Be open to the possibility of change*

Remember the goal:
To produce the best text possible

I really like your arguments. They support your opinion... You forgot to write a closing.

Thanks for the feedback!

The Paper Bag Princess
by Robert Munsch

Elizabeth was a beautiful princess. She lived in a castle and had expensive princess clothes. She was going to marry a prince named Ronald.

Unfortunately, a dragon smashed her castle, burned all her clothes with his fiery breath, and carried off Prince Ronald.

Elizabeth decided to chase the dragon and get Ronald back.

She looked everywhere for something to wear, but the only thing she could find that was not burnt was a paper bag. So she put on the paper bag and followed the dragon.

He was easy to follow, because he left a trail of burnt forests and horses' bones.

Finally, Elizabeth came to a cave with a large door that had a huge knocker on it. She took hold of the knocker and banged on the door.

The dragon stuck his nose out of the door and said, "Well, a princess! I love to eat princesses, but I have already eaten a whole castle today. I am a very busy dragon. Come back tomorrow."

He slammed the door so fast that Elizabeth almost got her nose caught.

Elizabeth grabbed the knocker and banged on the door again.

The dragon stuck his nose out of the door and said, "Go away. I love to eat princesses, but I have already eaten a whole castle today. I am a very busy dragon. Come back tomorrow."

"Wait," shouted Elizabeth. "Is it true that you are the smartest and fiercest dragon in the whole world?"

"Yes," said the dragon.

"Is it true," said Elizabeth, "that you can burn up ten forests with your fiery breath?"

"Oh, yes," said the dragon, and he took a huge, deep breath and breathed out so much fire that he burnt up fifty forests.

"Fantastic," said Elizabeth, and the dragon took another huge breath and breathed

---

breath: air that is inhaled and exhaled through respiration.
knocker: device (usually metal and ornamental) used to knock on doors.

out so much fire that he burnt up one hundred forests.

"Magnificent," said Elizabeth, and the dragon took another huge breath, but this time nothing came out. The dragon didn't even have enough fire left to cook a meatball.

Elizabeth said, "Dragon, is it true that you can fly around the world in just ten seconds?"

"Why, yes," said the dragon, and jumped up and flew all the way around the world in just ten seconds.

He was very tired when he got back, but Elizabeth shouted, "Fantastic, do it again!"

So the dragon jumped up and flew around the whole world in just twenty seconds.

When he got back he was too tired to talk, and he lay down and went straight to sleep. Elizabeth whispered, very softly, "Hey, dragon." The dragon didn't move at all.

She lifted up the dragon's ear and put her head right inside. She shouted as loud as she could, "Hey, dragon!"

The dragon was so tired he didn't even move.

Elizabeth walked right over the dragon and opened the door to the cave.

There was Prince Ronald. He looked at her and said, "Elizabeth, you are a mess! You smell like ashes, your hair is all tangled and you are wearing a dirty old paper bag. Come back when you are dressed like a real princess."

"Ronald," said Elizabeth, "your clothes are really pretty and your hair is very neat. You look like a real prince, but you are a bum."

They didn't get married after all.

Culture

Robert Munsch is a well-known Canadian author who loves storytelling. Munsch has published dozens and dozens of books in many different languages. His stories tend to challenge perceptions and stereotypes.

o Do you consider this story a fairy tale? Why or why not?

---

to shout: to speak very loudly.

to whisper: to say something softly in a very low voice.

mess: not arranged.

Cinderella

January 19

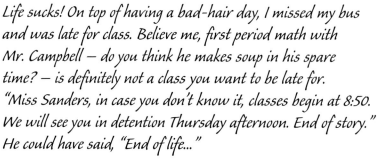

Dear Diary,

Life sucks! On top of having a bad-hair day, I missed my bus and was late for class. Believe me, first period math with Mr. Campbell — do you think he makes soup in his spare time? — is definitely not a class you want to be late for. "Miss Sanders, in case you don't know it, classes begin at 8:50. We will see you in detention Thursday afternoon. End of story." He could have said, "End of life..."

I also had a stupid fight with Molly, and now she's not speaking to me. I feel so bad. So much for best friends!

And, to top it off, I forgot to put Sherman in the basement before I left for school. You wouldn't believe the mess he made! Not to mention the big hole he chewed in Mom's brand new angora sweater. She went ballistic! "Laurie, how many times do I have to tell you... If you want a dog, you have to learn how to... etc., etc. When are you going to learn some responsibility? You're grounded*."*

Whatever. Maybe she should just lock me in the basement with Sherman. No, but she's always on my case *for something. "Laurie, let the dog out. Laurie, the dishwasher needs emptying. Laurie, could you please..."* Nag, *nag, nag. Maybe from now on, I'll just answer to Cinderella... Whatever happened to fairy godmothers and magic wands anyway? Where's the Prince Charming that's supposed to come and rescue me?... So much*

---

grounded: punished by not being allowed to go out socially.

on someone's case: after someone for something.

to nag: to be on someone's case; to annoy or to find fault with constantly.

for fairy tales and all that *crap* about high school being the best days of your life...

Cinderella, formerly known as Laurie

January 21

Dear Diary,

Well, I made it through detention this afternoon. Actually, it was kind of fun. Carey, this new kid, was also there. He's so-oo-oo cute! Every time he looked at me I almost died. I'm sure my face was beet red... Oops, gotta run! The nag's calling me to set the table for supper. Here we go again!

Cinderella

January 29

Dear Diary,

Guess what! Today after history class, Carey asked me to the school dance! I still don't believe it!!! It isn't exactly the glass slipper ball, but wow! I'm sooo excited!!! Tomorrow Mom and I are going shopping and I'm getting my hair cut and Molly's coming over and we're going to do each other's nails and...

Wow! I feel like I've been *sprinkled* with *stardust*! Think I'll go see if Mom needs any help with supper.

Later!

L.

○ What is the twist in this story?

---

crap: ridiculously false statement; bull; bunk (*very informal*).
to sprinkle: to scatter particles on.
stardust: magic or romance.

Unit 4 ■ Once Upon Another Time

111

 Goldilocks with a Twist

Hold on a second! Read this version of the story and tell me if your perception of Goldilocks has changed.

Goldilocks and the Three Bears
by Roald Dahl

This famous wicked little tale
Should never have been put on sale.
It is a mystery to me
Why loving parents cannot see
That this is actually a book
About a brazen little crook.
Had I the chance I wouldn't fail
To clap young Goldilocks in jail.
Now just imagine how *you'd* feel
If you had cooked a lovely meal,
Delicious porridge, steaming hot,
Fresh coffee in the coffee-pot,
With maybe toast and marmalade,
The table beautifully laid,
One place for you and one for dad,
Another for your little lad.
Then dad cries, "Golly-gosh! Gee-whizz!
"Oh cripes! How hot this porridge is!
"Let's take a walk along the street
"Until it's cool enough to eat."
He adds, "An early morning stroll
"Is good for people on the whole.
"It makes your appetite improve
"It also helps your bowels to move."
No proper wife would dare to question
Such a sensible suggestion,
Above all not at breakfast-time

When men are seldom at their prime.
No sooner are you down the road
Than Goldilocks, that little toad,
That nosey thieving little louse,
Comes sneaking in your empty house.
She looks around. She quickly notes
Three bowls brimful of porridge oats.
And while still standing on her feet,
She grabs a spoon and starts to eat.
I say again, how *would* you feel
If you had made this lovely meal
And some delinquent little tot
Broke in and gobbled up the lot?
But wait! That's not the worst of it!
Now comes the most distressing bit.
You are of course a houseproud wife,
And all your happy married life
You have collected lovely things
Like gilded cherubs wearing wings,
And furniture by Chippendale
Bought at some famous auction sale.
But your most special valued treasure,
The piece that gives you endless pleasure,
Is one small children's dining-chair,
Elizabethan, very rare.
It is in fact your joy and pride,
Passed down to you on grandma's side.

---

wicked: evil, cruel.
brazen little crook: shameless young criminal.

---

nosey: too curious.
thieving: adjective for someone who steals.

But Goldilocks, like many freaks,
Does not appreciate antiques.
She doesn't care, she doesn't mind,
And now she plonks her fat behind
Upon this dainty precious chair,
And crunch! It busts beyond repair.
A nice girl would at once exclaim,
"Oh dear! Oh heavens! What a shame!"
Not Goldie. She begins to swear.
She bellows, "What a lousy chair!"
And uses *one* disgusting word
That luckily you've never heard.
(I dare not write it, even hint it.
Nobody would ever print it.)
You'd think by now this little skunk
Would have the sense to do a bunk.
But no. I very much regret
She hasn't nearly finished yet.
Deciding she would like a rest,
She says, "Let's see which bed is best."
Upstairs she goes and tries all three.
(Here comes the next catastrophe.)
Most educated people choose
To rid themselves of socks and shoes
Before they clamber into bed.
But Goldie didn't give a shred.
Her filthy shoes were thick with grime,
And mud and mush and slush and slime.
Worse still, upon the heel of one
Was something that a dog had done.
I say once more, what *would* you think
If all this horrid dirt and stink

Was smeared upon your eiderdown
By this revolting little clown?
(The famous story has no clues
To show the girl removed her shoes.)
Oh, what a tale of crime on crime!
Let's check it for a second time.
Crime One, the prosecution's case:
She breaks and enters someone's place.
Crime Two, the prosecutor notes:
She steals a bowl of porridge oats.
Crime Three: She breaks a precious chair
Belonging to the Baby Bear.
Crime Four: She smears each spotless sheet
With filthy messes from her feet.
A judge would say without a blink,
"Ten years hard labour in the clink!"
But in the book, as you will see,
The little beast gets off scot-free,
While tiny children near and far
Shout, "Goody-good! Hooray! Hurrah!"
"Poor darling Goldilocks!" they say,
"Thank goodness that she got away!"
Myself, I think I'd rather send
Young Goldie to a sticky end.
"Oh daddy!" cried the Baby Bear,
"My porridge gone! It isn't fair!"
"Then go upstair," the Big Bear said,
"Your porridge is upon the bed.
"But as it's inside mademoiselle,
"You'll have to eat *her* up as well."

---

lousy: in poor condition.
skunk: mean, unworthy person; a rat (*slang*).
bunk: to leave in a hurry (*British slang*).
to not give a shred: to not care in the least.

eiderdown: a quilt made with goose feathers.
clink: prison.
scot-free: totally without punishment or consequences.

Culture

Roald Dahl (1916–1990)

Roald Dahl was a prolific British author born of Norwegian parents. At home he spoke Norwegian and his mother often told his sisters and him tales of Norwegian trolls and other mythical creatures.

Dahl is famous for his novels and short stories for both children and adults.
His works for children are generally told from a child's point of view. They often involve an adult villain who hates children, but they usually also contain at least one good adult to counteract this villain.

Dahl was the author of the script of the well-known James Bond movie *You Only Live Twice* and the stories behind the films *Charlie and the Chocolate Factory* and *James and the Giant Peach*, among others.

In addition to being a writer, Dahl was a pilot in the Royal Air Force in World War II. He was married to the American actress Patricia Neal, with whom he had five children. He died of leukemia at home on November 23, 1990.

OTHER THINGS TO DO

1 Turn *The True Story of the Three Little Pigs* or another fairy tale into a play or a trial.

3 Write your own fairy tale to portray specific stereotypes or an original point of view.

2 Draw a comparison between the traditional version of the fairy tale *Cinderella* and the movie *Ever After*.

4 Practise storytelling. Record a favourite fairy tale for a younger audience.

Look Back

Look back at the illustration on pages 88-89. You should now be able
to locate and explain some of the stereotypes presented.

Think About...

○ Think about all the stereotypes and perceptions seen and discussed.

- You should be able to identify a few and talk briefly about those that
  you find in fairy tales and the media.

- You should be able to make the distinction between a protagonist
  and an antagonist.

○ Think about how your own perceptions influence your decisions.

Now What?

○ Can you answer the questions on page 89?

○ At this point, are you able to recognize the stereotypes and perceptions
depicted in stories and differentiate fiction from reality?

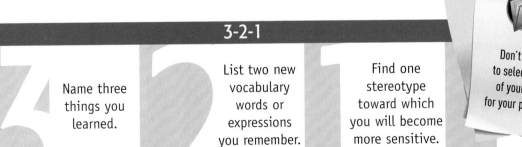

3-2-1

Name three things you learned.	List two new vocabulary words or expressions you remember.	Find one stereotype toward which you will become more sensitive.

Don't forget
to select some
of your work
for your portfolio!

UNIT 5

In White Ink

IN THIS UNIT...

In this unit, you will explore Black history in a Canadian context and beyond. You will learn how to organize an information log. As a final task, you will reinvest your knowledge and challenge your classmates with the game "Freedom Bound."

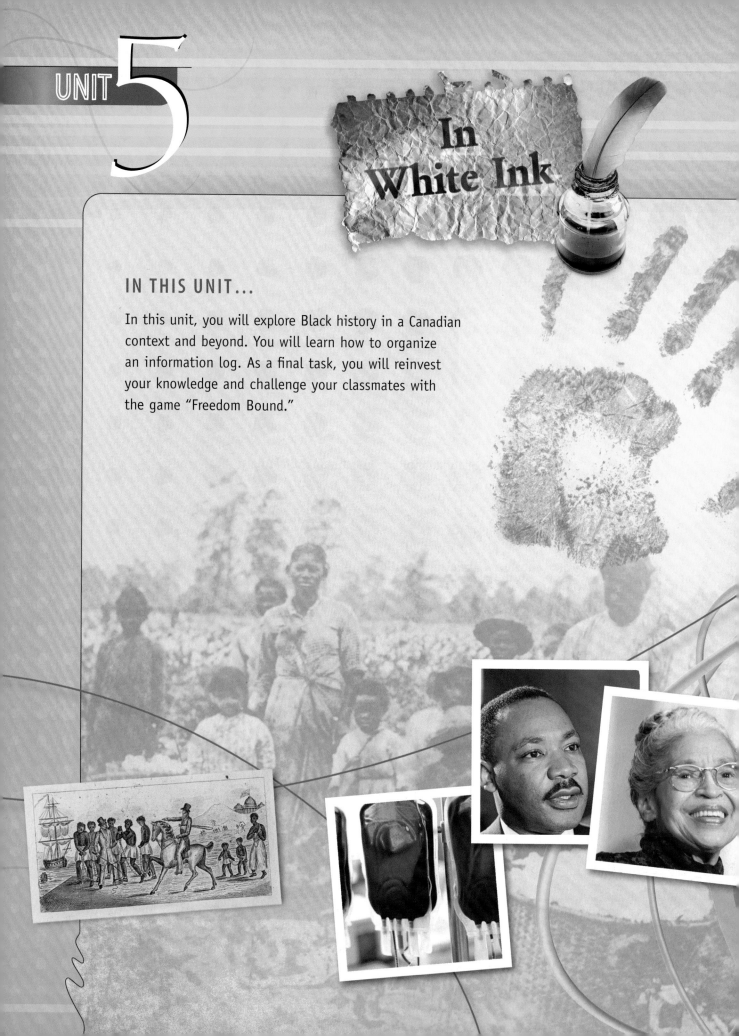

Guiding Questions

○ What do you know about Black history?

○ How can learning about Black history help cultivate a culture of peace?

In **TASK 1**, you will begin exploring Black history and some of the contributions made to Canadian society and the world by members of the Black community.

Did you know that there have been inventors, scientists, explorers, historians, artists, athletes, politicians, translators, teachers, educators, musicians, writers, mathematicians and astronomers of African heritage? In this task, you will become familiar with some of these people and their stories.

Forgotten Portraits

Get ready to discover some facts about Black history. Take the "Did you know that...?" quiz and start exploring. You will uncover a lot of new information.

Making Sense of the Title of This Unit

If you use white ink to write on white paper, then you see nothing: the words are invisible. This image helps us to understand how Black history has been neglected. Although it exists, we could not see it. Together we will uncover some of that hidden history.

1. First look at the pictures. They all depict people who have played a role in Canada's history.
   ○ Which ones do you know?

2. Take the quiz.

3. Write your answers on the handout.

4. Compare your answers with a classmate.

Don't worry if you don't know the answers. These facts are part of our missing heritage. The stories are real, but they have been written in white ink...

By the end of the unit, you will be able to pass this quiz with flying colours!

Did You Know That…?

1. …a black man was interpreter to Samuel de Champlain in the early 1600s?

2. …a woman escaped slavery and became a "conductor" on the Underground Railroad?

3. …a Montreal slave lit a fire that burnt down part of the city in 1734?

4. …an African-American Arctic explorer was one of the first people to reach the North Pole?

5. …an African-Canadian inventor patented over 57 inventions in his lifetime?

6. …an African-American scientist, who studied at McGill University in Montreal, found a way to preserve and store blood?

7. …one of Canada's legendary cowboys was a former slave?

8. …an escaped slave became the first female police officer in Canada?

9. …something called the "colour barrier" blocked Blacks from playing professional sports until this man struck down that barrier in 1946?

10. …the first female newspaper publisher in North America was African-American?

11. …an African-Canadian woman, the first black woman elected to Parliament, also successfully petitioned the Canadian government to recognize February as Black History Month. It became official in 1995.

12. …a female journalist from Radio-Canada was the first person of African-Caribbean heritage to serve as Governor General of Canada?

---

to patent: to obtain recognition and protection as the inventor of something.

to store: to put away and save for another time.

ACTIVITY 2

In Black Ink

Find the answers to the quiz. Learn about people who accomplished great things.

1. Read the twelve following texts. Each text contains clues that should enable you to match it to the previous quiz question.

2. Work together to match each text to one of the quiz questions.

3. Write your answers on the handout.

4. Go back and have another look at the pictures. Can you now match faces to stories?

A **Michaëlle Jean** was born in Port-au-Prince, Haïti, in 1957. Her family moved to Quebec in 1968 to escape the violence of the dictator Francois (Papa Doc) Duvalier. Jean studied at the Université de Montréal. She is fluent in five languages. She has worked in the field of journalism as a TV anchor, reporter, broadcaster and documentary filmmaker.

B **Matthew Henson** left the U.S. capital Washington, D.C. when he was only 12 years old. He was so determined to get a job on a ship that he told the captain he was an orphan. He was hired as a cabin boy. He learned about math, navigation, history, map reading and more. Henson became a remarkable man, well loved for his exceptional kindness. He developed a special rapport with the Inuit people of the Canadian North, who referred to him as "Matthew the Kind One," and became something of a legend.

C **Mathieu Da Costa** played an important role in the early exploration of Canada. There is not very much historical evidence, but we know that he was a free Black man who worked as a translator and interpreter for both the French and the Dutch during voyages to North America. He spoke several languages, including French, Dutch, Portuguese and Mi'kmaq, an Eastern Algonquian language still spoken in Canada's Maritime provinces.

---

fluent: able to express oneself with ease.

orphan: a child whose parents are dead.

D **Marie-Joseph Angélique** was a slave in Montreal. When she learned that her master was going to sell her, she set fire to his building. In so doing, she sparked a series of other fires. She was caught, tried and convicted of arson. Her sentence included torture and death by hanging.

F **Charles R. Drew** developed the first blood plasma bank. His idea revolutionized the medical profession. It helped save innumerable lives. He became director of the first American Red Cross blood bank.

E **Jackie Robinson** was the first Black man to participate in professional sports. In 1946, he played for the Montreal Royals for one year. The next year, he moved to New York to join the Brooklyn Dodgers. He became the first African-American to play Major League Baseball. In his debut season, he was named Rookie of the Year.

G **Rose Fortune** was born into slavery in 1774. She escaped with her family when she was only 10 years old. Their escape to Canada, via New York City, led them to Nova Scotia. They settled in the town of Annapolis Royal. Fortune created and occupied the position of policewoman in the late 1700s. She had a mind for business and started a successful company that offered different services. She used a wheelbarrow to make deliveries from ships in the town port to various hotels around the city. She also offered a wake-up service to help travellers arrive on time and not miss their boats.

H **Jean Augustine** was born in Grenada and arrived in Canada in 1959. She worked for years as an elementary school principal before entering the world of politics in 1993. She was a Liberal member of the Canadian House of Commons until 2005.

---

to spark: to ignite; to set off; to cause.

to be tried: to be accused of a crime and put on trial in a court.

arson: the crime of deliberately starting a fire.

innumerable: very, very many; too many to count.

wheelbarrow: a wheeled container that can be pushed around to move heavy loads.

Harriet Tubman was born into slavery. After escaping, she decided to help others. Through a series of elaborate escape routes to the northern states and Canada, she led more than 300 slaves to freedom. She made 19 trips down south to rescue slaves. Since she helped so many people gain their freedom, she was often referred to as the "Black Moses."

> **Moses** is a key figure in the Old Testament of the Bible. He was chosen by God to free his people from slavery. He led the exodus out of Egypt.

Elijah McCoy was born in Ontario in 1843. His parents had escaped from slavery via the Underground Railroad. McCoy was a prolific inventor. His most famous invention was a lubricating system to help machines run smoothly. Other people tried to make something similar, but McCoy's invention was the best. It worked so well that people started calling it "the Real McCoy," which became a common expression used to refer to anything of very good or superior quality.

Mary Ann Shadd Cary was the first of 13 children born to Harriet and Abraham Shadd. Her father was a key figure in the Underground Railroad. When she was young, Mary Ann witnessed slavery. She was motivated and inspired by her family's dedication to freeing the slaves. She emigrated to Ontario in 1851 and became an educator. She taught the children of arriving refugees and distributed anti-slavery materials. She was an active abolitionist. She founded a newspaper called the *Provincial Freeman*. She was also a lawyer and writer.

John Ware was an ex-slave from Texas who came to Canada in the 1880s. He settled in Alberta, where he became well-known and well-respected for his skills, strength and decency. He also had the reputation of being an exceptional horseman.

---

to escape: to get free; to break loose from confinement.

to witness: to be present at something or to have personal knowledge of something.

abolitionist: someone who is against slavery and works actively to eliminate it.

to found: to establish; to bring into existence; to create and set up.

to settle: to make one's home; to establish residence.

skill: ability; talent.

Lessons Learned

So many new facts, so many incredible people! In this activity, you will share and discuss what you have just learned.

1. Stop and pause to think.

2. Reflect upon the new information you have read.
   - Are you able to make any links with things you already knew?

3. Complete the handout.

4. Share what you've learned and what you think.
   - Use the questions in the **Talk About It!** box to help you.

Talk About It!

- Which people or facts had you already heard about? Explain.
- If this is all new for you, then what bit of information surprised you most?
- What was the most interesting fact that you learned? Share your thoughts.
- Can you think of anybody to add to the list?

Culture

Two Other Black Inventors

They weren't Canadian, but you know their inventions well!

- Phillip Emeagwali, an African computer scientist, envisaged a super computer that he programmed to compute 3.1 billion calculations per second in 1989. That was a world record! It made the Internet a real possibility. This former high school dropout and war refugee from Nigeria is considered to be one of the fathers of the Internet.

Phillip Emeagwali

- Lonnie Johnson, a black engineer from Los Angeles, invented a new type of water gun. The Super Soaker® squirt gun was the first water gun to incorporate air pressure into its design. It was originally called the "Power Drencher."

---

drencher: something that wets completely (from the verb "to drench": to make completely wet; to soak).

You will be learning new information throughout this unit. In **TASK 2**, you will learn how to organize and process this information by creating an information log. Your log will be particularly helpful in the Final Task, when you play the game "Freedom Bound."

Keeping Track

One way of keeping track of lots of new information is by using an information log. An information log is a way of organizing and managing facts and ideas. It provides quick and easy access to selected information. Writing down information also helps us remember it.

1. Read the **How to Start an Information Log** box on the next page.

2. Read the suggested categories on page 126.

3. Use the handout to help you begin your information log.

4. Choose at least three pieces of information for your information log.

START AN INFORMATION LOG

There are **three keys** to keeping a good information log:

1 | **Selection**
- Don't write everything.
- Choose only the information you find most **interesting** and **pertinent**.

2 | **Recording** (writing down)
- Don't copy word for word.
- Go for **keywords** rather than complete sentences.
- Get the facts right.
  - Pay special attention to **dates** and the **spelling** of proper nouns.
- Write down all **sources**.
  - It's important to know where you got your information in case you need to double-check something.

3 | **Organization**
- Use a system.
  - You want to be able to find your information easily.

Remember to keep your log up to date. It will only be useful if it is complete.

---

to double-check: to check again; to verify.

Types of Log Entries

Follow these models for your log entries:

PEOPLE

Name	full name and any nicknames or aliases
Dates	birth, death, special event or discovery
Country or nationality	where the person comes from and where he/she lived
Profession	Sometimes one person may have many jobs. Make your entries as complete as possible.
Special role	2 or 3 important reasons for remembering this person

EVENTS OR PHENOMENA

Title	name of the event or phenomenon (Example: slavery in New France)
Dates	year or month of the event or time span of the phenomenon
Country or part of the world	where it happened or started
Importance in history	2 or 3 reasons for remembering this event or phenomenon

PLACES

Title	name of city, state, province, country or continent... (Example: Washington, D.C., U.S.A.)
Dates	(Example: 1963)
Details	why this place is important and your choice of pertinent information (Example: Martin Luther King Jr. delivered his famous "I Have a Dream" speech.)

CULTURE

Name	Name of the cultural element or movement (Example: Kwanzaa)
Place	country, continent or the part of the world
Description and details	description and explanation of the cultural element

Also, remember to:

• Write neatly. Leave several lines between entries.

• Add more information as you make your way through the unit.

• Date each new entry.

Writing the Entries

When writing your entries, it is important to use the correct verb tense. This activity will help you by focusing on the two tenses that you will use most often: the **simple past** and the **present**.

1. Review the **simple past** and the **present** tenses by reading the *Focus on the Simple Past and Simple Present Tenses* box below.

2. Look at the entries in your information log.
   - Did you choose the correct tense?

3. For more practice, complete the handout.

Focus on...

THE SIMPLE PAST AND SIMPLE PRESENT TENSES

The Simple Past Tense

Since most of your entries will be about **events that happened in the past**, they will be written using the **simple past tense**.

Regular verbs	Irregular verbs
Remember that regular verbs in the simple past tense end in **ED**. *Examples:* • *Nelson Mandela **worked** for freedom and equality.* • *Elijah McCoy **invented** many useful things.*	Irregular verbs have a completely different form from the infinitive. They have to be memorized or looked up. *Examples:* • *Harriet Tubman **went** back across the border to help other slaves escape.* • *He **became** a free man.*

There is a list of irregular verbs in the Toolkit at the end of the Student Book on pages 326-327.

The Simple Present Tense

If, however, an entry is a **fact that is still true today** or one that is **recurrent**, it will be written using the **simple present tense**.

Examples: • *They <u>originate</u> from Africa.* • *He come<u>s</u> from Madagascar.* • *February <u>is</u> Black History Month.*	Don't forget to add an "**s**" to the verb in the third person singular.

Can you even begin to imagine what it was like to be a slave? In **TASK 3**, you will hear about a special escape route that led many slaves to freedom in Canada. In this task, you will also learn about the important role that music played in this quest for freedom.

ACTIVITY 1

Steal Away!

In order to escape slavery in the United States, many people used the Underground Railroad. In this activity, you will learn a little more about this incredible network.

1. Read the song, the short text on the Underground Railroad below and the text on the next page.
2. Try to imagine what it was like being a slave.
3. Complete the handout.
4. Share your thoughts and impressions with your classmates.

*POPULAR
SLAVE SONG*

*I'm on my way to Canada,
That cold and dreary land;
The dire effects of slavery
I can no longer stand...
Farewell, old master,
Don't come after me,
I'm on my way to Canada
Where coloured men are free*

Did you choose some facts for your information log?

The Underground Railroad

The Underground Railroad was a network of clandestine routes, meeting points and safe houses organized to help slaves escape the southern states of the U.S. and find liberty in the free northern states or Canada. Although the fugitives sometimes travelled on railways, the usual means of transportation was by wagon or on foot.

Such escapes were dangerous and had to be carefully planned. During the night, a "conductor" would direct runaway slaves to the next safe house. They would travel about 15 to 30 km per night. Information was passed on from "station to station" by word of mouth only.

The Underground Railroad led thousands to freedom. Because the trip was so difficult, most of the fugitives were men under the age of 40. Many of them came back later as free men to purchase their mates and family members. Thus, the Underground Railroad helped many others besides those who actually made the voyage.

Music on the Road to Freedom

Music has played a major role in Black history in North America. It has provided inspiration and distraction, and allowed messages to be transmitted secretly.

Onlookers did not suspect that the lyrics of songs might be part of a sophisticated system designed to lead slaves to freedom. Slave songs, as they were called, were perceived rather as innocent spirituals sung to summon fortitude and courage, and profess belief in a wonderful afterlife. Yet these simple songs of faith contained an essential hidden message. That message was *"Freedom now!"* Codes disguised in these songs gave instructions: when and where to escape, who to contact along the way, what to avoid and how to navigate on the road to safety.

> **Stop for a moment and imagine that you were a slave who was "freedom bound."**

Imagine that you are running for your life. Angry men and vicious dogs are hot on your trail. You need to find out quickly who's on your side. Then, you must communicate with your fellow travellers, who are also trying to escape. Remember, everything has to be in code. Every reference, every bit of information, must be kept under wraps. As an escaping slave you must decipher – and, in turn, help others decipher – the meaning hidden in seemingly simple songs. The risks are incredible!

You must learn these spirituals by rote. Clear communication, through verbal codes, could be a question of life or death, safe escape or dreadful capture. The songs are your lifeline; they connect you to both your past and future. Back in Africa, oral tradition kept culture and history alive. It ensured the transmission of knowledge and information. As you follow the road to freedom, you are keeping that oral tradition (and yourself!) alive. Remember: songs leave no tracks, no paper trail.

---

onlooker: spectator; observer.

spirituals: religious songs that are usually deeply emotional.
This type of song developed mostly in the southern United States, particularly among slaves.

to keep under wraps: to keep secret or hidden.

by rote: by heart; from memory.

dreadful: terrible; horrible; abominable.

Songs of Freedom

As you have just learned, people who took the Underground Railroad often shared information about their pathway to freedom through songs. In Activity 2, you will listen to two of these songs and look at the hidden messages they contain.

The Oral Tradition

Most slaves could not read or write; they were illiterate. In fact, it was against the law to teach slaves to read and write.

This was yet another good reason for passing messages on verbally.

1. Read the lyrics while you listen to the following songs.
  - Which words do think might be code words?
  - What do you think the hidden message is?

2. Complete your handout with a partner.

3. Compare your answers with another pair of students.

4. Share your answers with the class.

5. Listen to the songs again.
  - Have the lyrics taken on a new meaning for you?

This song gives explicit directions for slaves to follow.

Follow the Drinking Gourd

Chorus:
Follow the drinking gourd.
Follow the drinking gourd,
For the old man is waiting
for to carry you to freedom
If you follow the drinking gourd.

The riverbank will make a very good road,
The dead trees show you the way.
Left foot, peg foot traveling on,
Following the drinking gourd.
The river ends between two hills,
Follow the drinking gourd,
There's another river on the other side,
Follow the drinking gourd.

When the great big river meets the little river,
Follow the drinking gourd.
For the old man is waiting
for to carry you to freedom
If you follow the drinking gourd.

drinking gourd: name given by slaves to the Big Dipper, the familiar configuration of stars in the constellation Ursa Major.

Unit 5 ▪ In White Ink

This slave song appears to speak of the Old Testament and the Exodus. What was the hidden message?

Wade in the Water

Chorus:
Wade in the water.
Wade in the water, children.
Wade in the water.

God's gonna trouble the water.
Well, who are these children all dressed in red?
God's a-gonna trouble the water
Must be the children that Moses led
God's a-gonna trouble the water.
(Repeat the Chorus)

Who's that young girl dressed in white
Wade in the Water
Must be the Children of Israelites
God's gonna trouble the Water.
(Repeat the Chorus)

Jordan's water is chilly and cold.
God's gonna trouble the water.
It chills the body, but not the soul.
God's gonna trouble the water.
(Repeat the Chorus)

If you get there before I do.
God's gonna trouble the water.
Tell all of my friends I'm coming too.
God's gonna trouble the water.
(Repeat the Chorus)

Culture

The Influence of Slave Songs

The repetition of words in a song, called the refrain or the chorus, dates back to the time of the Underground Railroad. The "call and response" method of singing used in slave songs is still popular today. Rhythmic sounds mixed with different chants can be found in both blues and jazz. Early R&B, followed by soul and funk, all show similar rhythmic roots. So do rap and hip hop. In fact, modern contemporary music owes a debt of gratitude to the slave song and its African origins.

R&B: usual way of referring to **R**hythm **and** **B**lues music.

TASK 4

I n **TASK 4**, you will continue your journey into the past. Starting with the advent of slavery, you will get a brief overview of 600 years of history. Certain key figures, events and phenomena will be presented. Modern-day heroes will then point to the future and you will be asked to envisage a better world and share a dream for the times ahead.

ACTIVITY 1

Imprints of Time

This overview of 600 years of Black history will help you gain some perspective by situating several major events on a timeline. It will be up to you to add the latest information.

1. Scan the timeline for keywords and names.
2. Take a few minutes to look at the handout before the listening activity.
   - What information do you think you will be asked to find?
   - How can you get ready to listen?
3. Listen to the script.
4. Complete the handout.

1444 The era of slavery begins. Tens of millions of Africans are enslaved by both Europeans and their fellow Africans. They are brought by force to the Americas and sold into slavery.

1605 First Black presence on record in Canada. Mathieu Da Costa accompanies Samuel de Champlain as an interpreter and translator.

1628 First recorded slave purchase in New France: Olivier Le Jeune, a six-year-old boy from Madagascar.

---

enslave: to capture and take into slavery; to make someone a slave.

fellow: belonging to the same group.

TASK 4

I n **TASK 4**, you will continue your journey into the past. Starting with the advent of slavery, you will get a brief overview of 600 years of history. Certain key figures, events and phenomena will be presented. Modern-day heroes will then point to the future and you will be asked to envisage a better world and share a dream for the times ahead.

ACTIVITY 1

Imprints of Time

This overview of 600 years of Black history will help you gain some perspective by situating several major events on a timeline. It will be up to you to add the latest information.

1. Scan the timeline for keywords and names.
2. Take a few minutes to look at the handout before the listening activity.
   - What information do you think you will be asked to find?
   - How can you get ready to listen?
3. Listen to the script.
4. Complete the handout.

1444 The era of slavery begins. Tens of millions of Africans are enslaved by both Europeans and their fellow Africans. They are brought by force to the Americas and sold into slavery.

1605 First Black presence on record in Canada. Mathieu Da Costa accompanies Samuel de Champlain as an interpreter and translator.

1628 First recorded slave purchase in New France: Olivier Le Jeune, a six-year-old boy from Madagascar.

---

enslave: to capture and take into slavery; to make someone a slave.

fellow: belonging to the same group.

Slavery becomes legal in New France. — **1709**

Marie-Joseph Angélique, black slave and martyr, sets fire to her owner's house. In an attempt to escape, she destroys 46 homes. She is caught, tortured and hanged. — **1734**

At the end of the American Revolution, about 3,500 Blacks flee to what is now Nova Scotia and New Brunswick. They fought for Britain in exchange for freedom and land. — **1782**

1785

The Underground Railroad is established. — **1786**

The Haitian Revolution begins as a slave uprising near Le Cap in the French West Indian colony of Santo Domingo. It leads to the establishment of the first free black nation, Haiti, in 1801. — **1791**

Official Declaration by the Attorney General of Upper Canada: all Blacks residing in Canada are free and protected by British law. — **1819**

The Life of Josiah Henson is written. It is the autobiography of the man who has been called "the most controversial former slave ever to make his way to freedom and safety in Upper Canada." — **1830**

Harriet Tubman escapes. — **1849**

Uncle Tom's Cabin is published. This novel by Harriet Beecher Stowe tells of the horrors of slavery. It is inspired by the memoirs of Josiah Henson. It sells 300,000 copies within the first year. — **1852**

1865 — Slavery is abolished in the United States.

1909 — Matthew Henson is part of the expedition that first reaches the North Pole.

1920 — Montreal's jazz scene starts to develop. Musicians from Africa, the Caribbean and South America bring the beats of the world to Montreal.

1946 — Baseball player Jackie Robinson signs with the Montreal Royals.

1963 — Martin Luther King Jr. leads a march in Washington, D.C. More than 200,000 people unite to protest against the unjust treatment of Blacks in the United States. King delivers his famous "I Have a Dream" speech.

1966 — The holiday Kwanzaa is created by Dr. Maulana Karenga, a Black Studies professor.

1990 — Nelson Mandela, who had been imprisoned in South Africa for 27 years, visits Canada shortly after his release from prison.
AND
Namibia, the last colony in Africa, becomes an independent state after nearly a century of rule by Germany and, later, South Africa. Sam Nujoma becomes the country's first President.

1996 — Donovan Bailey, a Jamaican-born Canadian athlete dominates the Olympics by winning two gold medals. He is referred to as "The World's Fastest Man." He later becomes a successful businessman.

1999 — Thabo Mbeki assumes the Presidency of South Africa from Nelson Mandela. It is the first democratic transfer of power in South Africa.

What a lot of great information to add to your log!

On this page you will find a variety of interesting facts. The information touches upon various subjects in the timeline. It has been organized into "bite size" capsules. Enjoy!

Kwanzaa is a week-long holiday observed from December 26 to January 1.

The word *kwanza* comes from the East African language of Kiswahili and means "the first" or "the first fruits of the harvest." Dr. Karenga added a second "A" at the end of the word to distinguish the holiday from the Kiswahili word.

Culture

FYI

Josiah Henson is the first black person to be featured on a Canadian postage stamp. It was a 32-cent stamp issued in 1983.

For Fun and Practice

By now, you can identify some of the people whose inventions are shown on the cover pages of the unit.

- Search the Web to find out who invented the other items.
- Share your answers with the class.

For Fun and Practice

- Find two recent events to add to the timeline.
- Share your answers with the class.

Culture

Two Little-known Facts

- People of African descent have been living in Nova Scotia for nearly 300 years. In the early to mid 1700s, more than 300 people of African descent lived at the French settlement of Louisbourg, Cape Breton. There is a notable Black presence in Acadia to this day.
- In 1783, over 5,000 Blacks left the United States. They moved to the Maritimes, Quebec and Ontario. They sided with the British during the American War of Independence and came to Canada as United Empire Loyalists. They were considered free men and women. They were promised land by the British but only got small parcels of poor-quality land or nothing at all.

SEARCH THE WEB

The easiest way to search on the Internet is to use a search engine.

Most current search engines are pretty effective and very powerful. Following these tips will help make your research even easier and more efficient.

For a simple search, identify **keywords**, **phrases** and the **subject categories** to use in your search.

- Play with your search terms.
- Think of as many ways to describe your topic as you can.
- Identify synonyms, distinctive terms and alternative spellings.

One word might be common in Canada but not necessarily in other countries.

- The Internet is international, and while your *truck* may roll on *tires*, British *lorries* roll on *tyres*.

For a more precise search, use **and**, **or** and **not**.

- Using **and** narrows the search results.

  Example: A search using the terms *black and history* will return documents that contain only both words.

- Using **or** broadens the search results.

  Example: A search using the terms *black or history* will return documents that contain either or both words. Only one of the words needs to be present to get a document.

- Using the **not** operator will drop any documents that contain the excluded term.

  Example: If you are looking for countries in West Africa (but not Senegal), write: *West Africa not Senegal*.

Use + and " "

- *slavery + Canada* will return documents that contain both words.
- Putting the term in **quotation marks** will return only documents containing **exactly** what you put in quotation marks: *"Black history"*

ACTIVITY 2

The Peaceful Struggle for Equality

Did you know that people did not always have the freedom to move around or even to sit where they wanted? Some people could not choose their own friends or even their own school. Fortunately, many brave people were determined to change things.

Sometimes simple acts of courage can change the world. Read on to discover how three people helped to change our world with dignity and without violence. These peaceful warriors never reacted with anger or violence even though they were threatened, arrested and physically mistreated. By maintaining discipline and a spirit of non-violence, they turned the violence of their opponents to their own advantage.

"When you control a man's thinking you do not have to worry about his actions."

"Father of Black History" Carter G. Woodson

1. Read the three short texts.
2. Complete the first part of the handout.
3. Share your answers with a partner.
4. Complete the rest of the handout together.

Nelson Mandela

Nelson Mandela dedicated his life to the struggle for racial equality in South Africa. He spent 27 years in prison for opposing the South African system of segregation called apartheid (a-par-tide). In 1990, he negotiated an end to apartheid. Then in 1994, he became the first-ever democratically elected president. He stepped down in 1999. He is still one of the most famous, respected and deeply loved figures in the world.

Rosa Parks

Rosa was a seamstress who lived in Montgomery, Alabama. One day after work, she was tired and decided to defy the unjust laws of the time. She refused to give up her seat on the bus to a white man. She was arrested and put in jail. Her arrest inspired people to protest. People decided

to boycott the buses until the laws were changed. The Montgomery bus boycott, led by Martin Luther King Jr., lasted for over one year. It was a powerful and peaceful way of objecting to discrimination. By refusing to ride the bus, the people of Montgomery almost put the bus company out of business. The laws were changed and Rosa Parks became "the mother of the civil rights movement."

Martin Luther King Jr.

Martin Luther King Jr. was a political activist, a minister of religion and the most famous leader of the civil rights movement. He advocated non-violence as a means of change. On August 8, 1963, Martin Luther King Jr. gave a speech that inspired a generation and the world. He spoke about a better world, a world of equality and respect. He said, "*I have a dream that my four little children will one day live in a nation where they will not be judged by the color of their skin but by the content of their character...*" Even though he always used peaceful methods, his work was ended violently when he was assassinated in 1968.

ACTIVITY **3**

"I Have a Dream"

In this activity, you will have the opportunity to listen to an excerpt from Martin Luther King Jr.'s most famous speech. Then you, too, will have the chance to express a dream for the future.

1. As a class, brainstorm about Martin Luther King Jr. and that period in history.

2. Look at the photos.
   ○ What do they tell you?

3. Listen to excerpts of Martin Luther King's famous speech.

4. Complete the handout.

5. Write about a dream you have for the future. Refer to the Write About It! box.

Write About It!

I Have A Dream That ...

1. Now it's your turn. Try to make a difference.
   • Imagine all the good things in our world.
   • Now consider the injustice that still exists.
   • What would you change?
   • What would be your dream for a better world?

2. Write a short paragraph about your dream. Remember to think beyond yourself. Consider the rights of others: basic human rights, animal rights, environmental rights.
   • What do you want to change?
   • What do you think has actually changed recently?

3. Start with "I have a dream that one day ... will ... "

4. Remember to use the future tense.

5. Express yourself. Then share your dreams with your classmates.

Martin Luther King Jr.'s famous speech

ASKING QUESTIONS USING QUESTION WORDS

Unit 2 focused on asking questions in the present tense. Asking questions in other tenses follows the same formula:

Tense	Q. word	Auxiliary	Subject	Verb	Rest of the sentence
Simple present	**What**	do	you	know	about the Underground Railroad?
Simple past	**When**	did	Nelson Mandela	come	to Montreal?
Simple future	**Where**	will	they	celebrate	Kwanzaa?
Present perfect	**How**	has	he	promoted	world peace?

Remember:

When asking questions with a question word, you **must use an auxiliary**. This auxiliary is the same one that figures in the affirmative form.

Affirmative	Interrogative
She **has** helped free many slaves.	How **has** she helped free many slaves?
We **will** understand more.	When **will** we understand more?

For questions in the **simple present** and the **simple past**, use the auxiliaries **do (does)** and **did**:

	Affirmative (no auxiliary)	Interrogative
Simple present	Slave songs influence modern music.	How **do** slave songs **influence** modern music?
Simple past	The slaves hid.	Where **did** the slaves **hide**?

EXCEPTION

When asking a question in the **simple present** or the **simple past** using the question word "**who**," there is no auxiliary:

Who	Verb	Rest of the sentence
Who	helped	many slaves escape to Canada?
Who	writes	about that in the information log?

For Fun and Practice

Read the two stories on pages 147-148. Prepare five questions about them to ask your classmates. Use a different question word for each question.

Remember, there is a list of irregular verbs in the Toolkit at the end of your Student Book, on pages 326-327.

I n this **FINAL TASK**, you will conclude your journey. As you travelled back in time, you learned many new and interesting facts. It's now time to share this knowledge and challenge your classmates. Get ready to play "Freedom Bound"!

Getting Ready to Play

Soon it will be time to test your knowledge of Black history against that of your classmates. This activity will help you prepare for this final challenge by giving you an opportunity to study your information logs and prepare questions to try and stump your opponents. Are you ready?

1. Consult your information log.

2. Take time to look through your entries. Do you have at least 12?

3. If not, go back through the unit and complete your log.

4. Look at the examples below. Think of questions you could ask. Try to use each of the "5 Ws."

5. Try to formulate clear questions that require precise answers.

6. Study your information log as preparation for playing the game.

Q Who was the Black athlete who broke down the "colour barrier"?
A (It was) Jackie Robinson.

Q What is Carter G. Woodson's middle name?
A (It is) Godwin.

Q When was slavery abolished in Canada?
A (It was abolished in Canada) in 1819.

Q Where did slaves try to escape to?
A (They tried to escape) to the northern states or Canada.

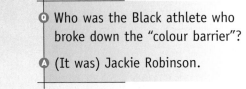

Q Why was Harriet Tubman called the "Black Moses"?
A (She was called the "Black Moses") because she helped many people escape to freedom like Moses during the exodus from Egypt.

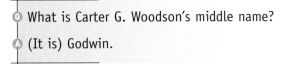

Q How did slaves escape from hound dogs?
A They waded in the water. **OR** By wading in the water.

---

to stump (your opponents): to challenge them with a question they cannot answer.

Playing the Game

The time has come to put everything you have learned into practice. Take the challenge and be "Freedom Bound"!

1. Form teams and find opponents.

2. Read the rules of the game on the next page.

3. Make sure everyone understands the rules.

4. Make sure you have everything needed to play (a pile of tokens, a die, a marker and your information logs).

5. Make sure everyone has a chance to ask and answer questions.

6. Enjoy!

Culture

FYI

Die is the singular of *dice*.

How to Play the Game

- A die
- A pile of tokens in the kitty
- Your information logs
- A marker for each person

RULES

1. This game is for two to six players. It can be played "one-on-one" or as pairs working together.

2. Roll the die to see who goes first. (The highest number wins.)

3. Turns move clockwise.

4. The first person (or team) rolls the die and counts that number of spaces on the board.

5. You may move horizontally or vertically in any direction but you must NOT retrace your steps on the same move. You may NOT move diagonally.

6. No two players may occupy the same space.

7. When you land on a yellow space, ask the player of your choice a question with that specific question word.
   If your question is formed correctly, take a token from the kitty.
   If the person answers your question correctly, he or she also takes a token.
   If he or she answers incorrectly or does not answer, he or she gives you a token. If the person doesn't have a token, take one from the kitty.

8. *How* and *Why* questions (red spaces) are worth two tokens instead of one.

9. If you land on a blue space, roll the die again. If you roll a:
   1 or 2, take a free token.
   3 or 4, lose a turn.
   5 or 6, play again.

10. You may consult your information log at any time during the game.

WINNING THE GAME

1. Players must collect a **minimum of 12 tokens** before they can head for "Freedom."

2. The game ends when a player **reaches "Freedom."**

3. A player must have the exact number to land on "Freedom" and end the game.

4. Careful! The winner is the person who has the **most tokens**.

---

kitty: the pot; the bank.

FREEDOM BOUND

A Game of Discovery and Insights

What?		Where?		Freedom!
			Why?	
Who?	When?			
		Where?	What?	
Who?			How?	
	What?			Start

A Man, An Inspiration

Nelson Mandela has been an inspiration to many generations of people all around the world. His strength and determination provided hope to people striving for a better world for themselves and others. Looking further than himself and his individual needs, Nelson Mandela showed the world a way to reach beyond our differences in order to embrace our common humanity.

Jean Chrétien and Nelson Mandela

He demonstrated a strong faith in democracy and equality. His conviction to his ideals was most impressive. He was ready to surrender his own life for the betterment of others. Before he was sentenced to life imprisonment, he spoke at his own trial. He bravely articulated the strength of his conviction:

> *"I have fought against white domination, and I have fought against black domination. I have cherished the ideal of a democratic and free society in which all persons live together in harmony and with equal opportunities. It is an ideal which I hope to live for and to achieve. But if needs be, it is an ideal for which I am prepared to die."*

Nelson Rolihlahla Mandela was born to a noble Thembu family on July 18, 1918. His father was a tribal chief. Mandela himself was supposed to one day assume a role as a tribal leader. Although he wanted to respect his elders and serve his country, he had a different idea of how to do that. He wanted to become a lawyer.

At this point in his life, he met Walter Sisulu. Sisulu, an inspirational man of wisdom and inner strength, became Nelson Mandela's mentor and lifelong friend. Sisulu introduced Mandela to some people at the law firm where Mandela ended up working while attending university. He obtained both a Bachelor of Arts and a law degree. During this same period of time, Mandela joined the African National Congress (ANC). The ANC, which was founded the same year that Mandela was born, was a political party

---

conviction: fixed or very strong belief.

betterment: improvement; the making of something better.

elders: people who are older or superior in rank.

whose goal was to put an end to white domination in South Africa.

South Africa was an unjust society that segregated people, giving full rights to some and very limited rights to others. The ANC and other political organizations were outlawed because they spoke out against injustice, inequality and discrimination. The members of various groups were silenced; some went into exile, some "disappeared" and others were put in prison. Mandela became the most prominent political prisoner in the world. He could not be silenced, not even from behind bars. He continued to work for his cause from his prison cell. He advocated equal opportunity and human dignity.

After almost 30 years in prison, the tide started to change. In 1989, Mandela had several productive meetings with the South African President, Frederik DeKlerk. A couple of months later, President DeKlerk spoke to the country's parliament and announced his intention to decriminalize the ANC and other political organizations. About one week later,

Mandela was released from prison. People sang and danced in the streets in South Africa and all over the world. There were tears of joy and hope as Mandela walked out a free man.

After 27 years of imprisonment, he started his life anew. His time was occupied by visiting old friends and supporters across the globe, becoming deputy president of the ANC and eventually the first black President of South Africa. In the summer of 1990, he visited Montreal. It was a joyous occasion as thousands of people met up in Old Montreal to hear the brave and noble man speak. Everyone was in a festive mood, full of optimism. Nearly 10,000 people assembled to listen to musicians and see dancers perform in honour of Nelson Mandela's historic visit. It was an incredible day. When Mandela finally stepped out on the stage, there was a moment of silence and then rejoicing. Some people cheered and whistled while others cried tears of joy.

o **Why do you think some people are ready to go to prison for a cause?**

---

segregated: discriminated against; separated.

released: allowed to go free after a period of time in prison or captivity.

Oral Tradition

The oral tradition is deeply ingrained in African history and culture. It was transplanted to the Americas along with slavery. Storytelling, an active way of keeping history alive, teaches basic human values by referring to both mythical and real events. Traditional storytellers (also known as *griots*) still occupy a special and respected place in African society. Many *griots* come from generations of storytellers, proud to uphold the traditions of their families and the history of their people. Stories may refer to historical events or special celebrations. They may also teach morals and values through folktales.

The animal-trickster tale is the most common and well-known type of African folktale. In the eastern, central and southern parts of Africa, the trickster is generally represented by the hare. In most of West Africa, it is the spider or the tortoise. Anansi, the spider-trickster, is even found in the folktales of Jamaica.

The various animals represent different human qualities and frailties. By showing us a character's shortcomings, they encourage us to look at ourselves. The stories can teach by example, showing both appropriate and inappropriate behaviour. They may also be considered morality tales.

 ○ Why is oral tradition important?

---

trickster: a special creature found in the mythology and folktales of various indigenous peoples. It is usually a mischievous or cunning animal used to teach a lesson or present a moral.

frailties: flaws, defects or weaknesses.

shortcoming: a fault or flaw, weakness or weak point.

Here are two examples of stories from the African-American and African oral tradition.

Why the Rabbit Has a Short Tail

Once upon a time the rabbit had a long bushy tail. Every time he saw the fox, he would take his tail and wave it in the fox's face. The fox thought about how to get even with the rabbit. One day he went fishing and had good luck. On his way home, he saw the rabbit who said, "Dear Fox, how did you catch all those fish?" The fox thought, "Now is my time to get even with the rabbit." So he answered, "On any cold night, all you have to do is to go down to the river and hang your tail in the water. Let it hang there from sundown to sunrise, and the next morning you'll have more fish than you can imagine."

Of course, he meant for the rabbit's tail to freeze in the ice. "Great!" said the rabbit. "I believe I'll go fishing tonight." So he took a blanket and went down to the river, where he sat on a log with his tail hanging in the water all night long. It got so cold that he began to shiver. All night he sat there shivering and thinking about all the fish he would have in the morning. The sun finally began to rise and the rabbit tried to pull out his fish but his tail was frozen tightly in the ice. He pulled and he pulled, but his tail was stuck. The rabbit got scared. He feared that he would freeze to death so he started calling

for help. "Help! Help! Help!" he cried.

The owl heard the rabbit's cries and flew down to the river. There he found the rabbit sitting on a log with his tail frozen tightly in the ice. The owl grabbed onto the rabbit's right ear and began to pull. It grew longer and longer, but his tail did not move. Then the rabbit said, "Why don't you try my left ear instead?" So the owl took the rabbit's left ear, and he began to pull. He pulled and pulled, but it too grew longer and longer. Finally the rabbit said, "Dear Owl, look what you have done. You've pulled so hard on my ears that now even my best friend won't recognize me. Why don't you try pulling on my tail?" So the owl grabbed hold of the rabbit's tail and began to pull. He pulled and pulled, and off came the rabbit's tail. Ever since that day, the rabbit has long ears and a short tail.

---

bushy: thick and shaggy; hairy.
to shiver: to shake and tremble from the cold.

The Tortoise and His Calabash of Wisdom

The tortoise was known to be the wisest of animals. He was wise enough to want to become even wiser. So he decided to collect all the wisdom in the world and keep it for himself in a hollow gourd, or *calabash*. His intention was then to hang the calabash high up in a tree for safekeeping.

For a long time, the tortoise travelled the world, collecting all the wisdom that he could find and stuffing it into his calabash. When he could find no more, he tied the calabash around his neck and found a tree. But each time he started up the tree, the calabash got caught between him and the tree trunk and he fell to the ground. This happened many times. A man came by and suggested, "Why don't you hang the calabash on your back so that it will not get in the way?"

The tortoise followed the man's advice and was able to climb to the top of the tree. Before hanging the calabash on a branch, however, he thought about how foolish he had been. The tortoise realized that if the man had been able to show him wisdom, it was because he had missed some in his travels. With all hope of collecting all the wisdom in the world gone, the humbled tortoise broke his calabash and let the wisdom go back into the world again.

OTHER THINGS TO DO

1 Do some research to find out more about any of the people mentioned in this unit. Write a short biography.

2 Learn more about African oral tradition. Search for information about *griots* and traditional storytelling or make up your own animal trickster tale.

3 Work with a partner to create a skit about any event in Black history. Practise and present it to the class.

4 Make up a scavenger hunt on Black history. Ask questions and present Internet sites where people can find the answers and more details.

hollow: empty; with nothing inside.

In White Ink

Look Back

○ Look back at the pictures on pages 116-117.

○ You should be able to explain why each photo is there.

○ You should also be able to answer the Guiding Questions.

Think About It...

○ Think about the different figures and events discussed.

○ You should be able to name a few and talk briefly about those you find the most interesting, most surprising, etc.

○ Think about some of the things that so many people went through to gain the rights that we often take for granted.

Now What?

○ Can you answer most of the questions in the original quiz, on page 119?

○ Is there a person or event you would like to learn more about?

Don't forget to select some of your work for your portfolio!

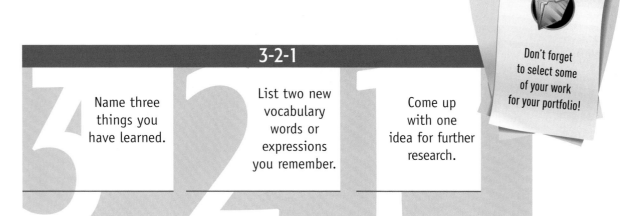

3-2-1

3 Name three things you have learned.

2 List two new vocabulary words or expressions you remember.

1 Come up with one idea for further research.

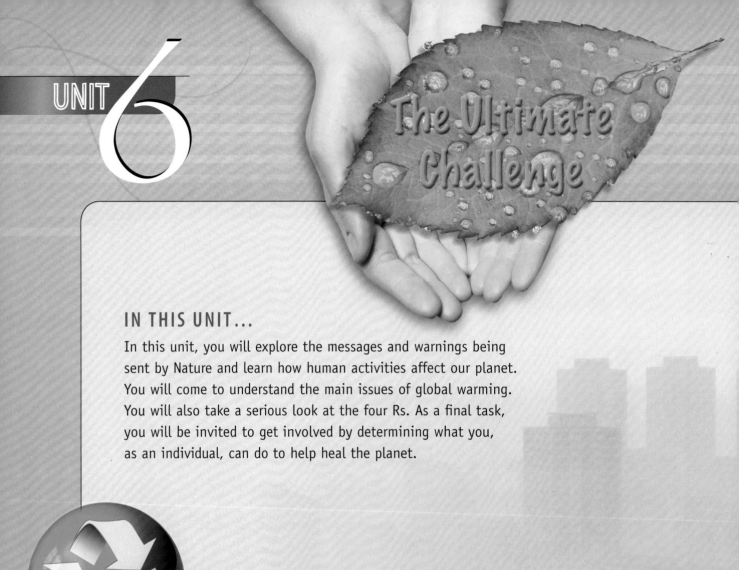

UNIT 6

The Ultimate Challenge

IN THIS UNIT...

In this unit, you will explore the messages and warnings being
sent by Nature and learn how human activities affect our planet.
You will come to understand the main issues of global warming.
You will also take a serious look at the four Rs. As a final task,
you will be invited to get involved by determining what you,
as an individual, can do to help heal the planet.

○ What is the ultimate challenge?

○ What can you, as an individual, do to help protect the environment and be a responsible resident of planet Earth?

What a wonderful world we live in! Such a strong will to survive and prosper; such a difficult balance to maintain! All over the world, scientists agree that human activities are affecting the health of our planet. Do you know what is at stake? In **TASK 1**, you will take a look at modern inventions and become knowledgeable about global warming.

In the Name of Progress

From domesticating animals and mastering fire, to understanding science and reaching out for the stars, humankind has always shown great ingenuity. Ever since the Industrial Revolution, which started over 200 years ago, human beings have become more and more dependent on machines. Today, our fast-track lifestyles require more and more energy. We are draining our resources.

Part A

1. Brainstorm as a class about the meaning of the title of this unit.
   ○ What do you think it means?

2. Read the description of Task 1 and the title and the description of Activity 1.
   ○ How do you think they are connected to the title of the unit?

3. Together, list all inventions that you can think of that you have come in contact with since waking up this morning.

4. Individually, make a Top-Five list of the greatest inventions ever, a Top-Five list of the most polluting inventions and a Top-Five list of eco-friendly alternatives. Write them on the handout.

Part B

1. In groups of four, compare your lists.

2. Together, answer the questions in the **Talk About It!** box.

3. Discuss and agree on the top three winners for each category and award them as follows: Orange prize (for the best invention), Lemon prize (for the most polluting), Green Apple prize (for the most eco-friendly alternative).

4. Present your choices to the class.

5. Finish completing the handout.

---

at stake: important; at issue.

eco-friendly: good for the environment.

The word **ecology** refers to the interaction of living things with their environment and with each other. It comes form the Greek words *oikos* (habitat) and *logos* (study).

It is the science of studying these interactions, especially from the point of view of prevention and conservation. Ecology is also sometimes called **environmental science**.

The prefix **eco-** is used in forming many words, such as: ecological, eco-friendly, ecosystem, eco-chic, eco-warfare, ecotourism...

For Fun and Practice

This Morning...

In your groups, answer these questions orally to find out how "eco-friendly" you were this morning.

1. What did you eat and drink?
2. How was it packaged?
3. What was the format of the packaging?
4. Is all of the packaging used recyclable? Are you sure?
5. If you had an orange or a banana, what did you do with the peel?
6. Did you eat white bread or brown bread? Ecologically speaking, what's the difference?
7. Did you leave the water running while you brushed your teeth? Did you use an electric toothbrush?
8. Did you use a hairdryer?
9. Did you turn off your computer?
10. Did you pack a lunch?
11. How did you get to school?

Talk About It!

- What are the benefits of all of these inventions?
- What negative consequences does each of them have on the environment?
- What are some eco-friendly alternatives? Why aren't they very popular?
- Do all the gadgets we use represent "progress"? What is progress anyway?

Nature Reacts!

In this activity, you will learn some basic facts about the greenhouse effect and what it has to do with global warming.

1. Read the article *Grassroots **Facts on the Greenhouse Effect***.

2. Validate your understanding with a partner and complete the handout.

Grassroots Facts on the Greenhouse Effect

Imagine that the Earth is wrapped in a blanket, a thin layer of carbon dioxide (CO_2) and other gases. This blanket retains just enough heat from the sun to keep us comfortable. This CO_2 is produced by the natural decomposition of organic matter. Our survival depends on this warmth. Mother Nature is taking good care of us!

Unfortunately however, human activities produce too much additional CO_2 by burning fossil fuels like coal, gas and oil. Power plants, cars and logging are the main sources of abuse. The gaseous blanket above the Earth is becoming too heavy and the planet is slowly suffocating! Too much of the sun's heat is being absorbed. Consequently, our planet is overheating and reacting strongly to all the irritants we are producing. Remember this principle: the more CO_2 there is in the atmosphere, the faster our environment will change. This is the greenhouse effect.

The effects of global warming on the planet are spectacular. Increases in the frequency and intensity of hurricanes, heat waves, higher sea levels, floods, droughts, the extinction of animal and plant species, the spread of tropical diseases... Earth is becoming fed up with us! It's almost as if

---

grassroots: basic; fundamental.

coal: black, combustible material made of carbon.

power plant: used to produce electricity.

logging: cutting trees; harvesting the forest.

drought: a long period with little or no rain.

to be fed up with: to have enough of; to be disgusted or disappointed with.

the planet were taking revenge! Scientists do not necessarily agree on how much time it will take to reach the limit, but they do agree that there is no time for procrastination. We must act now.

In most of North America, "greenhouse gases" are sent into the atmosphere whenever people use electricity, because it comes mainly from coal – or oil-fired power plants. This does not apply to Quebec, because electricity is produced using water (or hydro) power. Most factories also burn lots of coal or oil in order to produce the products we buy every day.

Have a look at your Top-Five lists. Do you want to make any changes or switch anything you have listed to another category?

Culture

Brr!

Over the next 100 years, the Earth's average global temperature could increase by 6°C.

This might not seem like a big deal, but 18,000 years ago the average global temperature was only 4°C colder than today, and most of North America was covered by glaciers!

Culture

Greenhouses and the Greenhouse Effect

Greenhouses that we grow plants in work by trapping heat from the sun. The glass panels of the greenhouse let sunlight penetrate, but keep heat from escaping. Gases in the atmosphere act like the glass panels of a greenhouse. They trap the energy of the sun inside the atmosphere. This causes the world to heat up. This process is called the greenhouse effect.

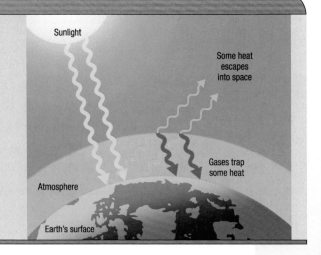

A Sense of Urgency

 Jim Warren is an American artist who was born in 1949. Two of his most powerful paintings are shown here. Their titles speak for themselves. On the left is **Earth... Love It or Lose It**, which has often appeared on billboards and magazine covers. It represents a child's vulnerability in an uncertain world. On the right is **Don't Mess with Mother Nature**. It depicts the risks of messing around with the environment.

 Think About It!

• Is Mother Nature taking revenge? Are human beings ready for the challenge?

Write About It!

The Paintings

Vulnerability, fragility, force, strength, uncertainty, fear, danger, hope, beauty, faith...

• What words come to mind when looking at these paintings?
• What emotions do you feel?
• Use the handout to write about these paintings.
• Use a dictionary or thesaurus to help you.

---

billboard: large sign along the road or on buildings.

to depict: to show; to portray.

USE A DICTIONARY

Dictionaries can be used to check spelling, learn new words, find or double-check the meaning of words, or simply find the right word to use. How to best use a dictionary depends on what you are doing with the words in question.

For spelling

Once you have found the word you are looking for and know how to spell it, don't stop there:

- *Check to see if the word is invariable. If so, it will not take the plural form. That is, ... no "s."*
- *Some verbs are irregular. The dictionary will give you this information and perhaps save you from making a mistake.*

For accuracy

When speaking or writing, you need to use the right word. Your dictionary can help:

- *Once you have found the word, read all its definitions.*
- *Choose the one that best represents what you want to say.*
- *Look for synonyms you know. Try replacing the unknown word in the sentence with a synonym to see if it makes sense.*

For creativity

For pronunciation

Your dictionary is a great companion to help you stretch your vocabulary. Most dictionaries will give you lots of keywords, phrases, synonyms and antonyms to vary your vocabulary.

Once you have found your word, don't stop there:

- *Keep on reading.*

   You will find tons of useful information. If you're looking for a special saying or expression, you're sure to find the one you're looking for to make your statement.

It's true! See for yourself:

- *Beside each word, you will find brackets [...] with a code to help you figure out the correct pronunciation of the word. Give it a try!*

A type of dictionary called a **thesaurus** is the best tool to help you find synonyms and antonyms.

Mother Nature Speaks

In ancient times, Greeks separated nature into four elements: earth, air, fire and water. In this activity, you will read about the effects of global warming on the four elements.

1. In groups of four, divide up the following pages so that each of you has one element to read about and report on to your group.

2. Take notes on your text using the handout.

3. Refer to *How to Take Notes* on the next page to help you.

4. Take turns explaining what you have read.

5. For each element, complete a section of the handout.

6. Discuss the questions in the Talk About It! box.

Talk About It!

• What are the main problems stated in the articles?

• Do you know any other problems that are not mentioned?

• Did the articles suggest any solutions? What are they? Do you believe the solutions given are sufficient and realistic? Can you come up with any alternatives?

Earth
+
Air
+
Fire
+
Water

Life

"We are the environment because we are the Earth and we're made of the four sacred elements, earth, air, fire and water."

David Suzuki, in the film *David Suzuki Speaks*

---

to state: to declare; to put into words.

TAKE NOTES

Taking notes is not always an easy task. It takes practice. Following these steps will help you:

1. Don't try to write everything down. Focus on the main ideas mentioned. Add more specific sub-ideas to them later.

2. Don't write complete sentences. Use keywords.

3. Know in advance what information you need and write only that information. If possible, use a graphic organizer.

4. It's okay to use personal symbols and abbreviations. Just make sure you understand them later on! If you can't read them, they will not be very useful.

5. If you are taking notes from a book or an article, remember to note the source. If you copy exact words or text from anywhere, remember to use quotation marks.

Good notes:
- are **short** and **precise**
- use **keywords**, not complete sentences
- use a **graphic organizer**
- can be **personalized**
- list the **source**

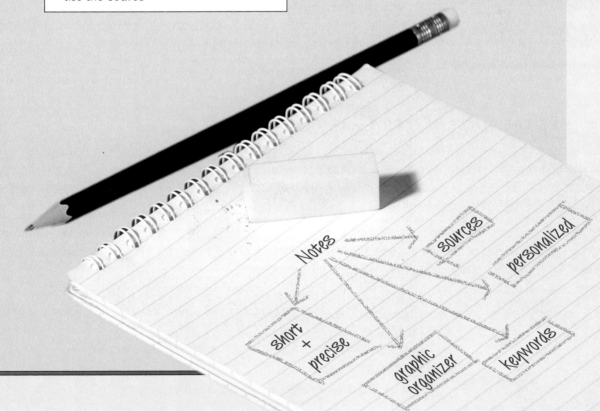

Element: Earth

TRUE OR FALSE?

China, India and the United States are the worst polluters on the planet.

True. Coal is a low-cost and abundant source of fuel in these countries and, traditionally, it has been used to produce energy. Unfortunately, it also pollutes the atmosphere extensively.

Global warming causes tsunamis.

False. Earthquakes are the real cause of tsunamis. However, melting glaciers could change the pressure at certain points of the globe, causing the underwater disruptions responsible for tsunamis.

World grain production will satisfy the demand for the next 20 years.

False. In Northern Europe, Asia and the United States, heat, storms and depleted water reserves threaten harvests year after year.

> In 2004, an earthquake in the Indian Ocean triggered a tsunami that killed more than 200,000 people.

For Fun and Practice

Wow!

The prefix *giga-* means one billion, so 800 gigatons is 800 billion tons!

Just how many kilograms would that be anyway?

(One ton = 2,000 pounds or 907.18 kilograms)

PERMAFROST

Permafrost is what we call land that has remained frozen for two years or longer. In some cases, it may even have been frozen for 8,000 years or more, but it won't stay like that for long! Global warming will see to that.

Permafrost contains organic matter rich in carbon. As it warms, it releases methane and CO_2. Do you remember what happens when there is too much CO_2 caught under the Earth's blanket? That's right, the planet gets warmer.

Now get this! Human activities produce about seven gigatons of carbon a year. In the Arctic soil alone, there are as much as 200 to 800 gigatons of carbon waiting to be released.

How hot do you like your tea?

"WE ARE THE GIANT METEORITE OF OUR TIME."

This quote from Edward O. Wilson, a renowned scientist, shows just how staggering the impact of our actions on the planet is. It is high time to invest in research on fuel-efficient cars and alternative transportation technologies, find low-cost green alternatives to fossil energy, reward eco-friendly industries and encourage dialogue with developing countries.

Did you know that there are billions of people who still do not have regular access to electricity? Caring for the natural world, being humble and adopting a healthier and simpler way of living could go a long way toward ensuring that our industrialized world has a future.

---

tsunami: a huge ocean wave caused by an underwater earthquake, volcanic eruption or landside.

depleted: showing a dangerous reduction in quantity.

to threaten: to menace.

staggering: huge, astonishing; difficult to believe.

Element: Air

TAKE A DEEP BREATH!

Sometimes, taking a deep breath isn't as healthy as it should be. Millions of people suffer from bronchitis, asthma and allergies. These illnesses are taking lives every day, all around the world.

When the air is too warm, many people find it very difficult to breathe. Did you know that a heat wave killed 30,000 Europeans in 2003? Cloudless skies and strong sunshine are hard on both people and crops.

Hotter record temperatures will be more frequent in the future. We will have to provide additional care for people who run the risk of dehydration and heatstroke.

By the year 2100, the Earth could be as much as 6°C warmer.

THE DAY AFTER TOMORROW

With global warming, there will be more water vapour in the air and this will increase the frequency of electrical storms and hurricanes. There will also be more fires and more air pollution.

Will tornadoes strike New York City and hail fall on Tokyo as seen in the movies? Perhaps, but severe climate change will take at least 20 years or longer to happen; it won't be as abrupt as shown in the movies.

And, because it takes a long time for oceanic circulation paths to change, climate change might also be counter-balanced by global warming.

LOOKING INTO THE GLOBE

In India, a few years back, a billion people had soot on their faces and clothes at the end of the day. The government then reduced smog by forcing buses, taxis and rickshaws to use cleaner fuel.

All countries should adopt ecological policies to curb the environmental damage being done to the planet. We should also fund research on climate change and improve weather forecasting. Giving timely alerts about impending disaster facilitates evacuation and can thus save lives.

Knowing, understanding and respecting Mother Nature are keys to adapting to global warming.

---

crops: products grown on farms.

hail: piece of ice falling from the sky.

soot: black dust produced by pollution.

rickshaw: a two-wheeled vehicle usually pulled by a man, but sometimes motorized.

fuel: a material used to produce energy.

to fund: to support financially.

forecasting: making predictions.

Element: Fire

Culture

Extremes!

The lowest temperature ever recorded on Earth was −89.2°C at Vostok, Antarctica, on July 21, 1983.

The hottest temperature on record was 56.7°C at Death Valley, California, on July 10, 1913.

BARBECUED FORESTS

It has been proven that there are more wildfires in warmer years than in cooler years. Thus, with the warming of the planet, we can expect an increased frequency of fires in coming decades. You should know by now that if there are fewer trees to absorb CO_2, it will mean a rise in the level of CO_2. Is it getting hot enough for you yet?

Every spring, snow starts melting earlier and earlier in mountainous regions. Winter is also arriving later. The accumulation of snow isn't as great as it used to be. The ground is becoming drier earlier and for longer periods of time. Summer, which is fire season, also lasts longer. Do you like your forests roasted or rare?

THE EARTH'S LUNGS

Would you like to live in the desert? That just might be the fate of millions of people...

Forests are our lungs. Trees catch CO_2 and transform it into oxygen. But due to human activities and mega-fires like those in the jungles of the Amazon, forests are rapidly thinning out and even disappearing completely.

When there are no trees, the sun bakes the ground, leaving it dry and parched. Drought is the result. Fire catches easily, scalding the ground and killing seeds that might have sprouted. The heat becomes overwhelming... And the desert grows, spreads, expands, multiplies... The planet's thermometer is about to burst!

HIGH UP IN THE MOUNTAINS

Forests need water and freshness as much as we do. Studies show that trees have started to move to higher elevations in order to escape heat and dryness. But there is only so far they can go before reaching the top of the mountains – and then disappearing.

Furthermore, every year, 5% of the world's forests are burned down to make room for cattle and crops. There's a lot of CO_2 in the atmosphere and fewer trees to absorb all the pollution. Helping Mother Nature should mean protecting the Amazonian and Congolese forests and investing in intensive reforestation programs.

---

parched: with no humidity.

scalding: burning hot.

furthermore: in addition.

cattle: bovine farm animals.

Element: Water

GLACIERS AND ICE SHEETS

Ice reflects about 90% of the energy radiating from the sun, whereas water absorbs 90% of this energy. Do you see the hitch? This means that the Earth will get warmer and warmer as more water and less ice lies on its surface. One of the consequences of this warming will be a rise in ocean levels. Why? First of all, warm water expands. Second, the melting of ice sheets, both in Antarctica and the Arctic, will pump huge amounts of extra water into the oceans.

Consequently, the oceans will eventually swallow up many costal regions, such as the city of New Orleans, the state of Florida and countries like Bangladesh. Lots of people will be left homeless. Some animal species will disappear. And the warmer the planet becomes, the faster we'll see our lives changing.

THIRSTY?

Many ski resorts, like those in Aspen, Colorado, have developed techniques for making snow without wasting too much water. Likewise, farmers now plant more and more varieties of crops that are more tolerant to drought. But water is still being wasted in big cities that need to quench the thirsts of their growing populations. And what about the terrible African droughts?

People have started to protect water, but when are we going to see, as a standard, toilets that don't flush potable water and houses with plumbing systems that operate with recycled water?

DID YOU KNOW THESE WATER FACTS?

- It takes about 215,000 litres of water to produce a metric ton of steel.

- It takes about 35 litres of water to produce one can of fruit or vegetables.

- It takes about 45% more water to make a slice of white bread than a slice of brown bread because more flour is used and more processing is required.

WARMER OCEANS, COLDER CONTINENTS

Warm water is light and floats on the surface of the ocean. As it gets colder, it drops down to the bottom of the sea. This makes a loop, a movement called a *current*. Ocean currents, such as the Gulf Stream, carry heat from the equator and the tropics to colder regions, and then travel back in the depths of the sea. All the fresh water added from the melting of ice sheets dilutes the salty seawater, making it lighter. It then starts to float. The looping movement slows down and eventually, it could stop altogether. The Gulf Stream has already slowed down by about 30% since 1957! If it stopped bringing warm water to Europe, the climate of that continent would change dramatically.

---

whereas: while on the contrary.

hitch: an imperfection that will cause difficulties.

to swallow up: to engulf; to absorb.

to quench: to put an end to; to stop.

Nature Strikes Back!

You have learned about the four elements. Now it's time to differentiate between facts and opinions. Listen carefully! You'll hear two news reports about natural disasters.

1. Read **How to Recognize a Fact and an Opinion** on the next page.

2. Look at the illustrations and make predictions about the contents of the two news reports your will hear.

3. Listen to the reports.

4. Try to identify some markers for both facts and opinions. Jot them down on the handout.

5. Listen again and complete your list of facts and opinions.

6. In pairs, discuss the questions in the Talk About It! box.

Talk About It!

- Have you ever heard a similar news report? When? What was it about? How did it make you feel?

- What do you think the role of the media should be during a disaster?

- Have you ever witnessed a disaster?

Focus on...

EXPRESSING OPINIONS

With the Modal Auxiliaries COULD, MAY, MIGHT, WOULD and SHOULD

- Use *could, may* or *might* to show **possibility**.

  Example: Pollution **could** be a factor in his illness.

  Example: The increase in the number of ants **may/might** be due in part to lack of pesticides.

- Use *would* to show **hypothetical possibility**.

  Example: There **would** be less pollution problems if more people took the metro.

- Use *should* to express **advice.**

  Example: The media **should** act responsibly and not stir up panic.

How to...

RECOGNIZE A FACT AND AN OPINION

A FACT is *verifiable.*

There is proof from a reliable source to back it up.

It isn't fiction. It cannot be refuted unless you're an expert who has collected data yourself and done serious research on the topic!

An OPINION is *subjective.*

It is a reflection or a thought on a subject. It is not backed by proof.

It is about feelings and beliefs. What you think is right might actually be wrong for someone else.

There are different ways to express facts and opinions.
Here are some examples:

FACTS

- **It is a fact that** the climate is already affected by global warming.

- **It has been proven that** in Alaska, salmon populations are at risk because permafrost pours mud into rivers, burying the gravel needed by the fish to reproduce.

- Biologists have **observed that** in Costa Rica, 66% of the different species of frogs have vanished since 1975.

- **According to scientists**, the percentage of the Earth's surface suffering from drought has more than doubled since 1970.

- "We haven't yet used alternatives to fossil fuels because there are initial high-end costs. Economics always plays a key role," **says Professor Will Gosnold.**

OPINIONS

- **It is all right** to use animals in order to satisfy our needs.

- **It would be wrong** to say that oil will run out before today's students are 50 years old!

- **I don't think** there is anything we can do to make up for the harm already done to the environment.

- **We can trust** industry to stop polluting the atmosphere.

- **We should trust** industry to take stronger measures.

- **According to my parents**, keeping animals in zoos is inhuman.

- **I believe** that killing to eat is cruel.

- Hubert Reeves is **such a cool guy!**

- Protecting the environment is **easy as pie!**

E very year, new animals are added to the list of endangered species. Unless serious measures are taken to protect and preserve the environment, this list will continue to grow. Eventually, some of these animals may even become extinct, like the dinosaurs. In **TASK 2**, you will learn about how our lifestyles and choices affect the other inhabitants of our planet, and find out what you, as an individual, can do to help better the situation.

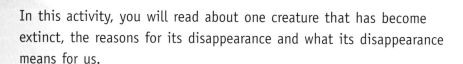

ACTIVITY 1

A Disappearing Act and a Warning

In this activity, you will read about one creature that has become extinct, the reasons for its disappearance and what its disappearance means for us.

Think About It!

Why is it important to protect and save all animals and plants? What impact does this have on our future?

1. As a class, brainstorm about the issue of endangered species.
   - How many animals can you think of that are presently considered to be endangered?
   - Do you know of any animals that have become extinct?
   - Do you know of any animals that were once considered endangered but are now off the list?
   - What is being done to protect endangered species and get them off the list?

2. Read the text **The Golden Toad** on the next page.

3. Work with a partner to complete the handout.

Mind Boggler

How many plants and how many animals do you think were on the endangered species lists in 2006?

(The answer is on page 179.)

 Culture

FYI

The Golden Toad measured only 2 cm. The female did not share the bright orange colouring of the male, but was deep olive green or black with scarlet spots with yellow rings.

The Golden Toad was first discovered in 1966 by the herpetologist Jay Savage. Most of what we know about this toad was documented by the American ecologist and herpetologist Martha Crump.

herpetologist: zoologist who studies reptiles and amphibians.

The Golden Toad

With its brilliant yellow-orange colouring, the Golden Toad (*Bufo periglenes*) was considered to be one of the shiniest and most brightly coloured toads on Earth. Although it had always been rare, and its habitat limited to a single mountain in Costa Rica, every year for a few weeks in April, hundreds of these toads would leave their underground burrows to breed. At the close of the dry season, when the forest had become wet again, males would gather in large numbers near ground puddles to wait for the females. They would fight each other for opportunities to mate until the end of their short mating season, then retreat. The eggs were laid in the pools in clutches that averaged more than 200 eggs. The tadpoles would then emerge nearly two months later.

Unfortunately, the Golden Toad no longer exists. Its population declined sharply from over 1,500 observed in 1987 to just 10 in 1988, none of which was breeding. In 1989, only one toad, a male seeking a mate, was observed. This was reported to be the last Golden Toad on Earth. No Golden Toads have been seen since. The disappearance of the Golden Toad is particularly significant because its habitat is located in a protected area, the Monteverde Cloud Forest Preserve.

So why did it disappear? Global climate change, increased UV rays and fungal disease are cited as probable causes.

What does this mean on a larger scale? The extinction of the Golden Toad reflects what may one day become the fate of other amphibians all over the world. The decrease in their populations should be regarded as an initial warning sign. Because most amphibians breathe at least partially through their skin, they are constantly absorbing the substances found in the environment. Because they live both on land and in water, they are doubly affected. The buildup of pollutants, changes in weather patterns and thinning of the ozone layer are all starting to take their toll. The time to act is now, before there is a large-scale breakdown of our ecosystems.

---

burrow: a hole in the ground made by an animal for shelter.

puddle: an accumulation of rainwater.

clutch: a set of eggs produced at one time.

tadpole: a larval toad or frog; a pollywog.

to take a toll: to be damaging or harmful; to cause loss or destruction.

ACTIVITY 2

History of Extinction

Previous periods of extinction were triggered by physical causes like the movement of tectonic plates and volcanic activity, without human intervention. However, current extinctions of animals and plants are not due to natural causes or natural selection. They are being caused mainly by human beings. With the birth of agriculture some 10,000 years ago, humans began destroying local ecosystems by removing existing vegetation and breaking the existing food chain in order to plant crops. Today, we continue to violate our environment on a much larger scale by virtue of deforestation, the introduction of alien species into established ecosystems, pollution, greenhouse gases and so on. Never before has the Earth been at such risk!

1. Brainstorm about the different ways humans have been violating the environment.

2. Read the text *One of These Days* on the handout.

3. Answer the questions on the handout.

Culture

Did you know...?

Each species carries unique genetic material in its DNA. A weed called *sweet wormwood* grows in central China. This plant is the only known source of a drug that is nearly 100% effective against malaria. If this plant were to become extinct, then our ability to control malaria would diminish.

There are innumerable other examples of chemicals unique to a particular species, whose only source is that species. Think what might happen if they were to become extinct?

Mind Boggler

How many species do you think may become extinct in the next 100 years?

(The answer is on page 179.)

---

to trigger: to initiate; to cause.

tectonic plate: segment of the Earth's crust that moves and has volcanic activity around its margins.

ecosystem: an ecological community and its environment functioning together as a unit.

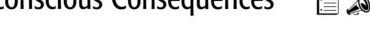

Unconscious Consequences

Pollution is killing our birds and destroying our marine life, that we all know. It's easy to blame industry. For sure, most industries cause a lot of pollution and it impacts our environment, but as individuals, we must also share at least part of the responsibility. Sometimes the little things we do, often without a second thought, can have serious consequences.

Mind Boggler

How long do you think it takes for a plastic bag to decompose?

(The answer is on page 179.)

1. Look at the pictures and the title of the activity.
   ○ What do you think the text will talk about?
   ○ What type of pollution do you think will be exposed?

2. Listen to the text.

3. Complete the handout.

Culture

Butt Facts

- Cigarette butt litter is the world's greatest environmental litter problem.

- It can take up to 12 years for a cigarette butt to break down and disintegrate, yet after only one hour of contact with water, it can leak harmful chemicals, such as lead, arsenic and cadmium, into a marine environment.

- Cigarette butts have been found in the stomachs of birds, whales, fish and other marine animals.

Mind Boggler

How many cigarette butts do you think are left to litter the world every year?

(The answer is on page 179.)

(cigarette) butt: the end; the part of a cigarette that is not smoked (the filter).

litter: papers, plastic, etc. thrown into the environment.

TASK 2

ACTIVITY **4**

Small Gestures

Once in a while, an individual gets the chance to do something extraordinary to save an animal or a plant. Most of us, however, will never have this opportunity. It's rather through the things we do every day that we can make a difference. Saving the planet is a collective and concerted effort, so, although they may seem insignificant, these small gestures do count!

1. Read the article below about "an extraordinary turn of events."
2. Read **The Starfish Story** on the next page.
3. Discuss both texts in your groups, using the Talk About It! box.
4. Complete the handout.

A Helping Hand

Although it sounds more like a children's fairy tale, the following event happened for real. It's the amazing story of how some great ingenuity and one man's height saved two dolphins.

On December 14, 2006, in China's Royal Jidi Ocean World aquarium, two dolphins became very sick after ingesting plastic litter that had accumulated near the edge of their pool. Veterinarians were unable to remove the plastic through surgery without the risk of tearing the animals' stomachs. They brainstormed and came up with a very creative solution. They requested the help of Bao Xishun, the world's tallest man, who measures 2.325 metres. He stuck his long arms into both dolphins' mouths and was

---

once in a while: occasionally.

to ingest: to eat.

able to physically pull out most of the garbage. The dolphins were able to digest the small pieces that remained and they survived! The dolphins were saved by a very clever idea, an unconventional tactic — and the help of some very long arms!

The Starfish Story

There are numerous versions of this story, often presented without any credit given to its author. Sometimes the person throwing the starfish back into the ocean is portrayed as an old man, and sometimes a young girl. Yet, what really matters is the message it carries.

One day, an old man was walking along the beach when he noticed what he believed to be a dancer. As he got closer, however, he realized that it was not a dancer at all, but a boy repeatedly picking something up and gently throwing it into the ocean. Approaching the boy, he asked, "What are you doing?"

The youth replied, "Throwing starfish back into the ocean. The surf is up and the tide is going out. If I don't throw them back, they'll die."

"Son," the man said, "don't you realize there are miles and miles of beach and hundreds of starfish? You can't possibly make a difference!"

After listening politely, the boy bent down, picked up another starfish, and threw it back into the sea. Then, smiling, he said, "I made a difference for that one."

Adapted from *The Star Thrower*
by Loren Eiseley (1907–1977)

Talk About It!

- Do you know any other true stories about spectacular events?
- What small gestures can teens make to help make a difference in saving animals or plants?
- If you had the choice, would you rather be a big environmental star like the man in the article or a starfish thrower like the boy in the story? Explain your choice.

Cues

- *I would rather be... than...*
- *If I could, I would...*
- *I would like to be famous for... because...*

---

to throw: to pitch; a thrower is a person who throws something.

tide: the periodic rise and fall in sea level under the gravitational pull of the moon.

W e have all heard of the three Rs: Recycle, Reduce, Reuse. In **TASK 3**, you will take a closer look at some astonishing facts and hopefully add the fourth R, Recover, **to your lifestyle.**

The Facts Speak for Themselves

In this activity, you will read about all kinds of facts about resources, energy and the environment. Some of them are quite shocking and certainly make us think.

Talk About It!

- Which facts surprise you most? Why?
- Which one do you find the most troubling?
- What actions could and should be taken?

1. Read the facts listed below.

2. Discuss them in your groups with the help of the **Talk About It!** box.

3. Complete the handout.

- Use **could** for possibilities.
- Use **should** for suggestions or advice.

Residents of the industrial world comprise 20% of the global population but consume about 80% of the world's aluminum, paper, iron and steel and timber.

•••

By the age of only six months, each Canadian has consumed as many resources as the average person in the developing world consumes in his or her entire lifetime.

•••

Twenty-seven percent of all food produced in North America is wasted.

•••

In Quebec, 36 million plastic bags are distributed in supermarkets every week.

•••

The typical computer is replaced after five years. Unfortunately, most of the time it ends up in a landfill, where the plastics and other materials can last for 450 years or more. Only about 20% of computers are currently being recycled. Also, it is estimated that every month, over 45 tons of CDs are destined for disposal.

Aluminum cans can be recycled endlessly. One such can take 100 years to disintegrate. Recycling one can saves enough energy to power a television for three hours.

•••

It takes approximately 1 million years for a glass bottle to break down by natural processes. Recycling one glass bottle into a new glass container saves enough energy to keep a 100-watt light bulb burning for four hours.

•••

Aerosol cans cannot be recycled, so not only do they contribute to air pollution, but they are also guaranteed to end up in landfills. It is estimated that if all aerosol cans in North America were recycled, there would be enough steel to make 160,000 new cars.

•••

It is estimated that 13 billion pieces of mail are delivered in Canada each year. This represents between 1,000 and 2,000 pieces per residence and 4 to 5 million trees. How much of this mail do you think was actually opened and read?

What's in the Big Black Bag?

In this activity, you will be asked to take a really close look at wasting and recycling. Be warned! It's not an activity for the faint of heart! Yet garbage is a serious business: our planet's health is at stake.

1. Before it goes out on garbage day, take your garbage bag (you know, one of the green or black ones or the equivalent...) and analyze its contents.

2. Classify what has been thrown away using the graph on the handout.

3. Compare your findings with the members of your group.

4. Discuss this issue using the **Talk About It!** box.

5. Compile class statistics. If you're up to it, try the experiment again, seeing how much you can reduce, recycle, reuse and recover.

For Fun and Practice

Make Every Day Earth Day!

Make a Commitment!

- Find at least three actions that you can make part of your everyday routine.

- Make the commitment to carry out these actions for a whole month.

Culture

The *Möbius strip* is used as the international recycling symbol. When it is on a light background, it means that the product can be recycled.

On a dark background, it means that the product contains recycled materials. Next to the symbol should be figures indicating what percentage of the recycled content is from post-consumer waste and what percentage is post-industrial. Post-consumer waste content is preferred because it has already been used by consumers at least once.

According to statistics compiled in the 1990s, each Canadian throws out about one ton of garbage every year! Each person in Canada produces 2.2 kg of garbage per day.

Talk About It!

- What could have been recycled?

- What could have been recovered for other uses?

- How could you reduce your garbage?

- Do you think people should be limited to the amount of garbage they can throw out each week? If so, what would be considered fair?

Mind Boggler

How many litres of water does the average Canadian use per day?

(The answer is on page 179.)

Throughout this unit, we have been learning about the negative effects of human activity on our planet and what we can do to help reverse these effects. In the **FINAL TASK**, you will have the chance to express what you can do as an individual. The fate of the Earth is in your hands.

ACTIVITY 1

What you can do

1. Read the six quotes below.

2. All of them hold a message concerning responsibility and, with that responsibility, a glimmer of hope.

3. In your groups, answer the questions in the **Talk About It!** box.

4. Then, choose one of the quotes and write a personal commentary. Refer to the guidelines on the next page to help you.

5. Follow the Writing guidelines closely.

6. Use the graphic organizer on the handout to structure your ideas.

7. Use the Toolkit to help you edit and revise your text.

Talk About It!

- Why could it be said that each of these six quotations contains a message of responsibility?

- And a glimmer of hope?

Cues

- I can help take care of the Earth by... (recycling my soda cans)
- As a caretaker of the planet, I will... (organize a clean-up of the school grounds)
- As part of the crew, I will...
- I can do my part by... (not buying aerosols)
- I will try to...
- I will not... any more.
- I will quit... (throwing out plastic bottles)

"We do not inherit the earth from our ancestors, we borrow it from our children."

Native American Proverb

"We are caretakers of this planet."

Brooke Medicine Eagle

"There are no passengers on spaceship earth. We are all crew."

Marshall McLuhan

"Take care of the Earth and she will take care of you."

Author Unknown

"We abuse land because we regard it as a commodity belonging to us. When we see land as a community to which we belong, we may begin to use it with love and respect."

Aldo Leopold

"Humankind has not woven the web of life. We are but one thread within it. Whatever we do to the web, we do to ourselves. All things are bound together. All things connect."

Chief Seattle, 1855

---

glimmer: a small ray of light.

Guidelines for Writing Your Commentary

PREPARATION

1
Choose one of the quotations to write about.

2
Decide upon an audience for your commentary.
Deciding first about the people you wish to address may
help you choose the final format of your work.

3
Choose the final format for your work. You can publish
your text as a letter, a PowerPoint presentation, a brochure,
a poster or simply as a long paragraph or short essay.

4
Use a graphic organizer to help you structure your ideas.

WRITING

1
Write a draft copy of your commentary.

2
Include all of the following:
- The quotation
- What it means to you
- At least two facts taken from information
  in the unit to support your ideas
- A commitment on your behalf with a list of specific actions
- A strong concluding sentence that summarizes what you have
  to say on the topic (this may be a kind of mantra or a slogan)

3
Revise and edit your work using the checklist in the handout to help you.

PUBLISHING

1
Make a polished copy of your text in the format you have chosen.

2
Present your work to your target audience.

Focus on...

TRANSITION WORDS

Try using some of the
following words to help
your commentary flow
from one idea to the next:

For a shift in time

At first; Initially

Before; Previously

After; Later;
Subsequently

Then; Next;
Consequently

To summarize

Briefly

In brief

Overall

To sum up

To conclude

Therefore

In conclusion

Thus

So

EXTRA READING

A Step in Time

According to anthropologists, climatic changes that began 24 million years ago are responsible for the development of the characteristics of humans. Our upright position, the way we walk, our large brains and our invention of tools are all landmarks in our history of adaptation. Have you ever heard about Darwin's theory of evolution?

Some Basic Elements of Darwin's Theory of Evolution

According to Darwin:
- All organisms are derived from a common ancestor.
- The world is constantly changing. Organisms today are not the same as those that lived in the past. Fossils prove this.
- All living species have descended with modifications from the species that lived before them.
- These changes were extremely slow and very gradual. They took place over a very long time.

Darwin believed in the process of natural selection:
- Natural selection explains how evolution occurred.
- Because of limited resources, more organisms are produced than are able to survive. Only the fittest survive. They pass on their traits to their offspring.
- Species whose individuals are the best-adapted survive; the others become extinct.

Although widely accepted as fact, some religious fundamentalists denounce Darwin's theory of evolution, claiming that it is in conflict with the teachings of the Holy Bible.

anthropologist: someone who studies the origins of human beings.
landmark: event that changed the course of history.
offspring: progeny; young; babies.

Culture

Charles Darwin (1809–1882) was an eminent English naturalist. He developed his interest in natural science while studying both medicine and theology. He was also the devout father of 10 children.

Darwin is well known for his theory of evolution. He believed that man descended from monkeys. His book *On the Origin of Species* was published in 1859.

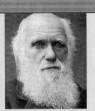

Charles Darwin

Many species and geographical locations have been named in honour of him. In 2000, the Bank of England put his picture on a 10-pound note.

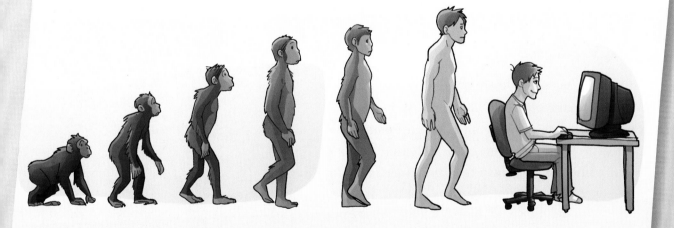

o What could the next possible step in our evolution be?

Trees

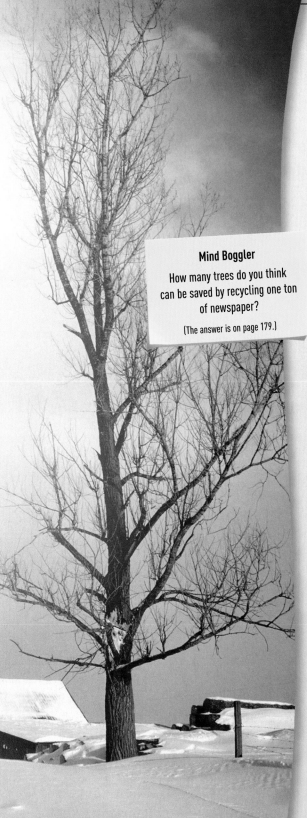

Trees are a source of beauty and pleasure. They are also extremely helpful. Trees provide humans with shade and privacy. They help reduce noise pollution. In addition to providing food and habitat for many animals, trees filter water and help prevent erosion.

Trees also produce oxygen. In fact, one large tree can provide enough oxygen for a day for up to four people. Furthermore, trees help the planet deal with climate change by removing carbon dioxide from the atmosphere through photosynthesis. As you know, CO_2 is produced by vehicles and other energy-consuming devices. Thus, trees play a key role in limiting global warming.

Trees are truly a blessing for cities, where pollution is often widespread. Did you know that a single tree can absorb as many as 7,000 dust particles per litre of air? In addition, by sheltering buildings in the summer, trees help reduce the need for air-conditioning. Evergreen trees planted in a

Mind Boggler

How many trees do you think can be saved by recycling one ton of newspaper?

(The answer is on page 179.)

Culture

Did you know that...?

You need 500 mature trees to absorb the carbon dioxide produced by a typical car that is driven 20,000 km a year?

row provide a windbreak, which can reduce winter heating costs significantly. Reducing the use of energy results in fewer greenhouse gas emissions.

We all benefit from trees, and we must do everything to protect them.

Celebrate the Earth! Plant a tree!

○ How are trees important to enhancing the environment?

Culture

"The End of the World"

In recent years, a movie genre has become increasingly popular: disaster movies. *The Day After Tomorrow* and many other disaster films take their roots from 1970s movies in which people try to survive catastrophes. Nowadays, very spectacular special effects and fast-paced suspense make such films extremely popular.

Some producers try to deliver an environmental message in their films, but disaster movies are not to be taken too seriously. Although they might look realistic, most of the time the facts are greatly exaggerated and the pace accelerated to attract an audience and please the box office. Nonetheless, they can be very entertaining to watch on the big screen.

The Day After Tomorrow, 2004

Mind Boggler
Answers

p. 166: 1,176 animals and 747 plants

p. 168: In 2002, E.O. Wilson, an eminent scientist, estimated that if human destruction of the biosphere continues at its present rate, one-half of all species of life on Earth will be extinct in 100 years.

p. 169: 400 years; 4.3 trillion butts

p. 173: 343 litres

p. 178: approximately 19

Culture

Did You Know That?

In the *Harry Potter* series, the four elements are represented in the four houses?

- *Slytherin* is water and its common room is situated under Hogwarts' lake.
- *Ravenclaw* is air. Its emblematic animal is the eagle.
- *Hufflepuff* is earth and it is located somewhere in the basement, near the kitchens.
- *Gryffindor* is fire. A large fireplace can be seen in the common area.

Do you know (or can you guess) what colours were used to represent each of these houses?

OTHER THINGS TO DO

1 A myth is a story about a real, natural phenomenon. Native Americans were very close to nature and loved to tell stories about nature. Write your own myth about one of the four elements.

3  Prepare a presentation based on your choice of an endangered or extinct species.

2 Do some research to learn about alternative forms of energy and present your findings to the class in the form of a quiz or a puzzle.

4  Write or record a review of a disaster movie. Give both facts and opinions found in the film.

The Ultimate Challenge

Look Back

○ Look back at the pictures on pages 150–151 and explain why they are there and what their link is with each other and the unit.

○ What are your answers to the questions on page 151?

Think About It

○ By now, you should know what global warming is and where it comes from.

○ You should be able to talk about the impact of global warming on the planet, and on the four elements and life itself.

○ Are you optimistic or pessimistic about our future?

Now What?

○ Think about what you should do if you want to live a long and healthy life.

○ Think about what we can do as individuals and as a society to help the planet.

○ Take action right now! Get involved!

Don't forget to select some of your work for your portfolio!

3-2-1

3	2	1
Explain what you understand by these three terms: clean energy forest ethics solidarity	Name two things that could change the future positively.	Find one action that you will put into practice.

UNIT 7

IN THIS UNIT...

In this unit, you will develop your media literacy by exploring the role of advertising in modern society. You will observe media messages and note where they appear. You will then analyze ads and exercise critical thinking skills. Finally, you will create your own advertisement, which you will present to your classmates.

Ads are everywhere!

Guiding Questions

- What does it mean to be media literate?

- How does learning about advertising help us become wiser consumers and more media literate?

As far as the eye can see.

In **TASK 1**, you will start thinking about ads and exploring their constant presence in modern society. You will investigate a variety of places where ads can be found.

Have a Look Around You

From the moment we wake up in the morning until we fall asleep at night, we are bombarded with publicity. It is present at our breakfast table, on our computer screens, on our clothing... Ads are everywhere!

1. Work with a partner. Brainstorm about all the different places where we might find publicity.
   - Can you list at least 10? Check pages 182–183 for ideas.

2. Write your answers on the handout.

3. Share your answers with your group.

4. Complete the handout.

Culture

Using the Right Word

Publicity is a general term for public information. *Ads* and *advertisements* are forms of publicity. They may appear in various media. *Commercials* are ads that are on TV or radio; they are broadcast. *Announcements* are public statements that teach or inform. This word is NOT used to refer to ads in general.

publicity: information about a person, group, event or product that is spread through various media to attract public notice.

advertisement: a notice, such as a poster or a paid announcement in newspapers and magazines, on TV, on Web sites, etc., designed to attract public attention or patronage.

ad: a synonym (and short form) for advertisement.

commercial: a paid advertisement on television or radio.

announcement: a brief message that is broadcast or made orally; a public statement.

---

to broadcast: to transmit information electronically.

Observe and Make Links

The term **media** is the plural form of the word **medium**. A medium is a means or instrument of communication. In Activity 2, you will begin constructing a word web of all the media used for advertising purposes.

1. Look at the answers you wrote in Activity 1.

2. Look at the word web below.
   ○ Do you understand how it is organized?

3. Read the examples that have been filled in.
   ○ What other words can you add?
   ○ Where will you put them? Why?

4. Work with a partner to begin building your word web. Add all the media you can think of on the handout. You will add new forms of media to your web throughout the unit. You may be surprised at how many different forms of advertising there are.

5. Validate your choices with the class.

Culture

A **word web** is a type of graphic organizer. It may also be called a *thought web*, a *mind map* or a *concept map*.

Although the name varies, the purpose is always the same.

It is a visual way of organizing words, thoughts and information.

It can help you understand and remember better. It can also help you organize your ideas before writing about them.

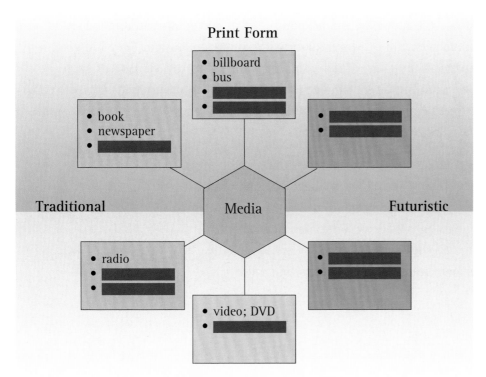

Print Form

- billboard
- bus

- book
- newspaper

Traditional

Media

Futuristic

- radio

- video; DVD

Broadcast Form

Perceiving the Unnoticed

Messages hidden inside messages, advertising you can't see or hear: Does this exist?

1. Listen to the audio text.

2. Follow along with the written text below. Pay attention to details.

3. Complete the handout.

Subliminal Messages

A **subliminal message** is created by an image or images that your unconscious mind detects but that you do not realize is there. It is conceived to persuade or induce. It is a signal that is hidden within another message.

People do not realize they are being manipulated because subliminal messages are below the normal limits of perception. Subliminal techniques have been used in both advertising and propaganda. They are also used in self-help tapes. Many people have debated the validity of such techniques. Some of the questions include: What is their purpose? How effective are they really? Could such techniques be used to manipulate our behaviour in a dangerous way?

Did you look carefully at the title of this unit on the opening page? Does it contain a "subliminal" message?

A market researcher named James Vicary was the first to introduce the idea of subliminal advertising. He became well-known in 1957 when he conducted an experiment in a movie theatre. Moviegoers were repeatedly shown rapid advertisements that were

to **induce:** to influence someone's actions or thoughts.

propaganda: a conscious effort by an institution to manage or control public opinion.

spliced into the film. According to Vicary, people were compelled to consume as a result. Even though they did not consciously perceive the messages, they bought more junk food. People around the globe were outraged. Several countries, including the United Kingdom, Australia and the United States, banned the use of subliminal advertising.

In 1958, Vicary conducted another experiment. This time it was a television test. During a Canadian Broadcasting Company (CBC) program, he flashed the message "telephone now" hundreds of times. There was no increase in phone calls. A few years later in 1962, Vicary admitted that the original study had been a fake. He had fabricated the results.

For Fun and Practice

How many sentences can you find in the passive voice?

- In the texts in this unit
- In various ads in magazines and newspapers

Focus on...

THE PASSIVE VOICE

The passive voice is used less frequently than the active voice, which is the "usual" voice.

How to form *the passive voice:*

Subject	Auxiliary (to be)	Verb (past participle)	+ Object
Many people	are	influenced	by publicity.
That ad	was	made	with teenagers in mind.
Some commercials	have been	banned	from airing.

When to use *the passive voice:*

1. When want to emphasize the object or give it importance:

Active Voice	Passive Voice
Millions of people watch the Super Bowl commercials.	The Super Bowl commercials are watched by millions of people.
The campaign committee paid for the ad.	The ad was paid for by the campaign committee.

2. When we do not know the subject:

Active Voice	Passive Voice
X uses publicity stunts to attract customers.	Publicity stunts are used to attract customers.
X will place the ad on a billboard.	The ad will be placed on a billboard.

---

spliced: joined, added or connected to something.

compelled: forced; obliged.

The Sky's the Limit!

Advertising seems to be going further and further. Consumers are pursued more and more actively. The line between private and public is getting harder to see. How far can publicity go? Where will it all end?

Talk About It!

- Which advertising gimmick surprised you most? Why?

- Would you consider shaving your head or getting a tattoo for advertising purposes? For what price?

- Do you know of any other new or very unusual advertising gimmicks?

- What do you think of these ideas? Are they fun and creative or simply strange and exaggerated? Explain.

1. Read the article below.

2. Complete Part 1 of the handout.

3. In your groups, answer the questions in the **Talk About It!** box.

4. Complete Part 2 of the handout.

5. Remember to add these new advertising media to your word web!

Space for Rent, Inquire Within

Talk about new – and different – directions in advertising!

Although fortunately the idea won't appeal to everyone, it seems that many people are ready to allow their bodies to be used for advertising. Did you know that some people are actually shaving their heads and renting out that space to advertisers? For real! And not just temporarily until the hair grows back... For terms of up to five years, with a signed contract! What do you think happens if the person dies in the meantime? Is that a breach of contract?

Also, numerous employees of a well-known sports company have had the famous company logo tattooed on their lower left legs. For sure, it's a way of showing company loyalty. Would you call that renting or buying?

This advertising craze has spread to animals as well. For a long time, farmers have rented the sides of their barns to advertisers, but now some farmers are allowing the cattle to be branded with a company name and

---

gimmick: innovative means of promoting a product.

logo! Somehow, that takes the romance out of what used to be a nice Sunday-afternoon drive down a quiet country road.

Eggs! Oranges! There's even advertising on food! And not just the peel-off labels you find on bananas. As you crack open your hard-boiled egg in the morning, you may have to face advertising. A major broadcasting company has run ads for a TV series stamped on eggs and well-known images of popular cartoon characters have been stamped on oranges, apparently as a way of encouraging youngsters to eat more fruit.

These are but a few examples. There are dozens more. If there is even the slightest chance of turning "unused" space into advertising, you can be sure that a clever marketer will find a way to do so. That's all part of creativity in advertising: attracting the consumer's attention and then pushing the limits! But at what cost? And to whom?

Culture

FYI

Did you know that there is a Quebec company that specializes in putting advertising on eggs as well?

Recycle Today's Newspaper!

For Fun and Practice

Can you find the brand names of the products and companies mentioned in the article?

By using a search engine and typing in keywords, you should be able to pull them up on the Internet. If you need help, see to *How to Search the Web* in the Toolkit page 262. While surfing, you may come across other examples of innovative places for publicity. Share your findings!

Culture

On the Money

Did you know that even currency has been used for advertising purposes?

American currency was twice transformed into ads. At one time, peel-off ads were put on 25-cent coins to promote savings bonds.

On another occasion, peel-off ads were placed on the back of one-dollar bills to promote a television miniseries.

---

brand name: distinctive name that identifies a product or manufacturer; trademark.
peel-off ad: sticker with advertising on it.

We have already taken notice of the fact that ads are everywhere. In **TASK 2**, we will now explore how they originated. Then we'll have a look at where publicity may be heading.

Where Did It Start?

In our modern technological society, we are confronted with a barrage of media messages each and every day. We are used to seeing advertisements when we watch television or go on-line or to the cinema, and when we read newspapers or magazines. We see ads on the way to work or school, in and on buses, metros and taxis. Advertising is pervasive. Its history is linked to human communications, and, as you will see, it didn't start yesterday.

1. Look at the illustrations and read the text below.
   ○ How did advertising begin and how has it evolved?
   ○ What effects does this have on us?

2. Complete the handout.

From the Ruins of Babylonia to Text Messaging in Your Room

The first evidence of advertising was uncovered among the ruins of several ancient civilizations. This evidence dates back to 3000 B.C in ancient Babylonia (present-day Iraq). Outdoor displays were among the first recorded means of advertising. Signs painted on the sides of buildings were discovered by archaeologists in the excavated ruins of Rome and Pompeii. Some of these signs advertised land and buildings for rent, while others promoted taverns in nearby towns.

barrage: an overabundance, like a deluge.

pervasive: ever present, everywhere.

outdoor displays: outside or exterior announcements or exhibits.

excavated: dug up or uncovered.

Culture

Being literate used to just mean being able to read and write. Our modern technological society has transformed that notion of literacy. Being "literate" in modern society now involves **media literacy**.

Today, it is essential to be able to understand the power and influence of multimedia messages.

Multimedia is no longer merely a part of our culture; it has become our culture.

Town criers became popular during the Middle Ages. Their role was to communicate information to the people. They would move about town and make public announcements, shouting loudly so that everyone could hear them. Not only did the criers read official public notices, they also encouraged people to visit certain merchants and buy their goods.

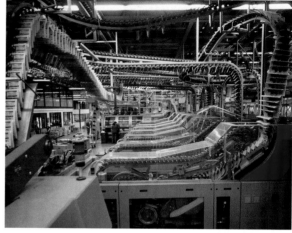

A modern printing press in action

Paper, still an important and widely used material today, was invented in the year 105 A.D. (or C.E. for Common Era). Tsai Lun, an official in the Chinese Imperial Court, developed an effective technique for making paper. His technique was kept secret for many centuries, but once out, it spread like wildfire. Printed newspapers, books, magazines and advertising followed much later, after Johannes Gutenberg invented the movable-type printing press in 1450.

The array of inventions and technological developments has continued to expand for almost 600 years. Human ingenuity has developed many ways to communicate, inform and entertain, including the telephone, movies and television, computers and the Internet, MP3 players and video consoles, as well as wireless phones and text messaging. And, of course, along with these new inventions come new ways of advertising.

Albert Einstein once said, "Imagination is more important than knowledge, for knowledge is limited while imagination embraces the entire world." One can't help but wonder where, in terms of advertising, the combination of the two will take us next.

---

to spread like wildfire: to circulate quickly.

array: wide selection or large quantity.

ingenuity: inventiveness, intelligence.

TASK 2

What's Next?

What will advertising be like in the future? Only time will tell for sure; however, a look at the latest trends may cue us in.

1. Have a look at your word web and all the various places, forms and ways used to get a message across.
   ○ Are there any places left on Earth not yet invaded by ads?

2. Brainstorm about the latest technological developments and gadgets.
   ○ What are they?
   ○ Has the advertising industry gotten hold of them yet?
   ○ How could they be used for advertising?

3. Prepare to listen to the text by reading the short introduction below and looking at the illustrations.
   ○ What is the meaning of **high tech**?

4. Listen to the text.
   ○ Focus on new places and ways to advertise.

> Remember to add any new media you come across to your word web.

5. Complete the handout.

6. In your groups, use the **Talk About It!** box to discuss the ideas presented in the text.

Talk About It!

- Are there places that should be "off-limits" to publicity?
  (For example: places of worship or schools...?)
  Use the cues to help you.

Cues

- I think that (I don't think that...)
- I feel that (I don't feel that)...
- It's important (essential) that...
- Publicity should be allowed in...
- It must be allowed in...
- It should not be permitted in... because...

High Tech

We may not know for sure what form advertising will take in the future, but you can be sure that it will be something high tech. Consider these recent trends and the impact they may have on the future of advertising.

---

trend: tendency; style.

to cue in: to give clues or information.

to get hold of: to gain possession of; to find.

off-limits: banned; not allowed or permitted.

place of worship: a place for religious assembly: a church, mosque, synagogue, etc.

USING MUST AND SHOULD

Must is used to show obligation by law. It is also used for what the speaker thinks is necessary or essential.

Examples:

- You must be 16 to have a driver's license.
- I must go or I will be late for class.

Should is used to give advice. It is used for a recommendation.

Examples:

- You should watch that ad; it's great!
- You shouldn't let yourself be influenced by that publicity.

Write About It!

The Future of Advertising

- Complete the following statement:
  In the future, advertising will...
- Write a paragraph using that sentence as your topic sentence. Include as many details as possible.
- Remember to use the future tense. If you need help, refer to the Toolkit page 316.
- Correct your text with a partner.
- Share your vision of the future of advertising with the class.

We have explored the idea of how pervasive advertising is in modern society. We have also explored how it started and where it's headed. Now it's time to dig deeper and have a look at the way ads work. In **TASK 3**, you will learn how to deconstruct media messages.

Learning to Deconstruct

Have you ever stopped to really look at ads? What makes an ad effective?

1. Read the text below.

2. Read the *How to Analyze an Ad* box on the next page.

3. Bring in two ads from a magazine and work with a partner to deconstruct them.

4. Complete the handout.

Behind What You See

All media messages are designed to appear natural, but all of them are, in fact, constructed to reach a *specific* audience for a *specific* reason. Most media messages are made to gain profit or power, or both. Understanding this allows you to take a giant step toward media literacy.

Media messages play on human perceptions. It is important to realize that *who you are* may affect *the way you perceive* the message. Building on what we learned about perceptions in Unit 4 on fairy tales, for example, it is easy to understand why selling something to Little Red Riding Hood would not be approached in the same way as selling the same thing to the Big Bad Wolf.

Media messages are constructed using the language, techniques and tricks of the trade. To be effective, they are constructed using specific types of words and expressions. The images are carefully selected, so is the mood; nothing is left to speculation. Commercials may also make use of other elements like a catchy jingle, ambient music or special effects.

Media messages have values embedded in them. Remember, being media literate involves using critical thinking to see beyond first-level representations. It involves looking at what the ad is trying to make us believe and understanding how this was done.

By taking the time to pick ads apart, by deconstructing them, we become more aware of the influence publicity can have on us and learn to make responsible choices.

Making responsible choices is a key to media literacy.

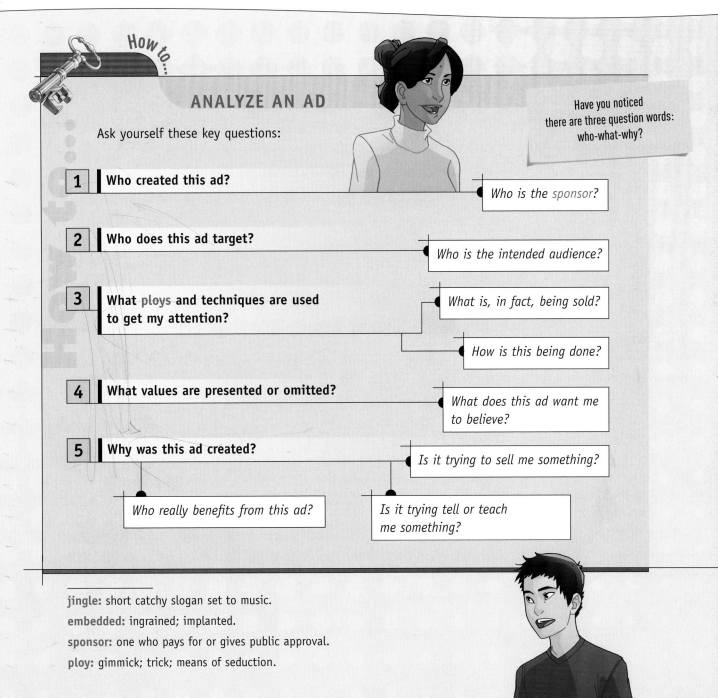

How to...

ANALYZE AN AD

Ask yourself these key questions:

Have you noticed there are three question words: who-what-why?

1 | **Who created this ad?**

Who is the *sponsor*?

2 | **Who does this ad target?**

Who is the intended audience?

3 | **What ploys and techniques are used to get my attention?**

What is, in fact, being sold?

How is this being done?

4 | **What values are presented or omitted?**

What does this ad want me to believe?

5 | **Why was this ad created?**

Is it trying to sell me something?

Who really benefits from this ad?

Is it trying tell or teach me something?

jingle: short catchy slogan set to music.

embedded: ingrained; implanted.

sponsor: one who pays for or gives public approval.

ploy: gimmick; trick; means of seduction.

ACTIVITY **2**

The Power of Words

New and improved! Incredible! All natural... When deconstructing ads, it's important to examine the words used. You can be sure that each one has been carefully and artfully selected. In this activity, we will look into word associations and how they are used to influence our perceptions.

Talk About It!

- What associations do advertisers want us to make with the product being advertised?
- What do they want us to believe?
- How do the words used appeal to the ad's target audience?

1. Brainstorm together to come up with a list of expressions that are often heard or seen in advertising.

2. Read the text below and the *Focus on Using Adjectives to Compare Things* box on the next page.

3. In your groups, have a look at your ads.
   ○ Do they use the comparative and superlative forms of adjectives?
   ○ Do they use words like those listed in the text below?
   ○ What words or expressions are recurrent?

4. Use the **Talk About It!** box to discuss the choice of vocabulary found in ads.

5. Complete the handout.

For Fun and Practice

Words That Sell

- Keep an ongoing list of all the comparatives and superlatives used in ads.
- Keep a list of power words and expressions you come across in ads.
- Share them with the class.

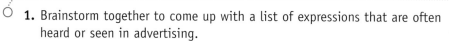

Power Words, Words with Punch

Ads are carefully constructed to entice their targeted audiences. The words and expressions used have been carefully selected to appeal to their emotions and connect with their prior experiences.

Bigger and better! Faster! More economical! Products to make your clothes *whiter*, your breath *fresher*, your body *healthier*... The use of the comparative form of adjectives is common. Superlatives are also widely used. *The best choice! The greatest adventure! The most incredible product!*

Advertisers favour adjectives like *super, outstanding, incredible, fabulous, rare, revolutionary, exclusive...* nouns like *breakthrough* and *miracle...* and verbs like *outrank, outlast, prove, reveal, surpass...* They like words with power, words with punch.

If only everything were as great as they claim!

USING ADJECTIVES TO COMPARE THINGS

THE COMPARATIVE FORM OF ADJECTIVES

How to form the comparative:

A) SHORT ADJECTIVES (1-2 syllables)	Add "**-er**"	*faster, richer, cleaner, bigger, easier*
B) LONG ADJECTIVES (over 2 syllables)	**more** + the adjective + *than*	**more** *effective,* **more** *incredible,* **more** *expensive* **than** *the other one*
Exceptions:	good ⟶ **better** bad ⟶ **worse**	
Some adjectives use either form: *quieter, more quiet; simpler, more simple...*		

When to use the comparative form:

Use the **comparative** form to compare **two** things.

> *Example:* Brand X is cheap. Brand Y is cheaper.
> Brand Y is cheaper than Brand X.

THE SUPERLATIVE FORM OF ADJECTIVES

How to form the superlative:

A) SHORT ADJECTIVES (1-2 syllables)	the + adj. + "**-est**"	*the fastest, the richest, the cleanest, the biggest, the easiest*
B) LONG ADJECTIVES (over 2 syllables)	the + **most** + the adjective	*the* **most** *effective, the* **most** *incredible, the* **most** *expensive*
Exceptions:	good ⟶ **the best** bad ⟶ **the worst**	
Some adjectives use either form: *the quietest, the most quiet...*		

When to use the superlative:

Use the **superlative** form to compare **three or more** things.

> *Example:* Brand X is cheap. Brand Y is cheaper. Brand Z is the cheapest.

See the Toolkit for variations and exceptions page 307.

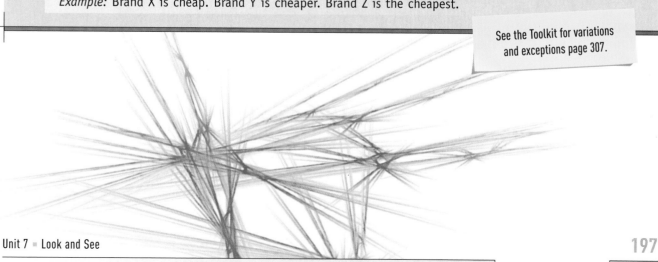

ACTIVITY 3

And the Power of Pictures

Words... Pictures... Pictures... Words... Is one more effective than the other?

1. There is a saying, "A picture is worth a thousand words."
   - What does it mean?
   - Is it true?
   - What do you think is more effective in advertising: words or pictures?

2. Look at the picture on the next page.
   - Why is it effective? What is more important: the picture or the caption?

3. As a class, hold an informal debate on the subject by trying to find examples of ads that support each side.

4. Complete the handout.

Remember: Media literacy involves constantly developing your critical eye. Ask yourself questions. Look for the hidden messages.

Culture

"A picture is worth a thousand words."

Some people believe that this popular saying is an ancient Chinese proverb. Others say that it comes from a Chinese advertisement. There is also some confusion about the translation. Apparently, the Chinese proverb states that "One picture is worth ten thousand words" and **not** "a picture" and "a thousand."

Many people believe that it was Fred Barnard, an advertising executive from the 1920s, who coined the phrase. Trying to convince advertisers to use images in their ads, he suggested that pictures would grab people's attention more than words.

---

caption: title or short description that accompanies an illustration or a photograph.

to coin a phrase: to invent an expression.

The Language of Ads

Advertisers use words and images to capture the attention (and wallets) of their audiences. They also use other elements, techniques and ploys. This activity will help you focus on some of them.

1. Think for a minute about the techniques and ways advertisers try to "suck you in."

2. Read each of the statements.

3. In your groups, find examples in ads of each of the ways mentioned.

4. Complete the handout.

❶ *That could be you!*
Advertisers associate their products with an **appealing lifestyle**. People in ads are attractive; they live in nice homes and do fun stuff.

❹ Commercials choose their **background music** very carefully to evoke a specific mood. Music for a funeral parlour will not be the same as music for a product aimed at selling snacks to young kids.

❷ *Using our product will make you rich, smart, sexy... It will bring you **instant success**.* This technique puts people in the wishful thinking mode.

❺ **Freebies.** Everyone likes getting something for nothing. Advertisers entice customers with toys in boxes of cereal, discount coupons, 2-for-1 sales and other free stuff. They also hold **contests**.

❸ *Everyone's doing it, eating it, playing it... You should, too. Don't be left out! Come on, **join the club**!*
Advertisers try to influence people by making them feel that they are the last people on Earth not using their products.

❻ Some ads use **humour**, funny situations gone wrong, etc. to grab the consumer's attention and sell their products.

❼ *Nine out of 10 dentists recommend...* Advertisers influence people with advice from **experts**, **survey results** and endorsement by **celebrities**.

to suck someone in: to take advantage of someone.

endorsement: public support.

DISTINGUISHING BETWEEN FACTS AND OPINIONS IN ADVERTISING

Advertising plays with fact and fiction. In fact, it often confounds fact with opinion:

FACT

A fact is a statement that **can be proven.**
A fact is **objective.**

> *Example:* BMW is a German car company.
> Honda is a Japanese car company.

- Use or look for nouns like *research* and *researchers*, *studies* or *surveys*... and verbs like *to prove* when discerning or expressing **fact.**

OPINION

An opinion expresses a person's **feeling, belief, viewpoint, idea** or **judgment.**
An opinion is **subjective.**

> *Example:* He thinks that they make the best car in the world.

- Use or look for verbs like *to think, to believe, to seem*... when discerning or expressing **opinion.**

Check back in Unit 6 for more on facts vs. opinions.

No, that cereal won't give you the power to fly.
No, Johnny, that car doesn't really have a lion in it.
No, that soup won't...

> *"Advertising may be described as the science of arresting the human intelligence long enough to get money from it."*
>
> Stephen B. Leacock

For Fun and Practice

Work with a partner to find examples of facts and opinions in newspaper or magazine ads. Explain why they are facts or opinions.

---

to discern: to distinguish.

From everything discussed and explored so far, it might appear that ads are "bad." They seem to corrupt our minds and pollute our environments. But are they really all bad? In **TASK 4**, you will explore a different type of advertising, one that tries to lend a helping hand.

Selling vs. Saving

Do you know what a public service announcement is? What about sponsorship? In Activity 2, you will learn something about these forms of publicity. Later, you will be asked whether they go hand in hand.

1. Read the definition of a public service announcement at the bottom of the page.

2. Brainstorm with a partner about public service ads.
   ○ How many can you come up with?

3. Jot them down on the handout.

4. Compare your lists in your groups.

5. Read the short definition about sponsorship.

6. Read and listen to some PSAs.

7. Discuss in your groups using the questions in the **Talk About It!** box.

8. Finish completing the handout.

PUBLIC SERVICE ANNOUNCEMENT

A public service announcement is also referred to by its acronym, PSA. It is a short message that is usually produced on film or video, or using an audio recording medium. There are also print PSAs. The ad on page 199 is an example of a print PSA. Since the goal of a PSA is to inform and educate the public, many public service announcements are about health and safety.

SPONSORSHIP

Sponsorship is the act of financing and promoting a product, person or cause.

hand in hand: together; in co-operation.

Heaven Can Wait. Buckle Up!

Picture this: An announcement warning people of the dangers of not buckling up.

The setting is a car crash. We see a motionless driver and a passenger in a crashed car. The music is celestial. We see shadowy figures rise up out of the bodies. Suddenly, the music stops.

One of the shadowy figures quickly returns into the passenger's body. He appears to suddenly awaken from a deep yet disturbed slumber. He reaches for his seat belt. We see his hand touching the buckled belt.

Then the words "Heaven can wait. Buckle up!" float across the screen.

Love. It Comes in All Colours

This was a television commercial and print advertisement produced by the National Urban Coalition in 1970 as part of a campaign to promote racial harmony. The TV commercial featured political figures and celebrities from sports and show business singing the chorus to *Let the Sun Shine In* from the famous musical *Hair*. It ended with the words "Love. It Comes in All Colors" superimposed across the screen. It was broadcast as a public service announcement during several shows, including the popular *Ed Sullivan Show*.

Think About It!

- What do you think about this description? Does it sound effective?
- Would it make you think twice about not wearing your seat belt?

For Fun and Practice

- Make a list of three causes or issues that you feel should be the subject of public service announcements at your school, in your community or at a higher level.
- Think of someone you would recommend to sponsor these announcements and why. These people do not necessarily have to be famous.

Talk About It!

- What celebrities or famous people can you think of who sponsor a cause or do PSAs?
- For what causes?
- For what reasons?
- Does having someone famous sponsor a cause help influence the public? How?

Cues
- I think that (I don't think that...)
- I feel that (I don't feel that)...
- I'm sure that...
- I'm not sure if...
- It seems to me that...

---

to buckle up: to fasten your seat belt.

Selling <u>and</u> Saving

Two things that appear to be opposite can sometimes meet and meld. A new age of advertising has arrived. A number of successful companies have launched ad campaigns that benefit certain causes, drawing attention to urgent social issues.

1. Read both questions.

2. Use the examples given in the texts as a starting point for a class discussion.

3. First discuss in your groups how you would answer each of the questions.

4. Fill in the first part of the handout.

5. Then continue the discussion as a class.

6. Complete the handout.

QUESTION 1

Is the Commercial World of Advertising Discovering the Benefits and Value of Public Service?

AIDS awareness has benefited greatly from this development. Famous actors and musicians are seen wearing decorative dog tags around their necks. In the photos, the celebrities have covered their eyes, ears or mouths with duct tape. The reference is obvious. It is the three wise monkeys' maxim, which says: "See no evil, hear no evil and speak no evil." The message that the ads are trying to portray plays on that theme and turns it around. Tape is used instead of hands to cover the eyes, ears and mouth.

Silence Kills!

The message is crystal clear: Ignoring AIDS and pretending it is not there will not make it go away. People need to speak out and get informed.

AIDS stands for Acquired Immune Deficiency Syndrome.

---

to meld: to blend or mix together; to merge.

What Other Conscious Commercial Ventures Are There?

The **Product Red** ad campaign was launched in 2006 to help women and children in Africa who are affected by HIV/AIDS, tuberculosis and malaria.

A percentage of the money generated by the sale of certain products is sent directly to the Global Fund. (The Global Fund was created in 2002 by the United Nations.) Several major retailers have become involved in this campaign by producing special "red versions" of their merchandise. This allows consumers to contribute to a worthwhile cause while enjoying their usual choices. This new form of advertising is known as "cause-related marketing" and the money raised so far has been substantial.

The pink ribbon is the breast cancer emblem. It is now found on a variety of products, and money for research has been flowing in. Maybe our spending will help find a cure.

Many people sport **silicone wristbands** as a way of showing support for a cause. One of the first ones was the yellow "LIVESTRONG" wristband

launched by the Lance Armstrong Foundation. Another example is the white "ONE" wristband to *Make Poverty History*.

For Fun and Practice

As a group,
- Choose a cause that you would like to bring to the public's attention.
- Explain your choice.
- Decide what kind of advertising campaign you would envisage.
- Present your ideas to the class.

Other major illnesses hold yearly campaigns to raise money to fund research.
How many can you recall?

worthwhile: valuable or important enough to be worth one's time, effort or interest.

ou have learned about the history of advertising and explored its role in modern society. You have also learned about the language of ads and how to deconstruct ads to determine hidden meaning. You will now have the chance to put all this new knowledge into practice. In the **FINAL TASK**, you will construct your very own ad and present it to your class.

Create It!

It's time to try your hand at making up your very own ad. Release your imagination! Get those creative juices flowing!

1. Think about everything you have learned about advertising and how an effective ad is constructed.

2. Choose a product that you would like to advertise.
   ○ It may be a real product or one you invent.
   ○ If you prefer, you may choose to do a PSA. If so, determine the message you want to get across.

3. Look at the various media listed on your word web.

4. Choose the media that will be most effective for what you want to say.

5. Plan your ad with the help of the handout and the **How to Create an Advertisement** box on the next page.

6. Read the handout carefully to make sure you understand how your ad will be evaluated.

7. Follow the steps in the **Production Process of an Advertisement** box, page 208, to help you create your ad.

8. *Go for it!*

---

creative juices: intellectual vitality.

CREATE AN ADVERTISEMENT
"THE SIX Ds"

1 **Decide** on the type of advertisement you would like to create:
- a commercial ad (to sell something)
- a public service announcement (to inform or educate people)

2 **Determine** your target audience.

3 **Define** your media.
- Choose the best means of getting your message across.

4 **Describe** your product.
- Choose keywords and catchy expressions.

5 **Devise** ways to get your message across.
- Choose techniques to establish atmosphere and support what you want your audience to believe.
- Make your product or cause irresistible!

6 **Do** it!

In Unit 2, you learned about mantras. Can you find at least two possible examples of mantras on these pages?

---

to devise: to come up with an idea; to think up or imagine.

The Production of an Advertisement

PRE-PRODUCTION

Brainstorm about the kind of ad you wish to create.

Determine the product or cause you wish to promote.
Remember to identify your target audience.

Define your media.

Decide what techniques you will use to entice your audience
in order to sell your product or advance your cause.

Find a name for your product and make a list of power words
to promote it.

Plan the layout or storyboard of your ad.

Validate your choices with your peers and the teacher.

PRODUCTION

Create your ad according to the layout or storyboard.

Use the checklist on the handout to make sure you have
not forgotten anything in your ad.

Make sure you have respected the requirements set forth
in the evaluation criteria.

Validate a preliminary version by presenting your work to
a sample audience.

Edit and add the final touches, taking feedback into account.

Present your ad to the class.

POST-PRODUCTION

Review the whole process.

Objectively evaluate your work and participation
as an individual and as a team.

In Unit 2, you learned how to design an effective poster. Many of the tips given may also apply to your ad. It may be helpful to go back and have a look.

Present It!

It's now time to present your ad to the class.

1. Decide on the form of your presentation, according to the medium chosen for your ad:
   - Will you showcase the ad, that is, show and explain it to the class, using visuals?
   - Will you "broadcast" your ad and then explain it?
   - Will you act out your ad "live" and then explain it?

2. Use the handout to help you plan and organize your presentation.

Tips and Hints
for Presenting Your Ad

- Know the date of your presentation and commit to it.
- Make sure you have all the necessary materials, props and equipment you need.
- Make sure you know how to use the equipment and that it is working properly.
- Practise!

In Unit 2, there is a list of tips and hints on how to communicate effectively...

Marshall McLuhan (1911–1980)

Marshall McLuhan was an influential Canadian and a man of many talents. He was a professor of English literature, a philosopher and a scholar. He was also a pioneer in media studies, exploring human communications in all its new and evolving forms. In the early 1960s, he popularized many expressions that are now commonly used, such as *the global village, food for the mind* and *the medium is the message.*

> *"Ads are the cave art of the twentieth century."*
>
> Marshall McLuhan

The *global village* refers to how our big world is becoming smaller and smaller. The globe is large, but varied media put us in contact with one another easily so we know what is going on in other parts of the world. Easy access to information makes a huge expanse feel more like a little village.

The image of *food for the mind* questions popular culture. It suggests that we need to nourish our brains with ideas and not simply "the flavour of the day." Pop culture may bombard us with new

> *"Advertising is the greatest art form of the twentieth century."*
>
> Marshall McLuhan

information, but media literacy can enlighten our thinking and help us work through these messages.

In modern society, a variety of media have their say. Even today, McLuhan's statement about how *the medium is the message* rings clearly. Do you think that a message comes across differently depending on the choice of medium? If you see an ad on TV, do you react differently than if you see it in a magazine? McLuhan suggested that the choice – television, magazine, billboard or whatever – actually does make a big difference. He believed that the message was actually transformed or adapted by the means used.

McLuhan gained the status of a cult hero. He had a keen intellect and critical eye. He was an avant-garde scholar who helped to create a new area of study. Today, years after his death, his many writings and sayings are still widely quoted. His contribution to modern society is immeasurable.

 o How does the choice of the medium have an effect on the message?

---

expanse: wide open area.

keen: fine, developed.

immeasurable: vast; impossible to measure; limitless.

Getting Attention!

Publicity is designed to attract public interest or gain public attention and support. A **stunt** is considered to be an unusual or challenging feat that requires skill or daring. The two words together create a modern-day phenomenon: **gaining media attention by any means necessary.**

A publicity stunt is a way of drawing attention to a person, product, cause or event. The person may be a new up-and-coming starlet, while the product may be the newest, smallest, cutest MP3 player ever. Events, such as the launch of a new CD, may be accompanied by a free concert by the actual artist. A special cause is brought into the public eye when environmentalists call reporters and then chain themselves to trees, protesting against the cutting of old-growth forests. All of the above are elements of publicity stunts.

Media-seeking stunts may be organized by professionals or set up by amateurs. Professionals, called public relations (or PR) agents, create a buzz around their famous clients by staging some kind of special event. Keep your eyes and ears open! There are publicity stunts going on everywhere.

○ Do publicity stunts work with teens?

---

feat: an extraordinary act.

daring: fearlessness.

starlet: a young actress who is considered likely to be a future star.

reporters: journalists.

buzz: excited interest or attention; rumour.

It Isn't There by Accident!

Product placement has probably been around longer than you think. In fact, John Huston's *The African Queen*, one of the great classics in the history of cinema, was the very first film to include product placement. In 1951, the film featured a scene in which Katharine Hepburn's character threw loads of gin overboard. The owner of a certain brand of gin paid for that privilege and started a trend.

In 1982, a specific brand of chocolates made product-placement history in Steven Spielberg's *E.T. the Extra-Terrestrial*. Elliot, the film's main character, used the candy-coated treat to coax a lost and frightened alien out of his hiding place. Sales of the candy went up 65 percent after the movie was released.

Television followed suit. Many commercial products, ranging from soft drinks to clothing, were placed in the decor of popular television shows. Brand names became more and more evident during the actual shows, not simply during commercial breaks. Advertisers actively pursued maximum screen time and exposure.

In 1989, video games also entered the world of product placement when a popular video game presented a certain gang of hungry young teens constantly ordering and eating pizza. A specific pizza company was featured prominently in that game. You probably know the game and which pizza company it was...

And then there were ads within ads. Flyers and catalogues featured products that were available or on sale, and, at the same time, they also showed other items. For example, a refrigerator ad may have had a well-known brand of orange juice prominently displayed. They became mini-ads inside larger ads. Strange, isn't it?

Music videos were originally conceived as musical advertisements for bands and solo artists, but have you ever noticed that they

---

overboard: over the side of a boat or a ship.

to coax: to persuade.

released: presented or made available to the public.

to follow suit: to follow the example.

to pursue: to try to obtain.

prominently: in a manner that is immediately recognizable.

now sell a variety of other products as well? Try counting the number of products you recognize in a video clip. You might be surprised by the number.

The next time you watch music videos, grab a paper and pencil. Jot down all the brand names that you notice. Make a check mark next to the product each time it appears. Then have a look at your results. Which of the products do you own? How many would you like to have? Remember: Every item you see (video console, beverage, watch, pair of sunglasses or whatever) has been placed there on purpose. In the world of advertising, nothing happens by chance. They are trying to sell you an image; they are the "merchants of cool."

It is thus important to keep in mind that product placement is a promotional tactic. It is beneficial for both parties involved. It is an exchange of goods or services. When a product name or logo appears on a TV show, in a movie or video clip, or within a video game, ask yourself: "Who placed that there and what did they have to do to get it there?"

Once again, product placement is a prevalent means of advertising. As a consumer, you see and recognize products, but do you realize that someone is trying to sell you something? Media literacy involves constantly developing your critical eye. Ask questions. Look for the hidden message.

 Why are advertising companies so interested in product placement?

prevalent: very common; widespread.

Smile!

It really is eveywhere!

OTHER THINGS TO DO

1
Design a collage of advertisements from various magazines. Present your collage to the class. Explain your choice of images and what they represent (the media message).

3 Compose a word puzzle based on media messages and other vocabulary or expressions from this unit.

2
Create a skit or prepare an interpretation of a television advertisement. Practise and present it to your class.

Remember: Include the different URLs with your questions so that people will know where to search for the answers. Don't forget to include an answer key.

4 Create an Internet scavenger hunt. Do an Internet search and find some sites that interest you. Then make up 10 questions based on information from those sites.

Look Back

- Go back to the pictures on the pages 182–183.

- In light of everything you have learned, how would you answer the questions on page 183?

Think About It

- Think about the various media messages we've explored.

- You should be able to name several places in which these messages appear.

- Talk briefly about those you find most effective or interesting.

- Has your opinion about advertising changed in any way after completing this unit?

Now What?

- Can you now see the hidden meaning behind certain media messages?

- Continue cultivating your critical eye.

- Keep observing and analyzing.

3-2-1

Write down the three key question words you should ask yourself when analyzing media messages.	List two new words or expressions you have learned.	Find one reason why advertising is a good thing and one reason why it is a bad thing.

Don't forget to select some of your work for your portfolio!

UNIT 8

WHODUNIT?

IN THIS UNIT...

You will become both a detective and a writer. You will take a quick look at mysteries in general and explore the mini-mystery as a genre. You will try your luck at cracking a few mini-mysteries and keep *The Mystery Writer's Journal* that you will use to help you structure and create your very own mini-mystery.

○ What makes a story a mystery?

○ How does understanding and solving a mystery develop logic and creativity?

In **TASK 1**, you will learn a bit about mysteries in general and mini-mysteries in particular. You will read and try to solve a mini-mystery and then have a look at how it was constructed. This will help you later on when writing a mini-mystery of your own.

Gumshoe Knowledge

In this warm-up activity, you will begin to explore the world of mysteries.

1. Brainstorm together about what you know about mysteries in general.
   - How many authors of mysteries can you name?
   - Do you know any famous detectives?

2. Make a list of vocabulary words often associated with mysteries.

3. Try to come up with your personal definition of a mystery.

4. With a partner answer the questions in the **Talk About It!** box on the next page.

5. Complete the handout.

Culture

- A **mini-mystery** is a short mystery, usually less than 1,000 words long.

- It is a detective story that actively involves the reader by providing clues from which he or she can deduce who committed the crime.

- Usually the detective is an amateur or semi-professional.

- The answer is given at the end.

- A mini-mystery is also known as a whodunit.

Culture

Mystery Facts and Firsts

- The first mystery was published in 1841. It is *The Murders in the Rue Morgue* by Edgar Allen Poe.

- The first mystery movie was made in 1903. It is *The Great Train Robbery*.

- *Perry Mason*, *Dragnet* and *Alfred Hitchcock* were among the first TV shows based on mysteries. They began during the 1950s and reruns can still be seen today.

- Today, mysteries and thrillers are still among the most popular TV shows, box office hits and best-sellers. Everyone seems to love a good mystery!

Alfred Hitchcock

gumshoe: detective.

Do You Know Your Mysteries?

Most mysteries fall into one of four general categories.

1. The Cozy Mystery

This kind of mystery is full of clues and a plot, but it is not loaded with action. It is an intelligent mind game between the criminal and the detective.

2. The Hard-boiled Detective Mystery

This kind of mystery is generally considered to be tough and violent. There is a lot of non-stop thrilling action. In a hard-boiled detective mystery, the crime takes place in a setting where the victim will have to act alone.

3. The Police Procedural Mystery

This kind of mystery includes a lot of police department rules, like making sure the accused has been read his or her rights. In a police procedural mystery, the detective is always a police officer. Today, more and more women play the role of detectives in literature and on television.

4. The Amateur Detective Mystery

In an amateur detective mystery, the detective is someone who becomes involved in the story by accident. The amateur detective solves the mystery by using good common sense and following his or her own instincts.

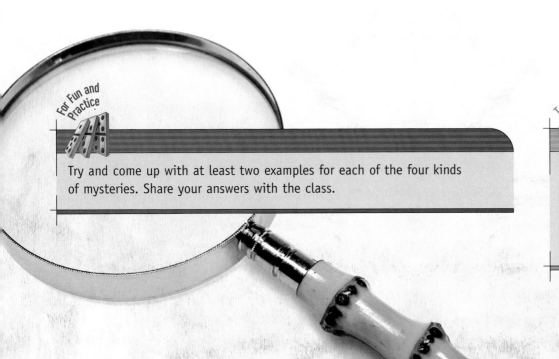

For Fun and Practice

Try and come up with at least two examples for each of the four kinds of mysteries. Share your answers with the class.

Talk About It!

- What kind of mystery do you prefer? Why?
- Which ones do you think are most popular on the big screen?

---

plot: the storyline; the sequence of events.

Solve It!

In this activity, you will read a mini-mystery and try your hand at solving it. Then you will try to extract the important elements that go into the making of a mini-mystery.

WARNING

There is a lot of vocabulary in this text. Remember, it is not necessary to understand every word. Go global!

1. Read the title of the story.
   ○ What is the meaning of the word *slip*?

2. Look at the illustrations.
   ○ Where does the story take place?
   ○ Can you make any predictions about what might have happened?

3. Share your answers with the class.

4. Read along as the story is read to you.

5. Work with a partner to complete the chart on the handout.

6. If necessary, go back and scan the text for specific information.

7. Finish completing the handout.

8. As a class, discuss what you think is the solution to the mystery.

The Big Slip

Olivia Clingstone and Jeremy Peach were students at Radville High. They had been best pals since childhood and now shared a mutual interest in crime solving. Olivia was an unusually tall girl with a gleaming mass of red curls, tons of freckles and a need to speak her mind at all times. Jeremy, on the other hand, was small for his age, wore thick Coke-bottle glasses and was naturally reserved, preferring the company of computers to people.

They were walking to the history class together when they ran into Jared Michaels, the school "hottie" who was as famous for his break-dancing as he was for his smart mouth. He was wearing the usual top-of-the-line hip-hop clothing, including a pair of oversized pants plastered with neon colours and various kinds of graffiti.

"Well, well, if it isn't the dynamic duo, Four-Eyes and Freckle-Face," he sneered.

"You should talk," Olivia shot back, "did you rob a clown to get those pants?"

Jared scowled at them and slunk off.

"Don't mind him," said Jeremy. "I happen to know he has a huge crush on you. He probably hates me because we hang out together so much."

Olivia rolled her eyes as they filed into the classroom and took their seats. The noontime bell rang an hour later and they headed off to get their lunch boxes. When they rounded the corner leading to their lockers, they saw the school custodian, Mr. Pool, looking disgruntled while mopping up a mess of dirty water from an overturned bucket.

---

pal: friend.

plastered: covered almost entirely.

to sneer: to show contempt or dislike.

to scowl at: to make a face of displeasure at someone or something.

to slink off: to walk off slowly and nonchalantly.

to have a crush on: to be in love with someone at a distance.

disgruntled: in a bad mood; in bad humour.

"Look at this!" growled Mr. Pool. "Someone spilled grape juice or something here. I cleaned it up and went downstairs to get a towel to dry the floor. I was coming back up when I heard the bucket going over and the sound of somebody falling down. But when I got here, no one was around and that locker over there was broken into."

Realizing in horror that the locker in question was his own, Jeremy checked inside only to find that his MP3 player was missing. He and Olivia started searching for clues right away. Who would want to do this to Jeremy? Three suspects came to mind. There was Viola Pierce, a "Goth" girl with an attitude that said: "Don't mess with me." Jeremy often caught her eyeing his MP3 player. Then there was Carter Evans, the school wrestling champ, who really resented the fact that Jeremy had been assigned to tutor him in math. And, of course, Jared Michaels.

"If the thief fell on the floor, he or she might be hurt," suggested Olivia. "Let's see who might be limping around the school like Quasimodo."

Sure enough, heading toward the cafeteria with a serious limp was Carter Evans. Jeremy and Olivia cornered him in front of the lunch counter.

"Hurt yourself, did you?" inquired Olivia insinuatingly.

Carter, a beefy guy with a shaved head, eyed them suspiciously. "Yeah, I got pinned down the wrong way in a match this morning," he told them. "My butt is killing me. Ask Coach if you don't believe me."

"Wrong!" Jeremy blurted out with uncharacteristic straightforwardness. "I know for a fact that Coach Clayton is out of town today with the track team."

Carter flushed, a deep red. "OK, so I got my days mixed up. I'm on painkillers. Go ask the other guys. They were there."

Just then, they spotted Viola Pierce moving casually toward a table, lost in her own little world. She was drinking juice and nodding to the sounds of... an MP3 player identical to Jeremy's! When Jeremy and Olivia confronted her, she was startled and defensive. "I got it for my birthday," she snarled. "What's your problem?"

"You asked me just this morning if you could borrow mine," said Jeremy.

"That's because I didn't have mine programmed yet, but now I do, OK?"

"You mean *re*-programmed, don't you?" probed the merciless Olivia, watching Viola turn a deeper shade of red than Carter.

Viola was about to yell out her protest when she was stunned into silence by the sight of a very peculiar-looking Jared Michaels walking right past them with a tray of hot dogs and fries.

"Look at that!" Viola burst out in complete surprise, "Jared Michaels is wearing a pair of *super* tight jeans! I can actually see what his body looks likes! He's usually swimming in those inflatable pants of his! Go figure."

"Jared Michaels could be wearing a gorilla suit for all I care!" snapped Olivia. "But I think I know which one of you is the thief. Come on, Inspector Peach, we've got some checking to do!"

Who did it?

Carter Evans?

Viola Pierce?

Jared Michaels?

---

to blurt out: to say without thinking.

straightforwardness: candour; frankness.

startled: scared; frightened momentarily.

go figure: Try and understand (*popular expression*).

TASK 2

In **TASK 2**, you will begin *The Mystery Writer's Journal*, which you will use to plan your mini-mystery step by step. This journal will not only help you keep track of all the important ideas and events you wish to include in your mystery, it will also help you organize your mini-mystery in a logical fashion.

ACTIVITY 1

Beginning with... the Crime!

Every mystery has a crime, or at least what appears to be a crime, that needs solving. What will yours be?

1. Take a few minutes to flip through *The Mystery Writer's Journal*.

2. Brainstorm with a partner about possible crimes for a mini-mystery.

3. Together make a list of your favourite ideas.

4. Write the four that appeal to you most in *The Mystery Writer's Journal*.

Focus on...

VOCABULARY BUILDING

to steal: to take property from someone without permission.

to rob: to take something with the use of force, violence or intimidation.

to break in: to force entry into a residence or building.

to burglarize: to break into a residence to rob it.

to hold up: to enter illegally with a weapon.

to swipe or **to cop:** to steal (*slang*).

to snatch: to rob from a pedestrian and run.

to embezzle: to take money in a fraudulent manner from a workplace.

For Fun and Practice

How many words do you know for *money*?

Here are some to start with: *cash, moolah, dough, bread, lettuce, green...*

224

Unit 8 ▪ Whodunit?

The Setting

Now that you have been thinking about, and perhaps already decided upon, the crime that will take place in your mini-mystery, it is important to start thinking about the setting. When and where will your mini-mystery take place?

1. Go back and look at **The Big Slip**, p. 221. Find all the words and phrases that describe the setting.
   - What do we know about the place?
   - What do we know about the time?
   - Is there anything said to describe the atmosphere?
2. Read the **Setting Tips** below.
3. Consider **where** and **when** you would like your mini-mystery to take place.
4. Share your ideas with a partner.
5. Complete the section on the setting in *The Mystery Writer's Journal*.

Setting Tips

- Try to make the reader feel that he or she is part of the story from the descriptions you give of the place.
- Don't just talk about what you can see, but also about the sounds and smells.
- Make sure you know why this particular setting is the one you need and make the reasons for your choice obvious in your writing. Build your story around the setting.
- Use the setting to create a specific mood or feeling. For example, tension will be increased if a story is set on a dark, windy, stormy night.

ACTIVITY **3**

Famous Detectives

In this activity, you will read short descriptions of some well-known detectives. In addition to learning a bit about some very famous crime solvers, you may get some ideas for the characters in your own mini-mystery. Pay attention to details as you read the texts.

Talk About It!

- Had you already heard of any of these detectives?

- From the descriptions, can you determine which of the four types of mysteries (see p. 219) each detective solves?

- Which detective would you most like to meet in person? Why?

1. Look at the pictures on the next three pages. You are sure to recognize some of fiction's most famous detectives.

2. Read the descriptions for each one.

3. Discuss them in your groups using the questions in the **Talk About It!** box.

4. Complete the handout.

Culture

A Detective by Any Other Name...

- *Gumshoe, private investigator, private eye, sleuth* and *dick* are all terms used to refer to detectives.

- The word **gumshoe** comes from the sneakers detectives often wore. These sneakers had soft, rubber heels that allowed them to move about without making any noise.

- **Private investigator** refers to a detective who works for a private company, rather than for the police. A private investigator is often referred to simply as a **P.I.**, as in the television series *Magnum, P.I.*

- A **private eye** is yet another way of referring to a private investigator. It became popular in the 1930s and is a play on the word **eye** and the letter **i** (investigator) and emphasizes the idea of a person "looking into things."

- A **sleuth** is usually reserved for an amateur detective.

- **Dick** is chiefly British slang. It comes from shortening and altering the word **detective**.

Some of the World's Most Famous Detectives

HERCULE POIROT

Hercule Poirot is the most famous character created by Agatha Christie. Poirot is a Belgian detective. He stands 5 feet 4 inches tall, has green eyes and an egg-shaped head. He has dyed black hair and his waxed moustache is always perfect. Poirot walks with a limp. He is always neatly dressed in the finest clothing. This famous detective loves luxury and the finer things in life. Poirot is known to be impatient, opinionated and direct.

This Belgian detective states that the greatest tool for crime solving is the mind, thanks to its "little grey cells" as he enjoys saying very often.

MISS MARPLE

Jane Marple, known as Miss Marple, is the second most famous of Agatha Christie's detectives. This nice, curious, elderly spinster is between 65 and 70 years old. She has snow-white hair, pale blue eyes and a pinkish wrinkled face. Always dressed in a lace cap and gloves, Miss Marple has a sharp, logical mind. She is an amateur detective who often embarrasses the local police by solving the crime.

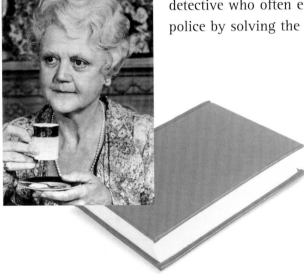

limp: with a difficult walk.

opinionated: insistent on maintaining his or her opinion.

little grey cells: brain cells.

spinster: an elderly woman who has never married.

SCOOBY-DOO

Scooby-Doo is a Great Dane detective with a tremendous appetite and the tendency to be a coward. Scooby-Doo has some difficulty with his pronunciation and begins most words with an "R."

The reason Scooby-Doo wasn't turned into a movie star until recently is mainly that computer special effects weren't advanced enough to make such a character look real.

THE SAINT

Simon Templar, also called the Saint, is a character created in the early 1930s. Templar has a number of aliases and often uses the initials S.T., introducing himself as "Sebastian Tombs" or "Sugarman Treacle" and so on. Blessed with a great sense of humour, he leaves behind his personal calling card on which there is a stick man with a halo, the logo of the TV series.

The Saint began his career as a criminal. He claims to be the Robin Hood of modern crime. He fights crime using criminal methods.

COLUMBO

This famous detective is from an American crime fiction TV series. It stars Peter Falk as Lieutenant Columbo of the Los Angeles Police Department.

Columbo appears as a shabby, slow-witted detective. However, his appearance is deceiving. Columbo uses his deliberately absent-minded character to give suspects a false sense of security. Columbo's signature technique is to exit the scene of an interview, only to return a moment later to ask "just one more thing" of the suspect. That "one more thing" always brings to light a key element in the case.

---

coward: person who is not courageous.

shabby: poorly dressed; unrefined.

slow-witted: not very bright.

deceiving: not as it appears to be.

SHERLOCK HOLMES

Sherlock Holmes is one of the best-known fictional detectives of the early-20th century. Holmes is famous for using logic and great observation skills to solve cases.

Holmes always wears a deerstalker and a cloak and has a pipe and a magnifying glass. He is described as a tall, lean gentleman with sharp, piercing grey eyes. His hair is black and he is always cleanly shaved.

Interestingly enough, Holmes inspired modern forensic science by:
- The use of fingerprints to free the innocent
- The use of typewritten letters to expose fraud
- The use of footprints, shoeprints and bicycle tracks to identify action at a crime scene

Holmes never acts alone, though. Dr. Watson, his assistant, is always close by.

JACQUES CLOUSEAU

The Pink Panther is a comedy series starring the French police detective Jacques Clouseau. Contrary to what many people seem to believe, Clouseau is not "The Pink Panther." The Pink Panther is a large, valuable, fictitious diamond. It bears its name because of the flaw in its centre. When looked at closely, it resembles a leaping pink panther.

Clouseau is seen as a bumbling, incompetent police officer whose investigations are marked by chaos and destruction, largely caused by himself. Immensely clumsy, he cannot interview a witness to a crime without falling down the stairs, destroying expensive objects or accidentally shooting another police officer in the rear. He often follows wrong leads. In spite of his apparent stupidity, Clouseau nevertheless always solves his cases and finds the culprits. He is immensely egocentric and convinced that he is a brilliant police officer. Clouseau is also known for his strong Parisian accent.

---

deerstalker: a tightly fitting hat with visors in the front and back.
cloak: a long coat without sleeves.
forensic: legal science used by police and detectives.
flaw: imperfection.
bumbling: clumsy; unskillful; uncoordinated.
clumsy: inclined to drop things or cause accidents.
culprit: a person who is guilty of a crime.

ACTIVITY 4

Your Characters

Your characters, from the sleuth and the victims to the suspects and the witnesses, are among the most important elements of your mystery. It is therefore a good idea to take the time to develop them carefully. In Activity 4, you will learn how to do so.

For Fun and Practice

Make a list of all the adjectives and expressions used to describe any of the characters in *The Big Slip*.

1. Read the ***How to Bring Your Characters to Life!*** box on the next page.

2. Work with a partner. Together, choose one of the main characters in ***The Big Slip***, page 221 and try to answer the questions in the **Talk About It!** box.

3. If there are questions that do not have answers, make suggestions.

4. Complete the handout together.

5. Start thinking about the major character in your mini-mystery and begin filling in the pages on the main character in *The Mystery Writer's Journal*.

6. Do the same on the following pages for any other characters you think you might include in your mini-mystery.

7. Continue working in your journal, adding new ideas and information as they come to you.

> You will probably be using lots of adjectives to describe your main character. If you need help in putting a string of adjectives in the right order, see the Toolkit, page 306.

Talk About It!

- Choose a character.
- Describe the size and shape, the hair colour and any other physical characteristics of this character.
- What are his or her favourite clothes?
- What is his/her favourite kind of music?
- Who are his/her best friends? Why?
- What are this person's favourite sayings or expressions?
- ....

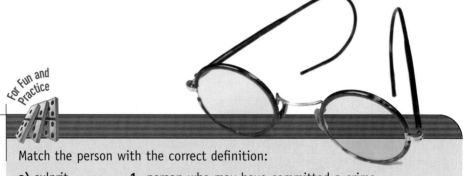

For Fun and Practice

Match the person with the correct definition:

a) culprit   1. person who may have committed a crime

b) witness   2. person who has first-hand knowledge of a crime

c) suspect   3. person who has committed a crime

d) victim   4. person who is suffering as a result of a crime

BRING YOUR CHARACTERS TO LIFE!

Describe Them in Detail!

Describe what you want the reader to know about your characters. Sometimes personality traits are sufficient. At other times, the physical description is required in order to be able to understand the true nature of the person.

Feel Good About Them!

- Your characters don't have to be perfect. In fact, perfect people are boring.
- Refer to the great detectives presented. They all have their qualities and flaws. Go for uniqueness.
- Play with their personality traits. Who knows, something quite interesting might come out of the exercise.
- The goal is to respect the true nature of your characters throughout your story.

Make Them Talk!

- Use dialogue to tell the reader more about your characters.
- And, of course, the dialogue must fit the character. Each character must have his/her own expressions that go with his or her personality and age.
- Remember, a 10 year old doesn't express himself the same way an elderly person does.

In Task 2, you laid the foundation for your mini-mystery. In **TASK 3**, you will first listen to a one-minute mystery. Then you will begin constructing your mini-mystery by determining the sequence of events. Finally, you will think up clues to help the careful reader solve the mystery and throw in at least one red herring to try and put the careless reader off-track.

Listen and Solve

In this activity, you will listen to a one-minute mystery. How did the daughter know who the thief was?

1. Before listening to the one-minute mystery, look at the illustration.
2. Listen to the one-minute mystery.
3. Complete the first part of the handout.
4. Share your answers with your groups. Use the **Talk About It!** box.
5. Finish completing the handout.

Talk About It!

- What clues does the author give to help the reader solve the mystery?

- Does logic play a role in this case? If so, how?

- How could this case have been made more difficult to solve?

- What would have made it easier?

- Do you think this is a good mini-mystery? Why or why not?

red herring: a false clue included to distract the reader.

What Happens

Before you actually begin writing your mystery, it is important to plan the actions step by step. You must first determine the plot, that is, the sequence of events. Then it will be easier to add details about the setting in order to create atmosphere, clues to keep the reader involved and a red herring or two to try and mislead him or her.

1. Think about the one-minute mystery you listened to in Activity 1.

2. Write five short sentences explaining what happened in the mystery, in sequence.

3. Compare your sentences with a partner.

4. Begin planning the sequence of events of your own mini-mystery.

5. Fill in the corresponding section in your journal.

6. Exchange journals with a partner and give each other some feedback about the sequence of events in your mysteries.

7. Make any desired changes.

8. Work on completing the previous pages of your journal.

For Fun and Practice

- Choose one of the mysteries presented in this unit and determine its sequence of events. Write the events out in short, simple sentences.

- Mix the sentences up and ask a partner to try and put them back in chronological order.

- Correct your work together.

ACTIVITY 3

Planting Clues

Part of the success of a mini-mystery resides in the way the author leaves clues that allow the reader to discover who committed the crime. The trick is to leave a sufficient number of clues to allow the mystery to be solved, without making it a dead giveaway. In this activity, you will explore the kinds of clues to leave and how to plant them effectively.

1. Read the mini-mystery on the handout.

2. Circle all the clues you find that help the reader crack the case.

3. Read **Planting Clues** below.

4. Complete the questions on the handout.

5. Begin working on clues for your mystery in your journal.

Think About It!

Which clue is most helpful in solving each of the mysteries presented in this unit?

Planting Clues

- There are three basic types of clues:
  - **physical clues** (fingerprints, personal items left in strange places, photographs...)
  - **verbal clues** (obtained through dialogue between characters)
  - **thematic clues** (black used as the colour of evil, a thunderstorm as a signal of danger, the lights going out as a symbol of something scary about to happen...).
- Sometimes the best clue is the absence of something (a dry car when it is raining outside, a dog that doesn't bark during a supposed break-in...).
- Clues can be subtle. If a person acts in a different way than he usually does, that becomes a clue.
- **Anything can become a clue.** It depends how it is presented. It's up to the writer to place clues in his or her text in such a way that they are never either too obvious or impossible to decipher.

---

dead giveaway: obvious clue.

Red Herrings

Every good mystery needs at least one red herring! In this activity, you will learn about red herrings and start thinking about one to include in your mini-mystery.

1. Read about the origin of red herrings.
2. Find examples of red herrings in the mysteries presented in this unit.
3. Think of possible red herrings you could include in your mini-mystery.
4. Take note of them in your journal.
5. Work on completing your journal.

Culture

Did You Know That...?

- In the *Scooby-Doo* series, there is a character named Red Herring who is often accused of being the criminal.

- In Dan Brown's *The Da Vinci Code*, there is a character named Bishop Aringarosa. He is a red herring in the story and his name means just that, "red herring" in Italian.

Culture

The expression **red herring** may have the following origin: Smoked herring is bright red and very smelly. It was sometimes used to train hound dogs to follow a scent. It was dragged across the trail of a hunted fox to create a new and useless scent in order to try and confuse the hound dogs. Only the best dogs were not duped and did not allow the fox to escape. Like the hound dogs, only clever readers will not be fooled by *red herrings*.

In the **FINAL TASK**, you will use all the information you have learned in this unit and the notes you have taken in *The Mystery Writer's Journal* to write your very own mini-mystery!

Writing Your Own Mini-mystery

1. Read through everything you have written in your journal.

2. Use your journal and the various tools presented in this unit to help you write the draft of your mini-mystery.

3. Use the checklist on the handout to make sure you have included everything in your draft.

4. Read the *Focus on Using Quotation Marks* box on the next page.

5. Scan the quotes in your mystery. Did you use quotation marks correctly?

6. Read the *Focus on Using the Correct Verb Tenses* box on page 238.

7. Reread your text just for the verb tenses.

8. Make any necessary corrections.

9. You are now ready to do some peer revising and editing. See page 241 for what to look for.

10. Make a polished copy of your mini-mystery.

For Fun and Practice

Match the word to the correct definition. Try to use some of these words in your mystery.

a) alibi   **1.** reason for committing a crime

b) motive   **2.** something used as proof of a crime

c) evidence   **3.** a feeling not based on facts

d) deduction   **4.** a fact used to solve crimes

e) hunch   **5.** logical reasoning

f) clue   **6.** an excuse for being somewhere else

Focus on...

USING QUOTATION MARKS

Quotation marks are punctuation marks used to quote a person's exact words when they are incorporated into your own writing.

Use the Proper Punctuation with Quotation Marks	
A comma introduces the quotation.	As Sherlock Holmes explains, "The evidence is clear."
Commas and periods go inside quotation marks.	He said, "I may forget your name, but I always remember a face."
Question marks and exclamation marks go inside quotation marks when they are part of the quotation, and outside when they are not.	The detective asked, "Did you see this man before?" Where is the "famous painting"?

Culture

"Elementary, my dear Watson."

This phrase is often attributed to Sherlock Holmes, the famous English detective. Holmes supposedly says this to his assistant, Dr. Watson, as he explains his reasoning in solving a crime.

The Hound of the Baskervilles, 1939.

For Fun and Practice

"Quote, Unquote"

1. Work with a partner.
2. Take turns writing out these quotations correctly. Help each other get it right.
   - Sherlock Holmes said Elementary, my dear Watson
   - Miss Marple asked What's your alibi
   - Columbo came back into the room and said Just one more thing Where were you last night at ten
   - Whose fingerprints are on the glass the detective inquired

Focus on...

USING THE CORRECT VERB TENSES

Verbs are divided into three distinct time frames: past, present and future.

• The **simple past**, **present** and **future** are the usual time frames.

• The **present perfect** is a verb tense in the **past** that carries over to the **present**.

• The **present continuous** is a verb tense of the **present** that carries on into the **future**.

Past	Present	Future
Simple past *Example:* I **played** tennis **last night**.	**Simple present** *Example:* I **play** tennis **every day**.	**Simple future** *Example:* I **will play** tennis **next year**.

Past continuous

Example:
I **was playing** tennis **when he called**.

> The action is finished. It was going on when something interrupted.

Present Perfect

Example:
I **have played** tennis **many times**.

> The action is finished, but there is a link with the present. There is more action to come.

Present Continuous

Example:
I **am playing** tennis **tonight**.

> The action is going on right now. Or, the action is going to happen in the near future.

Past Perfect

Example:
I **had** already **left** to play tennis **when he phoned**.

> Use the past perfect to show that an action in the past happened before another one.

For Fun and Practice

With a partner, read through one of the mysteries in this unit and find the verbs in the simple past, the past perfect and the present perfect. Explain why the tense used is the correct one.

Focus on...

CHOOSING BETWEEN THE SIMPLE PAST AND THE PRESENT PERFECT

If your mini-mystery is written in the past tense, you will have to know when to use the **simple past** and when to use the **present perfect**. Here is an easy way to go about it.

Ask yourself these questions:

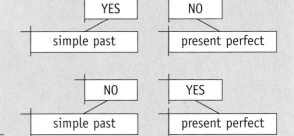

1 | Is the action over? Is it finished?

	YES	
simple past		present perfect

2 | **Do we know when in the past?**
Is the moment specified?
Example: The two friends left the park at **7 p.m.**

YES	NO
simple past	present perfect

3 | **Is there more of the same action to follow soon?**
Is there a marker like since, already or before?
Example: She has **already** solved the case.

NO	YES
simple past	present perfect

Since vs. For

- Use **since** with the **present perfect** to show when an action first started.

  Example: He **has been** a detective **since** 1978.

- Use **for** with the **simple past** or the **present perfect** to show the duration of the action:

  Examples:
  She **was** in prison **for** seven years.
  (She is out of prison now.)

  He **has been** in prison **for** two years.
  (He is still in prison.)

You may also need the past continuous.

The **past continuous tense** is used for actions in the past that were going on when something else interrupted.

Example: The lady **was playing** the piano **when the phone rang**.

The Golden Rules of Mystery Writing

From the beginning to the end, the reader must feel the satisfaction of being included in solving the crime.

There must be a crime and the reader is on the lookout for clues to solve it.

The criminal must be present from the beginning. He/she must not just "pop up" for no reason.

The writer must take an honest approach and make all the clues available to the reader.

The reader must know everything the protagonist knows.

With a Fine-toothed Comb

Wow! Your mystery is almost complete. Hold on though, not so fast! It's now time to work together to revise and edit your text in order to come up with the perfect story!

Work with a partner to:

Revise Your Mystery

- Have a second look at your **opening sentence**. Does it capture the reader's attention? What does your partner think?
- What about the **characters**? Did you include a clear and interesting description? Did you use dialogue? If so, did you think of personalizing the expressions and speech patterns to fit each character introduced in your story?
- Next, the **setting**! What's so special about your setting? Is it mysterious, strange or ordinary? The setting must nevertheless fit the mood of your story. Does it do that? If not, it's not too late to add or modify ideas to fit your initial intentions.
- Now the **plot**! Did you think of bringing in any surprise elements? Did you give the readers clues throughout the story to keep their minds busy trying to solve the puzzle? Ask your partner if your mystery is too easy to solve. If that's the case, then play with the clues and add elements to mislead the reader and make him or her suspect the wrong character.
- Finally, go back and look at the **dialogue** again. Does it fit with your characters? Read it out loud. Does it flow? Does it sound natural?

Edit Your Mystery

- **Read it aloud.** Maybe you will hear yourself say some funny sentences. Your ears will catch what your eyes didn't see. If a sentence is too long, it can be confusing. Shorten it.
- **Vary your vocabulary.** If the same word comes up many times in the same paragraph, do something about it. Look for synonyms. They are easy to find in a thesaurus.
- **Check for spelling** mistakes. Those are super easy to correct. Watch for the right definition, though. Be on the lookout for homophones. *Example: You're* and *your* have two different meanings.
  - Then, as far as **punctuation** goes, use exclamation points only when the character is exclaiming; otherwise use a period.

Skunked

Everybody loved Aunt Agatha. So, when a dead skunk turned up on her doorstep, no one could quite believe it. The first thought that came to mind was that the neighbour's cat had brought it to her as some kind of trophy. But surely, he would not have placed it in an old shoebox, now would he? No, this was definitely somebody's poor excuse for a joke.

Called to the scene by Aunt Agatha's niece Sarah, Inspector Bentley carefully examined the box and its contents. Some crumpled old tissue paper and the dead skunk was all there was: no note, no fingerprints. The box said "Soccer Shoes. White. Size 10." Maybe it came from one of the high school soccer players? It wasn't much to go on, but Inspector B, as he was affectionately known,

decided to drive over and have a little chat with Coach Watkins. He was about to enter the boys' locker room when he heard a loud string of profanities, followed by a tremendous bang that sounded very much like something heavy being hurled at the metal lockers. Cautiously, he pushed open the door.

"They're gone! My shoes are gone! Someone stole my shoes! I swear I'll get even with whoever took them!" Nick was in a rage and it took several minutes for him to calm down enough to talk to Inspector Bentley. It seemed that the lock on his locker had been picked and his prize shoes stolen. Everyone knew how much those shoes meant to Nick and how he kept them in their original box even though they were almost a year old. Now they were gone! The box, too.

Inspector B began taking notes in his little, black, spiral notebook with a cheap ball-point pen. Being the astute detective he was, he realized almost immediately that there was a connection here to Aunt Agatha's dead skunk.

"Well, son, I'm afraid I've got good news and bad news. The good news is that I have your box." Nick's eyes lit up. "The bad news is that your shoes aren't in it."

"Huh? Where did you find it? Can I have it back?"

"Not just yet. For now, it's evidence in another crime. Sorry I can't say anything else. It's privileged information... Any idea of who would want your shoes? Any enemies out there? Anyone jealous?"

Big John came over. "Hey, what about those two creeps yesterday?"

"These two gentlemen happen to have names?"

"No idea. But they were working for some sort of company. They were wearing grey uniforms and yellow safety hats. They saw Nick going through his usual pre-game ritual and began teasing him. We let it pass... Shouldn't have... Damn!"

Inspector B tapped himself on the belly, proud of the progress he'd already made on the case. He stuffed his notebook into his back pocket, placed his pen behind his right ear and looked at his watch: only 8:22, time for a cup of coffee and a doughnut.

He walked into Betty's Café and took his usual spot at the booth in the corner. The place was almost empty except for a group of teenage boys, an elderly couple, Mr. Greenwald (a regular) and two men from the cable company. Inspector B immediately picked up on their grey uniforms and yellow safety hats... He was about to go over and have a little chat with them when, for some reason, he turned his attention to the boys instead.

"What's a group of young bums like you guys doing hanging around here at this time in the morning? You should be sleeping or doing sports or something."

"Ain't against the law," replied the tallest one.

"No, it isn't, but if you're out looking for trouble, I'll guarantee that you'll find it." Inspector B looked the skinny one in the eye and added, "Been doing any hunting lately?"

"Ain't against the law to hunt rabbits," he smart-mouthed, turning beet red.

The boys had gotten up and were shuffling toward the door when Inspector B added, "Isn't against the law to hunt skunks either, but that doesn't make it right!"

This seemed to surprise the teens, who nearly froze in their tracks, causing the last one to trip over the leg of a chair. In doing so, he dropped his key chain and a long gold lace. Inspector B reached over and picked them up.

"Hey, that stuff's mine. Give it back…, sir." He added the "sir" at the last second.

"Yeah, well this lace happens to look exactly like something I'm looking for," he said, dangling the lace in his face. "You boys are going to have to come down to the precinct."

"What for? We didn't do anything."

"Good. Then you have nothing to worry about. Come on. Let's go."

The cable guys exchanged glances, paid for their breakfast and hurried out. Inspector caught sight of the badge number of one of the two, just in case. And, he couldn't help but notice that one of them was wearing white sneakers. Soccer shoes? He noted the information in his notebook.

At the precinct

"Okay, now suppose you guys tell me what you know about some missing soccer shoes, and cut the crap." The boys looked at each other uncomfortably, but said nothing.

"Fine, then we'll do it the hard way, starting with you." Inspector B pointed to a short kid with red hair and glasses and asked him to follow him into a small room. Now the others began getting nervous. Buddy didn't fare well under pressure.

"Man, we never should have gone into that stupid doughnut shop," commented Sam.

"What did you do with the shoes anyway?" Jake asked Fish.

"What do you mean? What shoes?" feigned Fish.

---

to shuffle: to walk without lifting the feet.

precinct: local police station.

"What do you mean 'What shoes?'"

"I don't know what you're talking about."

"Like hell, you don't!" And with that Jake gave Fish a big shove.

"What's wrong with both of you idiots? Cool it!" said Sliver, whose real name was Silver.

Inspector B came out of the little room and motioned for Fish and Jake to follow him to a second small room nearby. That left Sam and Sliver out in the lobby. After almost an hour, they had still not come out and Sam began to get really worried. He was sweating profusely and couldn't keep his legs from trembling. "Man, I can't take this any longer."

Finally, Inspector B came out. "Okay, so now why don't you tell me why you left the shoebox at Aunt Agatha's house?" Sliver and Sam looked at each other with genuine surprise.

"Who's Aunt Agatha?" they asked. And for once, they were telling the truth.

Inspector B put his pen behind his ear and read through his notes one last time. Buddy had told the truth when he said that he didn't know who took the shoes and that Jake, Sliver and Fish all liked hunting small animals. Fish was lying when he said that Sam took the lace from one of the soccer shoes, and Sam was telling the truth when he said that none of them knew Aunt Agatha. Last but not least, Sliver was lying when he said that Fish or Jake had taken the shoes and put the skunk in the box. Inspector B closed his notebook. Case solved. He patted his belly with satisfaction. Soon he would reward himself with another cup of coffee and doughnut. First though, he wanted to stop by and explain things to Aunt Agatha.

  o Who stole the shoes and left the shoe box with the skunk in it on Aunt Agatha's doorstep?

After Twenty Years

Slightly adapted from O. Henry

The policeman on the beat walked up and down the avenue. The time was barely 10 o'clock at night, but chilly winds with a taste of rain in them had kept people off the streets.

Trying doors as he went, twirling his club with many intricate and artful movements, the officer, with his stout form and slight swagger, made a fine picture of a guardian of the peace. The vicinity was one that kept early hours. Now and then you might see the lights of a cigar store or of an all-night lunch counter; but the majority of the doors belonged to business places that had long since been closed.

Halfway down a certain block, the policeman suddenly slowed his walk. In the doorway of a darkened hardware store stood a man with

beat: the area a policeman patrols, usually on foot.

swagger: walking in a way to attract notice; showing off.

an unlighted cigar in his mouth. As the policeman walked up to him, the man spoke up quickly.

"It's all right, officer," he said, reassuringly. "I'm just waiting for a friend. It's an appointment made twenty years ago. Sounds a little funny to you, doesn't it? Well, I'll explain if you'd like to make certain it's all straight. About that long ago, there used to be a restaurant where this store stands – 'Big Joe' Brady's restaurant."

"Until five years ago," said the policeman. "It was torn down then."

The man in the doorway struck a match and lit his cigar. The light showed a pale, square-jawed face with keen eyes and a little white scar near his right eyebrow. His scarf pin was a large diamond.

"Twenty years ago tonight," said the man, "I dined here at 'Big Joe' Brady's with Jimmy Wells, my best chum, and the finest chap in the world. He and I were raised here in New York, just like two brothers, together. I was eighteen and Jimmy was twenty. The next morning I was to start for the West to make my fortune. You couldn't have dragged Jimmy out of New York; he thought it was the only place on Earth. Well, we agreed that night that we would meet here again exactly twenty years from that date and time,

no matter what our conditions might be or from what distance we might have to come. We figured that in twenty years each of us ought to have our destiny worked out and our fortunes made, whatever they were going to be."

"It sounds pretty interesting," said the policeman. "Rather a long time between meets, though, it seems to me. Haven't you heard from your friend since you left?"

"Well, yes, for a time we corresponded," said the other. "Then after a year or two, we lost track of each other. But I know Jimmy will meet me here if he's alive, for he always was the truest, most faithful old chap in the world. He'll never forget. I came a thousand miles to stand in this door tonight, and it's worth it if my old partner turns up."

The waiting man pulled out a handsome silver watch.

"Three minutes to ten," he announced. "It was exactly ten o'clock when we parted here at the restaurant door."

---

chap: man.

"Did pretty well out West, didn't you?" asked the policeman.

"You bet! I hope Jimmy has done half as well. A man gets in a groove in New York. It takes the West to put a razor-edge on him."

The policeman twirled his club and took a step or two.

"I'll be on my way. Hope your friend comes around all right. Going to call time on him sharp?"

"I should say not!" said the other. "I'll give him half an hour at least. If Jimmy is alive on Earth, he'll be here by that time. So long, officer."

"Good night, sir," said the policeman, passing on along his beat, trying doors as he went.

There was now a fine, cold drizzle falling, and the wind had increased. The few people out hurried dismally and silently along with coat collars turned high and pocketed hands. And in the door of the hardware store, the man who had come a thousand miles to fill an appointment, uncertain almost to absurdity, with the friend of his youth, smoked his cigar and waited.

About twenty minutes he waited, and then a tall man in a long overcoat, with its collar turned up to his ears, hurried across from the opposite side of the street. He went directly to the waiting man.

"Is that you, Bob?" he asked, doubtfully.

"Is that you, Jimmy Wells?" cried the man in the door.

"Bless my heart!" exclaimed the new arrival, grasping both the other's hands with his own. "It's Bob, sure as fate. I was certain I'd find you here if you were still in existence. Well, well, well! Twenty years is a long time. The old place is gone, Bob; I wish it had lasted, so we could have had another dinner there. How has the West treated you, old man?"

"It has given me everything I asked it for. You've changed lots, Jimmy. I never thought you were so tall by two or three inches."

"Oh, I grew a bit after I was twenty."

"Doing well in New York, Jimmy?"

---

to get in a groove: to get stuck in a routine.

drizzle: steady rain.

"Moderately. I have a position in one of the city departments. Come on, Bob; we'll go around to a place I know of, and have a good long talk about old times."

The two men started up the street, arm in arm. The man from the West, his egotism enlarged by success, was beginning to outline the history of his career. The other, submerged in his overcoat, listened with interest.

At the corner stood a drug store, brilliant with electric lights. When they came into this glare, each of them turned simultaneously to gaze upon the other's face.

The man from the West stopped suddenly and released his arm.

"You're not Jimmy Wells," he snapped. "Twenty years is a long time, but not long enough to change a man's nose."

"It sometimes changes a good man into a bad one," said the tall man. "You've been under arrest for ten minutes, 'Silky' Bob. Chicago thinks you may have dropped over our way and wires us she wants to have a chat with you. Going quietly, are you? That's

sensible. Now, before we go on to the station, here's a note I was asked to hand you. You may read it here at the window. It's from Patrolman Wells."

The man from the West unfolded the little piece of paper handed him. His hand was steady when he began to read, but it trembled a little by the time he had finished. The note was rather short.

> Bob,
> I was at the appointed place on time. When you struck the match to light your cigar, I saw it was the face of the man wanted in Chicago. Somehow I couldn't do it myself, so I went around and got a *plainclothes man* to do the job.
>
> JIMMY.

 o What's the twist in this story?

---

to gaze upon: to look directly or closely.

plainclothes man: policeman not in uniform.

Culture

O. Henry

O. Henry

- O. Henry was the pen name of William Sydney Porter. He was born on September 11, 1862, on a plantation in North Carolina. In 1879, he started working as a bookkeeper in his uncle's drugstore, and in 1881 – at the age of 19 – he was licensed as a pharmacist. It was while in prison for embezzlement that O. Henry began writing short stories. He wrote some 300 stories in all. He died in 1910.

- O. Henry is known for his clever use of endings with a twist in his stories. You can find many of them on the Internet.

"There are stories in everything.
I've got some of my best yarns
from park benches, lampposts, and newspaper stands."

– O. Henry

OTHER THINGS TO DO

1 Produce a CD with the collection of mini-mysteries produced by your classmates.

3 Read a book by one of the authors mentioned in this unit.

2 Watch the movie *The Saint* and use a graphic organizer to show the parts of a mystery.

4 Turn your mini-mystery into a play.

Look Back

Look back at pages 216-217. You should be able to answer the Guiding Questions and explain why the title and the illustrations were chosen for this particular unit.

Think About It…

○ Think about mysteries you have read or watched on television and what made them good or lousy.

○ Think about the role logic plays in mysteries.

○ In a mystery, you should be able to create and describe a character, catch and hold the reader's attention, build suspense and bring in the unexpected.

Now What?

○ Consider finding some mini-mysteries on the Web and printing them out to read and solve.

○ Maybe you could start writing a new mystery. Why not?

3-2-1

Name three things you learned.	List two new vocabulary words or expressions you remember.	Name one mystery novel you want to read in English.

Don't forget to select some of your work for your portfolio!

Montreal, June 1

Dear Students,

Your first year in Cycle 2 is almost over. Before closing your books for the summer however, it's time to take a step back and reflect on everything you have accomplished in English throughout the year. What are you most proud of having accomplished?

Please take a minute to flip through the pages of your book... Which was your favourite unit? Why? In which one did you learn the most?

We're sure you realize that learning English will open the door to lots of opportunities. Don't be afraid to take the risks involved; you'll find it worth the time and effort...

It is our hope that you will continue exploring this fascinating world of ours by *Connecting Through English*.

Have a great summer!

Sincerely,
The Team

Elisa   Judith   Martine   Suzanne

Reference
Toolkit

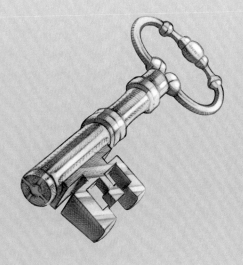

Grammar

Cross-Curricular Competencies

Cross-curricular competencies are competencies developed in all subject areas, not just in English. They play an important role in developing thinking and social skills. They are necessary tools to help you cope with the various situations that arise throughout your life and, as such, are considered essential in the working world.

There are nine cross-curricular competencies, organized into four distinct categories. As you do the tasks in your Student Book, you will be developing all of these competencies to some degree, and some more than others.

The cross-curricular competencies, or CCCs as they are often called in English, are:

Intellectual Competencies

- Uses information
- Solves problems
- Exercises critical judgment
- Uses creativity

These competencies help you develop your thinking.

Methodological Competencies

- Adopts effective work methods
- Uses ICT (Information and Communication Technologies)

These competencies help you develop strategies and tools in order to become better organized.

Personal and Social Competencies

- Achieves his/her potential
- Cooperates with others

These competencies help you develop personal and social skills for life.

Communication-Related Competency

- Communicates appropriately

This competency helps you develop various ways to communicate effectively in different situations.

In this section of the Reference Toolkit, you will find step-by-step procedures to help you develop particular aspects of a number of cross-curricular competencies.

START AN INFORMATION LOG

There are **three keys** to keeping a good information log:

1 | **Selection**

- Don't write everything.
- Choose only the information you find most **interesting** and **pertinent**.

2 | **Recording** (writing down)

- Don't copy word for word.
- Go for **keywords** rather than complete sentences.
- Get the facts right.
  - Pay special attention to **dates** and the **spelling** of proper nouns.
- Write down all **sources**.
  - It's important to know where you got your information in case you need to double-check something.

3 | **Organization**

- Use a system.
  - You want to be able to find your information easily.

Remember to keep your log up to date. It will only be useful if it is complete.

---

to double-check: to check again; to verify.

TAKE NOTES

Taking notes is not always an easy task. It takes practice. Following these steps will help you:

1. Don't try to write everything down. Focus on the main ideas mentioned. Add more specific sub-ideas to them later.

2. Don't write complete sentences. Use keywords.

3. Know in advance what information you need and write only that information. If possible, use a graphic organizer.

4. It's okay to use personal symbols and abbreviations. Just make sure you understand them later on! If you can't read them, they will not be very useful.

5. If you are taking notes from a book or an article, remember to note the source. If you copy exact words or text from anywhere, remember to use quotation marks.

Good notes:
- are **short** and **precise**
- use **keywords**, not complete sentences
- use a **graphic organizer**
- can be **personalized**
- list the **source**

Citing Sources and Making a Bibliography

Citing Sources

When citing someone else's work, there are two general rules to follow:

1. When you copy something directly, word for word, put it in quotation marks and state the source.

2. If you borrow ideas that are not general knowledge, without copying them directly, don't use quotation marks, but state the source.

Making a Bibliography

Formal writing should contain a bibliography of the sources used. It should give due credit to the authors involved and allow the reader to consult them if he/she wants or needs additional information.

This is how to make a list of your sources:

Book	Author. *Title: Subtitle*. Place of publication: Publisher, Date. Black, Simon. *The Pony Mystery*, New York: Winston Publishing, 1987.
Magazine or newspaper article	Author. "Title of Article." *Title of Periodical,* Volume # (Date): Pages. Dufour, James. "The Greenhouse Effect." *News Today,* Vol. 3 (Jan. 6, 2002): pp.11-15.
Web site	Author (if available). "Title of page." Editor (if available). Date (if available). Institution. URL. **(Omit any information not available.)** "Black History." 2004. [on-line] http://www...
Article from an encyclopedia	Author. "Title of Article." *Title of Encyclopedia*. Date. Munroe, Alfred. "History of Musicals." *New World Encyclopedia*. 2005.

The abbreviation for **page** is **p.** For **pages**, it's **pp.**

How to...

RECOGNIZE A FACT AND AN OPINION

A FACT is *verifiable*.

There is proof from a reliable source to back it up.

It isn't fiction. It cannot be refuted unless you're an expert who has collected data yourself and done serious research on the topic!

An OPINION is *subjective*.

It is a reflection or a personal thought on a subject. It is not backed by proof.

It is about feelings and beliefs. What you think is right might actually be wrong for someone else.

There are different ways to express facts and opinions.
Here are some examples:

FACTS

- ***It is a fact that*** the climate is already affected by global warming.

- ***It has been proven that*** in Alaska, salmon populations are at risk because permafrost pours mud into rivers, burying the gravel needed by the fish to reproduce.

- Biologists have ***observed that*** in Costa Rica, 66% of the different species of frogs have vanished since 1975.

- ***According to scientists***, the percentage of the Earth's surface suffering from drought has more than doubled since 1970.

- *"We haven't yet used alternatives to fossil fuels because there are initial high-end costs. Economics always plays a key role,"* **says Professor Will Gosnold.**

OPINIONS

- ***It is all right*** to use animals in order to satisfy our needs.

- ***It would be wrong*** to say that oil will run out before today's students are 50 years old!

- ***I don't think*** there is anything we can do to make up for the harm already done to the environment.

- ***We can trust*** industry to stop polluting the atmosphere.

- ***We should trust*** industry to take stronger measures.

- ***According to my parents***, keeping animals in zoos is inhuman.

- ***I believe*** that killing to eat is cruel.

- Hubert Reeves is ***such a cool guy!***

- Protecting the environment is ***easy as pie!***

ANALYZE AN AD

Ask yourself these key questions:

1 | **Who created this ad?**

> *Who is the sponsor?*

2 | **Who does this ad target?**

> *Who is the intended audience?*

3 | **What ploys and techniques are used to get my attention?**

> *What is, in fact, being sold?*
>
> *How is this being done?*

4 | **What values are presented or omitted?**

> *What does this ad want me to believe?*

5 | **Why was this ad created?**

> *Is it trying to sell me something?*
>
> *Who really benefits from this ad?*
>
> *Is it trying tell or teach me something?*

sponsor: one who pays for or gives public approval.

ploy: gimmick; trick; means of seduction.

How to...

SEARCH THE WEB

The easiest way to search on the Internet is to use a search engine.

Most current search engines are pretty effective and very powerful. Following these tips will help make your research even easier and more efficient.

For a simple search, identify **keywords**, **phrases** and the **subject categories** to use in your search.

- Play with your search terms.
- Think of as many ways to describe your topic as you can.
- Identify synonyms, distinctive terms and alternative spellings.

One word might be common in Canada but not necessarily in other countries.

- The Internet is international, and while your *truck* may roll on *tires*, British *lorries* roll on *tyres*.

For a more precise search, use **and**, **or** and **not**.

- Using **and** narrows the search results.

  Example: A search using the terms ***black and history*** will return documents that contain only both words.

- Using **or** broadens the search results.

  Example: A search using the terms ***black or history*** will return documents that contain either or both words. Only one of the words needs to be present to get a document.

- Using the **not** operator will drop any documents that contain the excluded term.

  Example: If you are looking for countries in West Africa (but not Senegal), write: ***West Africa not Senegal.***

Use + and " "

- ***slavery + Canada*** will return documents that contain both words.
- Putting the term in **quotation marks** will return only documents containing **exactly** what you put in quotation marks: ***"Black history"***

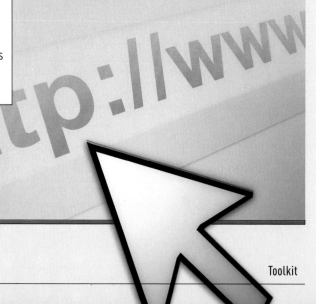

Determining the Validity of Information Found on the Web

It's important to realize just how easy it is to publish on the Web. That's great, because it means you can find out just about anything you are looking for. The whole world is right there at your fingertips, so to speak. There are, however, some downsides. Since anyone can put anything on the Web, how do you know if the information you find is true?

> Taking the time to check out a Web site before you use it as a reference can save you a lot of problems down the road!

One of the quickest ways to validate a Web site is to look at its URL or Web address. For example,

- Addresses that end in **.gov** or **.gouv** are government addresses.
- Educational organizations often end in **.edu** (US) or **.ac** (academic institution, outside the US).

These are generally considered to be reliable sources.

- Addresses that end in **.org** belong to organizations. They also tend to be reliable, although sometimes they may present biased information in order to promote their cause.
- Less reliable are those addresses that anybody can buy. Validity then depends on the author's credibility and the ways you have of checking the veracity of the information.

Ask yourself the following questions:

1. Is there a mission statement describing the purpose of the site?
2. Who sponsors the site?
3. Is it a personal site, created by an individual?
4. Is the author identified?
5. What information is given about the author? What are the person's credentials?
6. Are sources of information listed and documented?
7. Is the content biased or does the site attempt to present facts?

8. Is the "look" professional?
9. Are there lots of grammatical and spelling errors?
10. Is the date of the most recent site update indicated?
11. When was the content last updated?
12. Do the links work?
13. Is there a lot of distracting advertising or are there too many wild graphics "jumping around"?
14. Is there a site map?
15. Are you able to contact the owner or webmaster of the site?

You want to be able to answer <u>yes</u> to the questions in blue and <u>no</u> to those in pink. The answers to the other questions should also provide clues to the reliability of the site.

Fostering Cooperation and Collaboration

Things to Think About

When working together...

- Make sure that everyone gets a fair chance to speak, especially those who are less talkative or less fluent in English.

- Avoid interrupting when someone is speaking.

- Avoid changing the subject too abruptly.

- Indicate by your gestures, facial expressions and posture that you are interested in what is being said.

- Offer your help to someone trying to understand a text.

- Make sure you take the time to help everyone on your team.

- Offer constructive feedback, as opposed to negative feedback, before or after presentations.

- Encourage your team members.

- Take turns and equally share the work to be done.

- Pool your talents and resources.

- Do your part of the work.

- Respect deadlines for group work.

- Give credit where credit is due.

Working together is not necessarily *cooperating*.

"There is no I in team."

Communicating Effectively

Tips and Hints

1. Become familiar with the information. **Practice** giving it.

2. Prepare a short **introduction** and **closing**. This will contextualize your presentation and get your audience's attention.

> *A connection with current events, sharing a personal experience or even asking a question can help guarantee success.*

3. Watch the **tone of your voice**. You want to create a pleasant and relaxed atmosphere. This should also help you relax.

4. Practise **handling your support material**.

> *This part could get tricky if you haven't taken the time to synchronize everything!*

5. Also, whenever possible, **keep eye contact** with the audience and take pride in presenting your information. Your audience will certainly appreciate that.

Try practising in front of a mirror or even in the shower.

Use your best friend, your family, or even your teddy bear or dog as an audience. They'll give you practice and help boost your confidence.

Knowing How to Learn

Taking the time to stop and think about how you are doing is not a waste of time. On the contrary, it will help you gain confidence and become an independent learner.

Before, during and after a task, it's best if you pause for even a short moment to ask yourself the following questions. Depending on your answers, you can readjust your plan of action.

Before	While	After
• What do I already know about the topic or task? • What other information do I need and where can I find it? • Do I understand what I have to do? Do I know the requirements? • Why am I doing this? • Where do I begin? What do I do first? • How much time do I have to complete the task? • Etc.	• Am I on the right track? • Should I stop and do anything differently? • What are my options if I get stuck? • Where can I get help? • Etc.	• How well did I do? • Did I meet the requirements? • Did I respect the deadline? • What could I have done differently? And... • Look at what you did well and apply it to the next task. • Find ways to improve certain things or do them differently. • Fix a reasonable goal and aim for it! • Etc.

Interacts Orally in English

What It Means

To interact orally in English means to carry on a spontaneous conversation with one or more persons.

How to Go About It

To develop this competency, you must be able to do each of these four steps: Initiate, React, Maintain and End (IRME).

Initiate	• Start the conversation by saying something: - You can make a comment or ask a question
React	• React to what has been said: - Non-verbally with a gesture - Verbally by answering the question or responding with a pertinent comment
Maintain	• Keep the conversation going by: - Asking another question related to the subject - Giving your opinion on the subject - Asking someone else for his/her opinion - Changing subjects and starting over again
End	• Finish the conversation: - With a polite remark like: *Thanks for the idea!* - With a comment like: *Great! Let's do it.* - By leave-taking: *Bye! See you later!*

Use **IRME** to help you develop each of these four steps.

• Write language cues in each of the four sections.

• Refer to them when speaking in class.

Some strategies you can use are:
• Stalling for time
• Asking for help or clarification
• Using gestures and substituting words
• Taking risks

PARTICIPATE IN A DISCUSSION

When it's your turn, think of a sentence to **introduce** your point of view. Then **support** your opinion with an explanation, a fact or an example from your own experience or that of someone you know. Remember, you can also **react** to what someone else has said during the discussion. Finally, make sure you say something to **end the conversation**.

- *In my opinion...*
- *I think that...*
- *I really believe that...*
- Etc.

1 | **Introduce** your opinion or point of view.

- *I know that...*
- *I learned that...*
- *It happened to me.*
- *... because...*
- Etc.

2 | **Support** it with a fact, an example or a reason.

3 | **React** to the opinions of others.

- *I agree completely.*
- *I disagree.*
- *That's amazing (unbelievable, strange, incredible, crazy, ridiculous...).*
- *What you just said is...*
- *Wow! Fantastic!...*
- Etc.

4 | **End** the conversation.

- *Well, that's what I think.*
- *That's all I have to say.*
- *I want to hear what Eric has to say.*
- *It's Carolyn's turn to give her opinion.*
- Etc.

JORDAN: *What do you think about doing a PowerPoint presentation?*

LISA: *That sounds like a good idea, but I'm not very good at it.*

JORDAN: *No problem. I can take care of the technical stuff.*

LISA: *Perfect! I'll scan our illustrations.*

JORDAN: *Our presentation's going to be super.
Do you want to meet tomorrow after school?*

LISA: *Sure. We can work at my house, if you want.*

JORDAN: *Great! See you then.
Don't forget your memory stick.*

LISA: *I won't. Thanks.*

Maintaining the Conversation

Maintaining the conversation is the most difficult part of oral interaction because it requires you to build on what someone else has said in order to keep the conversation going.

The usual ways of maintaining a conversation include:
- Adding a comment.
- Asking a question.
- Elaborating on what has been said with an explanation or by adding a new idea.

A conversation may also be maintained by asking for clarification or precision. These may also include apologies.

Here are some useful expressions:

POLITELY INTERRUPTING
- *Excuse me for interrupting, but...*
- *May I please add something? (...)*
- *I'd like to add something, if you don't mind. (...)*
- *There's something I'd like to mention. (...)*
- *Excuse me, but the point is...*
- *That's not the point.*
- Etc.

- *Of course!*
- *Go ahead.*
- *By all means.*
- *Be my guest.*
- *Please do.*
- *Please feel free to jump in.*
- Etc.

ASKING FOR PRECISION
- *I'm sorry, but I don't understand...*
- *I'm sorry. I didn't catch that./I didn't get that.*
  (Could you repeat what you said?)
- *Could you please explain* (how that works)?
- *What are you referring to?*
- *What are we talking about here?*
- *What do you mean?*
- *What was that again?*
- *How do you spell that?*
- *Can you put it another way?*
- *Can you be less vague?*
- Etc.

- *Hold on a sec!*
- *Wait a minute, please.*
- *Just a minute.*
- *Not so fast!*
- *Give me a minute here.*
- *Let me think about it.*
- *Come again.*
- *Hmm... Let me see...*
- *Well...*
- Etc.

More Functional Language

SHARING YOUR OPINION

- *In my opinion, ...*
- *According to me, ...*
- *I think that...* (I don't think that...)
- *I believe that...* (I don't believe that...)
- *I feel that...* (I don't feel that...)
- *It seems to me that...*
- *It doesn't seem likely that...*
- *I wish that... would...*
- *I wonder if... will/would...*
- *I realize that...*
- *I prefer that...*
- *I'll admit that...*
- *Etc.*

> **The art of giving my opinion without really saying anything!**
>
> *According to me, they are aware of the problem. I feel that they understand what's going on, but I don't think that they want to change anything. I wish they did, but I'll admit that I don't believe they will. In my opinion, it doesn't seem likely...*

MAKING REQUESTS

- *Can you help me?*
- *May I help you?*
- *Could you please (turn the volume down)?*
- *Would you please (listen to me)?*
- *Would you mind if (I sat down)?*
- *Do you mind (me taking off my shoes)?*
- *Is it okay if (I call my mom)?*
- *May I (borrow your pencil)?*
- *Etc.*

EXPRESSING ASPIRATIONS

- *I would like.../I wouldn't like...*
- *I really hope that...*
- *It's my dream to...*
- *It's my life goal to...*
- *I wish I could...*
- *I am willing to sacrifice* (my free time) *for* (a dancing career).
- *I would give up* (chocolate for a year) *to* (meet him).
- *I would rather* (be rich and famous) *than* (poor).
- *If I could, I would* (travel all year long).
- *It's not important to me that* (you come with me to the show).
- *I don't care if...*
- *I have no desire to...*
- *Etc.*

AGREEING AND DISAGREEING

- *I agree/I don't agree.*
- *I believe you're...* (mistaken/right).
- *I don't think that's* (correct).
- *You're absolutely right.*
- *On the other hand, ...*
- *According to* (him), *that's not true.*
- *That's impossible because...*
- Etc.

ANSWERING
(BESIDES YES OR NO)

Affirmatively	Negatively
• *Right on!*	• *No way!*
• *Okay/OK*	• *Never.*
• *Sure!*	• *Never ever.*
• *Fine.*	• *Not on your life.*
• *Perfect!*	
• *Sweet!*	• *Under no circumstances.*
• *No problem!*	• *Absolutely not!*
• *No sweat!*	• *Of course not.*
• *All right.*	• *Nope.*
• *You bet.*	• *I don't think so.*
• *Of course.*	
• *Absolutely.*	• *I doubt it.*
• *Definitely.*	• *Forget it!*
• *Why not?*	• *Impossible!*
	• *I'd rather not.*

SHOWING UNCERTAINTY
OR POSSIBILITY

• *I'm not sure.*	• *Perhaps*
• *I don't know...*	• *Possibly.*
• *In a way...*	• *It's possible.*
• *Sort of...*	• *I guess so.*
• *Maybe.*	• Etc.

REASSURING

- *It doesn't matter.*
- *It's not important.*
- *Don't worry about it.*
- *Take it easy.*
- *Don't sweat it.*
- *Stay cool.*
- *Keep calm.*
- *Don't panic.*
- *So what?*
- *The same thing happened to me...*
- *You're not alone.*
- *You can count on* (me).
- Etc.

WARNING

- *Watch out!*
- *Watch it!*
- *Be careful!*
- *Hold it!*
- *Look out!*
- *Danger!*
- *Stand back!*
- *Watch your step!*
- *Wet paint*
- *Don't touch.*
- *Keep out!*
- Etc.

REACTING

- *I can't believe it!*
- *No kidding!*
- *Really?*
- *I've got to admit, ...*
- *Wow! That's...*
- *Huh? I don't get it.*
- *Come again.* (when you want someone to repeat)
- *Are you sure?*
- *What's the point?*
- *So what?*
- Etc.

WORKING TOGETHER

- *Let's do it together!*
- *Why don't we (start with that question)?*
- *Whose turn is it?*
- *It's (my) turn. It's (Carolyn's) turn.*
- *Who's next?*
- *How should we separate the work?*
- *Who wants to do (Part A)?*
- *Oops! Let's get back on task!*
- *Is everybody ready?*
- Etc.

PLAYING GAMES

- *Roll the dice.*
- *Move ahead* (4 squares).
- *Change places with* (Rob).
- *Go back to square* (17).
- *Take a chance.*
- *Take a risk!*
- *Lose a turn.*
- *Free turn!/Free spin.*
- *Play again.*
- *Shuffle the cards.*
- *Cut!*
- *Deal the cards.*
- *Draw (pick) a card.*
- *Lay down your cards.*
- *Winner/loser*
- Etc.

ENCOURAGING

- *Good job!*
- *Fantastic!*
- *You've got it!*
- *You did it!*
- *Yippee!*
- *You're the best!*
- *You're a genius!*
- *Come on, you can do it.*
- *We're with you all the way.*
- *Come on. Let's go.*
- *Go for it!*
- *Almost!*
- *You're getting there.*
- *Next time will be better.*
- *Don't give up.*
- Etc.

REFLECTING TOGETHER

- *What were our strong/weak points?*
- *We did great on* (respecting the time limits).
- *(Kenny), you did a great job* (on the poster)*!*
- *We need to improve on* (speaking only English).
- *We could do better at* (sharing the work).
- *Good! But I think we can* (share ideas even more).
- *Next time we'll* (plan more carefully).
- *Let's try to* (finish on time).
- Etc.

"TIME IS MONEY…"

- *Hurry up!*
- *Let's go.*
- *Come on!*
- *Shake a leg.*
- *Time!*
- Etc.

SOCIAL CONVENTIONS

- *Bless you!* (when someone sneezes)
- *Pleased to meet you/How do you do?* (when you meet someone for the very first time)
- *May I please speak to...?* (when you want to speak with someone else, not the person who answered the phone)
- *May I please be excused?* (when you want to leave the table after a meal)
- *No, thank you. I'm just looking.* (when a clerk in a store asks you if you need help and you don't)
- *Never mind.* (when you don't need someone's help after you asked for it) (Be careful though, this can be impolite...)
- *Best wishes* (when someone is sick or when you want to wish someone well)
- *Congratulations!* (when someone tells you some great news)
- *I'm sorry to hear that.* (when someone tells you some sad news)
- *That's too bad.* (when someone tells you some sad/bad news)
- Etc.

 Use *How do you do* only when you have just been introduced to someone.

It is incorrect to use it to mean *How are you*?

LEAVE-TAKING

- *Goodbye!/Bye!*
- *See you later/See you* (tomorrow).
- *Catch you later!*
- *Talk to you soon.*
- *Ciao.*
- *Take care!*
- *Say hello to* (your sister) *for me.*
- *See you later, alligator.*
- *After while, crocodile.*
- *Have fun!*
- *Good luck!*
- *Have a nice day!*
- Etc.

MAKING POLITE CONVERSATION

- *How are you?*
- *How's everything going?*
- *How's your ...* (mother, father, sister)?
- *How was...* (your trip, the party, the weather)?
- *What's up?*
- *What's new your way?/What's new with you?*
- Etc.

USUAL GREETINGS

- *Hello!*
- *Hi!*
- *Howdy!*
- *Good morning/Good afternoon*
- *Good evening*
- *Greetings!*
- Etc.

Ending a conversation doesn't always mean that you are leaving.

Sometimes we simply end a conversation because everything has been said.

 Good night is used when someone goes to bed or when someone leaves at night.

Don't use it as a greeting.

OVERCOME STRESS WHEN TALKING

1	Use the models, cues and examples given in class as a starting point.
2	Add a personal touch or comment.
3	Take a risk. Don't be afraid of errors.
4	Remember, the message doesn't have to be perfect to be understood.
5	Say something. Go for it!

"Practice makes perfect!" or so the saying goes.

At any rate, the only way to improve is to dare to say something, anything! You may be surprised at what comes out!

274

Reinvests Understanding of Texts

What It Means

To reinvest understanding of texts means that you read, listen to or watch authentic texts, try to understand them alone and with your peers and use knowledge from them to do a new task.

How to Go About It

To develop this competency, you must:

1. **Read**, **listen to** and **watch** a variety of authentic texts in English. These include stories, fairy tales and legends, poems, newspaper and magazine articles, songs, movies, radio and television programs of all kinds, jokes, cartoons and comic strips.

2. **Construct meaning** of the texts and **show what you understand** by:
   - Asking questions
   - Answering questions
   - Completing graphic organizers
   - Discussing with classmates, etc.

3. **Adapt or use the information and ideas** from one text or several texts in a new way.

4. **Reflect on your learning** to help you set new goals.

Strategies you can use:

Before reading, listening to or watching a text:
- Activate prior knowledge
- Predict
- Direct or focus your attention

While reading, listening to or watching a text:
- Pay selective attention
- Skim or scan a written text
- Take notes
- Ask yourself questions and use inference

After reading, listening or watching a text:
- Ask questions
- Restate what you have understood to validate your understanding

The Response Process

Many texts, especially stories and poems, naturally stir up feelings and make us think. One way of exploring these feelings and thoughts is through the Response Process.

The Response Process has three phases: **exploring the text, establishing personal connections with the text** and **generalizing beyond the text.** These phases help you gain a deeper understanding of what the text really means by going beyond answering simple Wh- questions.

When you use the Response Process, you make links with your personal experiences and with the world around you. You share your experiences and ideas with your peers and co-build your understanding. Doing this makes the texts both more meaningful and enjoyable.

Sometimes, the Response Process is approached very formally with the keeping of a journal or information log. At other times, it is done more informally. You should, however, take the time to jot down your impressions, feelings and questions about the texts you read, listen to or watch. This will help you organize your thoughts and make it easier to share them with your peers.

1. When EXPLORING TEXTS, you:

Before	While	After
• Make predictions about the content of the text. • Set goals for exploring the text. • Determine what strategies to adopt to help you understand the text. • Use guiding questions to help you know what to look for.	• Confirm or invalidate your predictions. • Try to answer the guiding questions. • Identify key elements that you believe are important.	• Answer the guiding questions. • Jot down any ideas you think are pertinent. • Support these ideas with direct links to the text. • Share your ideas with your peers. • Discuss the text with your peers using the prompts provided.

2. When ESTABLISHING PERSONAL CONNECTIONS WITH THE TEXT, you:
   • Relate what happens in the text to your own personal experiences or to those of someone you know.

3. When GENERALIZING BEYOND THE TEXT, you:
   • Deal with the issue mentioned in the text on a broader level. You might, for example, discuss how it relates to your school or community, or even decide to make it your cause.

Discussion Prompts

EXPLORING THE TEXT

- *From the title and the illustration, I think this text will talk about...*
- *I already know this about the subject: ...*
- *For me, the most important part of the story is when...*
- *I noticed that...*
- *I learned that...*
- *I understood that...*
- *I had trouble understanding...*
- *To understand the text, I...*
- *I found this idea very interesting because...*
- *That part makes me think of...*
- *I believe the author is trying to...*
- *The text is about...*
- Etc.

ESTABLISHING A PERSONAL CONNECTION WITH THE TEXT

- *I experienced something similar when I...*
- *I know how the character feels because I...*
- *The main character is exactly like my sister...*
- *The woman in the story reminds me of my mother...*
- *I find this character very interesting because...*
- *I heard about this before. ...*
- *If I were in the same situation, I would...*
- Etc.

GENERALIZING BEYOND THE TEXT

- *We can do something about it...*
- *I think we should...*
- *Maybe we could...*
- *I have an idea. Let's...*
- *What if we all...*
- Etc.

How to...

How to...

READ A STORY

Does reading a story in English seem like a big job?

When you see a whole bunch of text and lots and lots of words, do you tend to panic?

Here are some strategies to help you. With a little patience and practice, you'll find reading easier and maybe even fun! Give it a try. You can do it!

▶ Before you begin reading

1. Look at the **title** and **illustrations**.
   - What information do they give you about the story?
   - Can you make any predictions?

     Example: I think this story is about...

▶ While reading the story

2. If there is a word you don't know, **keep on reading**. You may get the meaning from the context, or you may be able to understand the text anyway. Read for the **general idea**.

3. Let yourself become part of the action. Imagine you are there. **Visualize** the story, like a film in your mind.

4. Don't try to read the whole thing at once. **Read a section and stop**.

   Think about what you do understand. Do you have any questions?

5. Stop and try to **predict** what might happen next.

   *Example: I think that (Parker will miss the shot because in the title
   it says "second chance").*

6. Make **connections** to the story:

   Example: (Parker) is like me. We both (play basketball and want to be great players).

   Example: (The game) reminds me of (a football game I attended).

▶ After reading the story

7. Try to make sense of the story: Identify **the beginning**, **the problem**, **the solution** and **the ending**.

8. Think about why the author wrote this story:

   Example: The message the author wished to convey is...

   Example: I think the author wanted to show that...

9. **Share** your opinions about the story:

   Example: I think this story is... because...

Understanding the Parts of a Story

All stories follow the same general pattern. It is called the plot line.

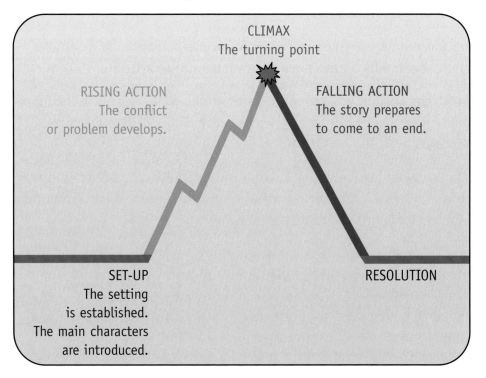

CLIMAX
The turning point

RISING ACTION
The conflict
or problem develops.

FALLING ACTION
The story prepares
to come to an end.

SET-UP
The setting
is established.
The main characters
are introduced.

RESOLUTION

If you are having trouble understanding a story, try establishing the plot line using the diagram above.

When writing a story, plan your action using a plot line.

The elements of a story include:

- **Setting** – It describes when and where the story takes place.

- **Characters** – The people in the story. The main character is called the protagonist.

- **Plot** – It is a series of events that make up the action of the story. The set-up, rising action, climax, falling action and resolution are all part of the plot.

- **Conflict** – This is the problem or sticky situation that the main character must deal with.

- **Climax** – This is the high point in the story. Something happens here that allows the conflict to end. It is the turning point of the story.

- **Resolution** – This is how the problem is resolved. It is the conclusion.

Reading Non-fiction

Non-fiction is information that is presented as being true. It is supposed to be factual information.

Documentaries, biographies, textbooks, scientific papers, news articles and encyclopedia entries are some examples of non-fiction.

Magazine articles, articles on the Internet and some articles in the newspaper may or may not be non-fiction, depending on the subject and how it is treated.

The purpose of reading non-fiction can be for pleasure, but often it is to obtain specific information about a specific subject. If that is the case, here are some tips and strategies to help you:

Read the answers to the five Ws:

Who?

What?

When?

Where?

Why?

and the one H:

How?

INFERRING INFORMATION

- Before you begin reading, look at the titles, subtitles and illustrations.
- Most non-fiction articles are divided into sections. The subtitles will give you an idea of what to expect in that part of the article.
- They can also indicate where to find specific information.

NOTE-TAKING

- When you find the information you are looking for, stop and write it down.
- Don't forget to write down the page number and the source. You may need them later.

PARAPHRASING

Paraphrasing is saying something using different words of your own.

- After you have read a factual article, you may find it useful to tell yourself what you have just read in your own words.
- If you get stuck, go back and read the difficult section again.

SCANNING

Scanning is a strategy you might find useful if you know exactly what you are looking for. Here's how to do it:

- Run your finger (and your eyes!) quickly down the article, looking for the desired information.
- When you find it, stop and read it to make sure it's what you want.

Reading a Newspaper Article

A News Article

The Dateline

The Headline
(It sums
up the article.)

The Placeline

The Lead
The most
important
information
is given at
the beginning
of the article.

In general, here
you will find out:
who
what
when
where

Daily Press

Thursday, May 27, 2004

Teens Tackle Thief

New Linton, NB. Late yesterday afternoon, two high school students found themselves the centre of attention. Gillian Carter, 16, and her friend Roxane Malone, 15, were coming out of the Mall when they heard a scream. At the same time, a tall man wearing a light grey hooded sweatshirt and navy sweatpants raced past them. "I noticed he was carrying a lady's purse and something just clicked. I stuck out my foot to trip him and Roxie kicked him in the groin. Real hard! He fell to the ground screaming obscenities. I snatched the purse and we hurried back inside the building

for help." A clerk called 911 and the police arrived and took the suspect into custody.

The woman whose purse had been stolen was elated. Thanks to some quick thinking and quick actions by the girls, she recovered everything. "These girls are my lifesaver; purse had my rent mo grocery money in it, r mention all my cards, 62 year old, who prefe remain anonymous.

The Body
It gives facts about an event that has recently taken place:
- The most important information is given in the first paragraph.
- Further details and additional information are given toward the end of the article.

Quotes by the people involved add interest and credibility to the article.

Newspapers also contain two other kinds of articles:
- **Feature Articles:** special, detailed reports on a person or event
- **Editorials:** articles expressing the opinion(s) of the editor(s) on a specific issue

Journalists put the essential information at the beginning; therefore, you may not need to read the entire article in order to find what you are looking for.

USE A DICTIONARY

Dictionaries can be used to check spelling, learn new words, find or double-check the meaning of words, or simply find the right word to use. How to best use a dictionary depends on what you are doing with the words in question.

For spelling

Once you have found the word you are looking for and know how to spell it, don't stop there:

- *Check to see if the word is invariable. If so, it will not take the plural form. That is, ... no "s."*
- *Some verbs are irregular. The dictionary will give you this information and perhaps save you from making a mistake.*

Use the guidewords at the top of the page of the dictionary to help you find your word quickly.

For accuracy

When speaking or writing, you need to use the right word. Your dictionary can help:

- *Once you have found the word, read all its definitions.*
- *Choose the one that best represents what you want to say.*
- *Look for synonyms you know. Try replacing the unknown word in the sentence with a synonym to see if it makes sense.*

For creativity

For pronunciation

Your dictionary is a great companion to help you stretch your vocabulary. Most dictionaries will give you lots of keywords, phrases, synonyms and antonyms to vary your vocabulary.

Once you have found your word, don't stop there:

- *Keep on reading.*
  You will find tons of useful information. If you're looking for a special saying or expression, you're sure to find the one you're looking for to make your statement.

It's true! See for yourself:

- *Beside each word, you will find brackets [...] with a code to help you figure out the correct pronunciation of the word. Give it a try!*

A type of dictionary called a **thesaurus** is the best tool to help you find synonyms and antonyms.

Writes and Produces Texts

What It Means

To write and produce texts means that you write various types of texts using the Writing Process to organize and structure your writing. If you are producing a media text, you will use the Production Process.

How to Go About It

To develop this competency, you must:

1. **Write often**, expressing yourself and your ideas.
2. **Explore** different types of texts, not always the same kind for the same audience and the same reason.
3. **Know what is involved** in the Writing Process and the Production Process.
4. **Follow these processes** closely.
5. Use **strategies** like planning and note-taking.
6. Use **resources** such as dictionaries, thesauruses, checklists and this Reference Toolkit.
7. **Reflect** on your writing and find concrete ways to **improve** specific points in future texts.

From the rough draft to the final copy, you must develop your own strategies and use the resources available to help you compose and improve your texts. For example, you should use a checklist to revise and edit your text. And you can ask for specific feedback from peers.

Using strategies and resources will help you communicate a clear message to your chosen audience.

The Writing Process

PREPARING TO WRITE

Be clear about the message you want to convey (the purpose) and the audience for which you are writing (the targeted audience).

Brainstorm for additional ideas with others.

If necessary, do more research and take notes.

Use examples provided in the unit to help you.

Organize your information using an outline or a graphic organizer.

WRITING THE DRAFT(S)

Concentrate on getting your ideas on paper; don't worry about mistakes yet.

Find and add information to support your point of view or opinion.

REVISING

Ask someone to give you feedback on:
The format of your text • The task requirements
• The logical sequence of the information
• Synonyms and your choice of words
• The variety of sentence structures used

Make changes, taking the feedback into account.
In case of doubt, ask for a second opinion.

EDITING

Ask someone to give you feedback on:
Punctuation • Spelling • Choice of verb tenses • Use of prepositions
• Use and placement of adjectives • Use of adverbs

Make proper corrections to your text.

Refer to the grammar toolkit to help you.

PUBLISHING

Add illustrations.

Make a polished copy.

Revising vs. Editing

Revise your text for clarity, organization and ideas.

Edit it for spelling and grammar.

It's not necessary to use the Writing Process for informal writing or short messages, like e-mails or quick notes.

In formal writing, however, using the Writing Process will help you come up with a better product.

284

PEER EDIT

One good reason for using peer editing or small group editing is to get feedback –
helpful feedback! Here's how to go about it.

TO GIVE FEEDBACK:

Listen *carefully:*
- *Don't interrupt*
- *If necessary, take notes*

Give feedback:
- *Use a checklist*
- *Mention strong points*
- *Offer suggestions*

Avoid:
- *Negative comments*
- *Automatic stamp of approval*
- *Getting off track*

TO RECEIVE FEEDBACK:

Read *your text to your partner.*

Listen *carefully:*
- *Don't interrupt*
- *Take notes*

Ask for help:
- *Ask for clarification if necessary*
- *Ask for help with specific things*
- *Don't make excuses*
- *Be open to the possibility of change*

Remember the goal:
To produce the best text possible

I really like your arguments. They support your opinion... You forgot to write a closing.

Thanks for the feedback!

WRITE A PARAGRAPH

A paragraph is a group of sentences that develops one idea or topic. This idea is expressed in one sentence called the topic sentence. All the other sentences in the paragraph explain or support this idea. The concluding sentence restates the topic sentence in different words.

To write a paragraph, try following these steps:

1 | **Choose the subject.**

2 | **Determine what you want to say about the subject in general.**

Choose a fact	or	Give your opinion
My bedroom is very small.		I think that my bedroom is too small.

3 | **Choose a fact or an opinion and write one sentence about the subject. This is the topic sentence.**

> *Examples:*
> ***Fact:*** *My bedroom is small.*
> ***Opinion:*** *I think I need a bigger room.*

4 | **Determine at least three ideas, arguments or examples to support the sentence.**

> *Examples:*
> - *I have to do my homework on my bed; there is no room for a desk.*
> - *I can't have more than one or two friends over; there is no room to sit.*
> - *I can't open the closet door very wide; my bed is in the way.*
> - *There is no room to put anything else.*

5 | **Write a one-sentence conclusion. This should repeat what you said in the topic sentence in a new or different way.**

Try this:
- If your first sentence is a **fact**, end with an **opinion**.
- If it is an **opinion**, end with a **fact**.

My room is very small. There is no room to do anything! I can't have many friends over, because there is nowhere to sit, and I can't bring in chairs, because there is no room. I can't even open the closet door all the way! My room is so small that there is no room for a desk so I have to do my homework in the kitchen or lying on my bed. I would like to have a TV in my room, but you guessed it – there is no room! I like my room, but it really is too small. Maybe I should move into the garage!

Writing Different Types of Paragraphs

All paragraphs are organized around **one idea or subject**. This is the **topic sentence**.

All the other sentences **explain or support the idea** expressed in the **topic sentence**.

All paragraphs finish with a **concluding sentence** that **restates the idea** of the topic sentence in **different words**.

There are many different types of paragraphs. The type you choose will depend on your purpose. Here are some possibilities:

 Each time you finish writing about one idea, stop.

Start a new paragraph for each new idea.

Your writing will be better organized.

Type of Paragraph/Purpose	What to Do	What to Include
DESCRIPTIVE • To describe a person, place, event or object	• Create a picture for the reader. • Make him/her feel, smell, see, etc. • Use lots of details. • Choose a mood.	• Vivid language • Lots of adjectives • Adverbs • Strong verbs
NARRATIVE • To tell a story about one event or sequence of events	• Use chronological order. • Use transition words like *first, then, later, finally*, etc. • Make sure there is a beginning, a middle and an end.	The principal elements of a story: characters, setting, conflict, climax and resolution
EXPLANATORY/EXPOSITORY • To give information or to explain something	• Use chronological order. • Or, show the relation between elements (*in between, next to, behind*, etc.). • Support with examples and facts.	
OPINION/PERSUASIVE • To convince the reader	• State your opinion clearly. • Justify it with facts, arguments and examples. • Explain why. • Use transition words like *in fact, furthermore, thus, however*, etc.	• Statistics • Quotations from experts • Reliable sources

WRITE A LETTER

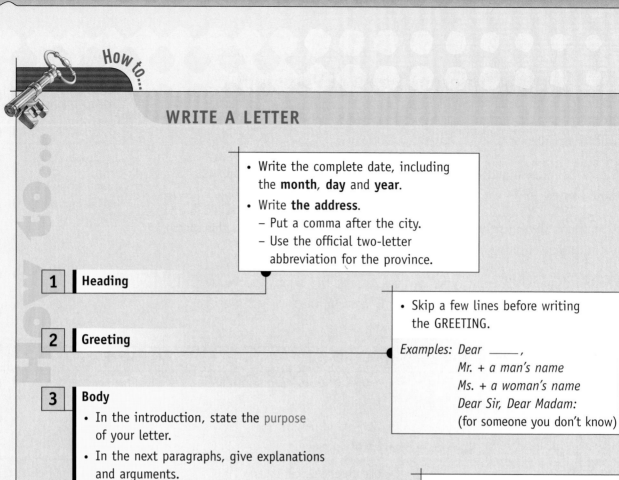

• Write the complete date, including the **month**, **day** and **year**.
• Write **the address**.
  – Put a comma after the city.
  – Use the official two-letter abbreviation for the province.

1 | **Heading**

2 | **Greeting**

• Skip a few lines before writing the GREETING.

Examples: *Dear* _____,
          Mr. + a man's name
          Ms. + a woman's name
          Dear Sir, Dear Madam:
          (for someone you don't know)

3 | **Body**

• In the introduction, state the purpose of your letter.
• In the next paragraphs, give explanations and arguments.
• In the last paragraph, summarize what you wish to accomplish by writing the letter.

BODY
This is the main part of the letter. It is the message.

4 | **Closing**

CLOSING
Depending on to whom you are writing, the closing will vary.

Examples: *Sincerely,*
          Your friend,
          With love,
          (or something creative)

Capitalize only the first word and put a comma at the end.

5 | **Signature**

Remember to sign your name under the CLOSING.

Did you forget to write something? If so, add a postscript by writing P.S. followed by your final message. Sign your initials to show that it comes from you.

purpose: reason; intention.

Writing a Mini-mystery

The mini-mystery follows the same plot line as all other short stories, but there is always a crime and a person who solves the crime. This person may be either a professional detective or an amateur sleuth.

The mini-mystery is written in such a way as to allow the reader to participate in the solving of the crime. In fact, it is important that the reader have the same information as the person who solves the crime. If he/she has too little or too much information, the mini-mystery will not be a success.

In a good mini-mystery, clues are planted very carefully. Often it takes an expert reader not to miss them. In addition, special clues, called red herrings, are artfully included to try and throw the detective (and the reader) off track.

Here are some tips to help you write a good mini-mystery:

1.	Use the **Writing Process** to structure, organize, revise and edit your story.
2.	Follow the **plot line**.
3.	Plan **details** very carefully.
4.	Use lots of **descriptive language**.
5.	Make your characters realistic. (Remember, **real people** aren't perfect!)
6.	Make the **crime** believable.
7.	Use the setting to add **suspense** and **establish mood**. For example, the atmosphere is not the same in a *bright cheerful room* and a *dark, dirty alley on a cold, rainy November evening*.
8.	Plant your **clues** carefully. They must be where they are for a reason.
9.	Add at least one **red herring**.
10.	Consider having at least **three likely suspects**; it will help make your mini-mystery more of a challenge.
11.	Make sure your mini-mystery presents a real **challenge**, but that it is **solvable**.

Use this as a checklist to help you plan and organize your mini-mystery.

Mini-mysteries often make use of deduction.

Don't tell the reader everything. Instead, require the reader to read between the lines.

If the solution to your mini-mystery is too simple, the reader will be bored. If it is too far-fetched or complicated, he/she will lose interest.

BRING YOUR CHARACTERS TO LIFE!

Describe Them in Detail!

Describe what you want the reader to know about your characters. Sometimes personality traits are sufficient. At other times, the physical description is required in order to be able to understand the true nature of the person.

Feel Good About Them!

- Your characters don't have to be perfect. In fact, perfect people are boring.
- Refer to the great detectives presented. They all have their qualities and flaws. Go for uniqueness.
- Play with their personality traits. Who knows, something quite interesting might come out of the exercise.
- The goal is to respect the true nature of your characters throughout your story.

Make Them Talk!

- Use dialogue to tell the reader more about your characters.
- And, of course, the dialogue must fit the character. Each character must have his/her own expressions that go with his or her personality and age.
- Remember, a 10 year old doesn't express himself the same way an elderly person does.

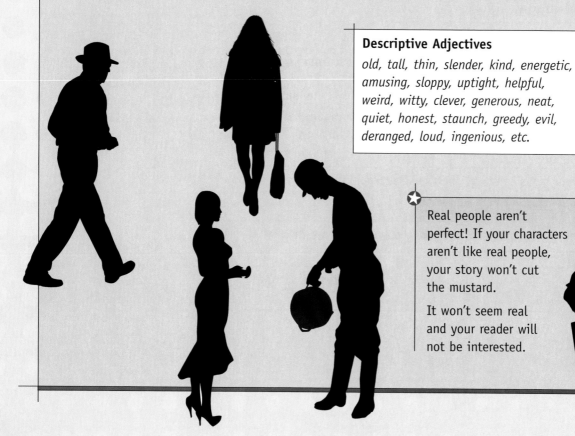

Descriptive Adjectives

old, tall, thin, slender, kind, energetic, amusing, sloppy, uptight, helpful, weird, witty, clever, generous, neat, quiet, honest, staunch, greedy, evil, deranged, loud, ingenious, etc.

Real people aren't perfect! If your characters aren't like real people, your story won't cut the mustard.

It won't seem real and your reader will not be interested.

Improving Your Writing with the Help of a Thesaurus

*Did you just use the word <u>good</u> for the third time
in your last paragraph?
Don't despair; there is hope!*

If your goal is to improve your choice of words and at the same time make your text more interesting for your reader, you can spice up your writing a little with the help of a thesaurus.

Using a thesaurus will help you add variety, personality and power to your writing.

A thesaurus is...

- A book of synonyms and antonyms.

- A thesaurus may also give a list of words related to a specific concept or subject.

The plural of thesaurus is thesauruses or thesauri.

How to say it:
thĭ-**sôr**′əs
(The accent is on the second syllable.)

A thesaurus is used to find...
- Synonyms, in order to avoid repeating the same words over and over again in your text
- Antonyms (words with the opposite meaning)
- The word that best suits the genre, purpose, intended audience and context of what you are writing
- Different expressions to help you avoid using clichés

If you don't have a thesaurus, you might try an **on-line** version:

- Just type the word in and a list of synonyms will appear.
- Make certain though that you know what the word means and that it goes with the context of your text.
- In case of doubt, consult a dictionary or choose a different word.

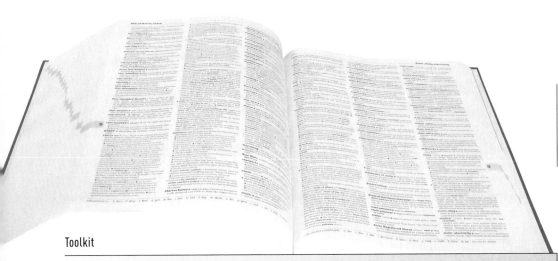

"What's another word for thesaurus?"

Steven Wright

PROOFREAD

It's okay to have your own personal proofreading strategies as long as they do the job.

If you have trouble staying on topic or your texts often fall short, the following tips may help you stay on top of things.

Tips of the Trade:

1 | **Read your text for the content.**

> Make sure all the required elements are present. Double-check everything!

2 | **Read your text out loud.**

> Reading and hearing every single word will help you notice awkward phrasing or incorrect use of words.
>
> If it doesn't sound right, then it must be wrong.

3 | **Try proofreading your text from the bottom up.**

> It will force you to pay attention to individual sentences.

4 | **Take a break!**

> In a rut? Even a five-minute break can help you get some distance and allow you to see your text in a new way.

5 | **Develop a buddy system.**

> Ask a partner to read your text. Having another person may help you locate the awkward or missing elements.
>
> Ask your partner to read for a specific task.

6 | **Stay focused.**

> Once you are satisfied with the content, check for spelling and grammar errors.
>
> Scan for one element at a time. Otherwise, it's easy to lose track of your intention.

The Production Process

PRE-PRODUCTION

Brainstorm about the media text you wish to create.

Determine the product or cause you wish to promote.
Remember to determine your target audience.

Determine your type of media.

Decide what techniques you will use to entice your audience.

Plan the layout or storyboard of your media text.

Validate your choices with peers and the teacher.

It's not necessary to make a production of everything you write. It depends on your purpose.

PRODUCTION

Create your media text according to the layout or storyboard.

Use a checklist to make sure you have not forgotten anything.

Make sure you have respected the requirements set forth
in the evaluation criteria.

Validate a preliminary version by presenting
your work to a sample audience.

Edit and add the final touches, taking feedback into account.

Present your media text to the class.

POST-PRODUCTION

Review the whole process.

Objectively evaluate your work and participation
as an individual and a team.

The Production of a Good Survey

PREPARE THE SURVEY

- Select the elements you want to investigate.
- Target your audience.
- Write your focus sentence stating the hypothesis you want to prove.
- Prepare your questionnaire.

CONDUCT THE SURVEY

- Interview people from your targeted audience.
- Initiate the conversation properly.
- Explain the purpose of your survey.
- Ask your questions.
- Conclude properly.

COMPILE THE RESULTS

- Organize your data.
- Calculate the percentages.
- Select the best kind of graph to use to present your data.
- Produce the graph accurately.

DRAW ACCURATE CONCLUSIONS

- Connect your conclusions to your initial hypothesis.

The Production of a Poster

PRE-PRODUCTION

1
Brainstorm about different ways to present the results on a poster.

2
Determine the elements you want to include.

3
Choose fonts and colours.

4
Plan the layout: position the title,
graphs and any other pertinent elements on the board.

5
Validate your choices with classmates and the teacher.

PRODUCTION

1
Mount the poster according to the layout.

2
Validate the preliminary version by presenting your poster
to a sample audience.

3
Edit and add the final touches, taking feedback into account.

4
Plan the presentation of the results.

POST-PRODUCTION

1
Review the whole process.

2
Objectively evaluate your work and participation
as an individual and as a team.

R.A.S.C.O

READABLE
Check it.

ATTRACTIVE
Choose a simple
concept.

SHORT
Keep it to
the point.

CLEAR
Choose the
fonts wisely.

ORGANIZED
Make it easy
to follow.

For a Poster
with Pizzazz!

CREATE AN ADVERTISEMENT
"THE SIX Ds"

1 **Decide** on the type of advertisement you would like to create:
- a commercial ad (to sell something)
- a public service announcement (to inform or educate people)

2 **Determine** your target audience.

3 **Define** your media.
- Choose the best means of getting your message across.

4 **Describe** your product.
- Choose keywords and catchy expressions.

5 **Devise** ways to get your message across.
- Choose techniques to establish atmosphere and support what you want your audience to believe.
- Make your product or cause irresistible!

6 **Do** it!

---

to devise: to come up with an idea; to think up or imagine.

The Production of an Advertisement

PRE-PRODUCTION

Brainstorm about the kind of ad you wish to create.

Determine the product or cause you wish to promote.
Remember to identify your target audience.

Define your media.

Decide what techniques you will use to entice your audience
in order to sell your product or advance your cause.

Find a name for your product and make a list of power words
to promote it.

Plan the layout or storyboard of your ad.

Validate your choices with your peers and the teacher.

PRODUCTION

Create your ad according to the layout or storyboard.

Use a checklist to make sure you have
not forgotten anything in your ad.

Make sure you have respected the requirements set forth
in the evaluation criteria.

Validate a preliminary version by presenting your work to
a sample audience.

Edit and add the final touches, taking feedback into account.

Present your ad to the class.

POST-PRODUCTION

Review the whole process.

Objectively evaluate your work and participation
as an individual and as a team.

Grammar

Numbers

✪ The short form of ordinal numbers is the numeral plus the last two letters of the ordinal number:

*1st, 2nd, 3rd,
25th, 50th, 75th*

✪ In British English, **hundreds** and **tens** are separated by **and**; in American English, the **and** is omitted:

123:
- one hundred **and** twenty-three (British)
- one hundred twenty-three (American)

2001:
- two thousand **and** one (British)
- two thousand one (American)

In Canada, we find both forms, but the British form is the official form.

	Cardinal	Ordinal
0	zero	--
1	one	first
2	two	second
3	three	third
4	four	fourth
5	five	fifth
6	six	sixth
7	seven	seventh
8	eight	eighth
9	nine	ninth
10	ten	tenth
11	eleven	eleventh
12	twelve	twelfth
13	thirteen	thirteenth
14	fourteen	fourteenth

	Cardinal	Ordinal
15	fifteen	fifteenth
16	sixteen	sixteenth
17	seventeen	seventeenth
18	eighteen	eighteenth
19	nineteen	nineteenth
20	twenty	twentieth
21	twenty-one	twenty-first
30	thirty	thirtieth
40	forty	fortieth
50	fifty	fiftieth
60	sixty	sixtieth
70	seventy	seventieth
80	eighty	eightieth
90	ninety	ninetieth
100	a/one hundred	

✪ Large numbers are written using commas as separators:

251,000   345,894,200

Large Number	Cardinal
1,000	a/one thousand
10,000	ten thousand
1,000,000	one million
1,000,000,000	one billion
1,000,000,000,000	one trillion

First, Second, Third...

These are called **ordinal numbers** because they show the specific position or **order** of something (the first/second/third one).

To show order, you can also use words like:
the next one: *I know the next answer.*
the one **after that**: *The answer after that is...*
the one **before that**: *The answer before that is...*
the **next to the last** one: *The next to the last answer is...*
the **last** one: *The last answer is...*

Names of Coins	
One cent	*penny*
Five cents	*nickel*
Ten cents	*dime*
Twenty-five cents	*quarter*
One dollar	*loonie*
Two dollars	*toonie*

Roman Numerals

I	1	XV	15	XC	90
II	2	XX	20	C	100
III	3	XXV	25	D	500
IV	4			M	1000
V	5	XL	40	MCM	1900
VI	6	L	50	MM	2,000
VII	7	LX	60	L̄	5,000
VIII	8				
IX	9				
X	10				
XI	11				
XII	12				

For large numbers (5,000 and up), a bar is placed over the base number to multiply it by 1,000.

Today, Roman numerals are still used on **clocks**, to identify **events** like the Super Bowl, for some **page numbers** and for **movie credits**.

Dates	*May 25, 2005* or *25 May 2005*
Years	*2006* • *1996–1999* or *1996–99* • *the eighties* or *the 1980s*
Time of Day	*6:00 a.m.* or *6:00 A.M.* • *11:45 p.m.* or *11:45 P.M.*
Address	*241 Marks Road* • *4683 42nd Street West*
Percentages	*70%* (seventy percent) • *65.5%* (sixty-five point five percent)
Large Round Numbers	*4 million* or *4,000,000* • *8.5 million* or *8,500,000*
Fractions	*1/2* (one half) • *1/4* (one fourth, one quarter)
Prices	*$46.34* (forty-six dollars and thirty-four cents)

The popular search engine **Google** took its name from a pun on the number googol. The difference in spelling was due to an error.

A Few Other Special Names

- for zero:
  - *nought* (chiefly British)
  - *oh* (when saying phone numbers)
  - *nil* or *nothing* (in sports scores)
    The score is 7-nil or *7 to nothing.*
  - *love* (tennis)
  - *zip, nada, zilch, nothing!*

- for twelve: *dozen*
- for thirteen: *baker's dozen*
- for 144 (used in commerce): *gross*
- for 10^{100} (1 + 100 zeroes): *googol*

Nouns

A noun is a person, place, thing, idea or quality. *Boys*, *park*, *pencil*, *music* and *happiness* are all nouns. Common nouns refer to things like objects, professions and locations, not names of people or places. They do not start with a capital letter.

<table>
<tr><td colspan="2">Proper Nouns (names of person, places or things like organizations)</td></tr>
<tr><td>• Proper nouns always start with a capital letter.</td><td>Columbo, Africa, Andy Warhol, James A. Naismith, the Underground Railroad</td></tr>
<tr><td colspan="2">Possessive Nouns (nouns that show ownership)</td></tr>
<tr><td>• Possessive nouns are formed by adding 's to nouns in the singular.</td><td>• Lisa's purse
• A baker's dozen</td></tr>
<tr><td>• For plural nouns, an ' is added.</td><td>• The neighbours' car
• the dogs' owner</td></tr>
<tr><td>• With words that end in an s sound, the possessive is formed by adding 's or just '.</td><td>• Charles'(s) car
• the princess'(s) crown</td></tr>
<tr><td>• For family names, the name is pluralized and an ' is added.</td><td>• the Johnsons' garden</td></tr>
</table>

Six general ways to make singular nouns plural:

Rule	Examples	Exceptions
1. For most nouns, add **s**.	*cars, horses, hats*	
2. If a noun ends with **s**, **ch**, **sh**, **x** or **z**, add **es**.	*buses, churches, bushes, taxes, quizzes*	When **ch** sounds like a **k**, only add **s**. (*Example: stomachs*)
3. If a noun ends with **f** or **fe**, change the **f** to a **v** and add **es**.	*scarves, loaves, leaves, knives*	*beliefs, chiefs, cliffs, gulfs, proofs, roofs, safes*
4. If a noun ends with a **vowel** and a **y**, add **s**.	*toys, birthdays, keys*	
5. If a noun ends with a **consonant** and a **y**, drop the **y** and add **ies**.	*bunnies, pennies*	
6. If a noun ends with **o**, we usually add **es**.	*tomatoes, potatoes, heroes*	music terms (*pianos, sopranos, altos, tangos, concertos, etc.*) and *zoos*

Articles

Indefinite Articles	
Singular	Plural
a/an	–/some
a book a mountain an apple an envelope	books mountains apples envelopes

Use indefinite articles for objects that are **not specific**.

Examples:
- She is reading **a** book.
  (a book in general)
- Apples are good for you.
  (apples in general)

Use the indefinite article the first time you speak of something:

Examples:
- She found **a** wallet.
- He is a busboy in **a** restaurant.

Definite Articles	
Singular	Plural
the	the
the book the mountain the apple the envelope	the books the mountains the apples the envelopes

Use definite articles for objects that are **specific** or **unique**. It is clear which particular objects are being referred to.

Examples:
- She is reading **the** book I gave her yesterday.
  (a specific book)
- May I have **the** green apple?
  (a specific apple)

Use the definite article the second time you speak of something:

Examples:
- **The** wallet contained a lot of money.
- **The** restaurant is downtown.

✪ In American English, we say: *in the hospital.*

In British English, we say: *in hospital.*

✪ **Some/Any**
- Use **some** for an indefinite number or quantity in an affirmative statement: *I need some help. We want some answers.*
- Use **any** with negative statements: *I don't have any money. They don't want any food.*

✪ **Do not use definite articles for:**
- Sports
- Hobbies, activities and school subjects
- Names of streets, roads, avenues, etc.
- Languages
- Names of continents
- Names of countries
- Names of provinces and states
- Names of lakes and bays
- Names of individual mountains

Use definite articles for:
- Names of rivers, oceans and seas
- Names of deserts, forests, gulfs, peninsulas and mountains

IN CONTEXT

Romano is originally from Italy, but now he lives in Quebec City near **the** St. Charles River. He speaks French at school and Italian at home. He attends **a** public high school where he is **a** good student. He prefers math and science to art. Romano plays sports, including soccer, basketball and tennis. He's also **an** excellent swimmer. He's on **the** school team. Romano likes watching TV and reading science fiction, but his passion is photography. He takes pictures of things all around **the** area. Last year, **a** photo of his taken at Mont-Sainte-Anne won **an** award. The prize was presented to him by **the** mayor.

Pronouns and Possessive Adjectives

Pronouns are words used to replace nouns. They act like nouns. Possessive adjectives and possessive pronouns are used to show ownership.

1. Here is a list of personal pronouns, possessive adjectives and pronouns and reflexive pronouns:

<table>
<tr><th colspan="2">Personal Pronouns</th><th colspan="2">Possessive Adjectives and Pronouns</th><th rowspan="2">Reflexive Pronouns</th></tr>
<tr><th>Subject Form</th><th>Object Form</th><th>Possessive Adjective</th><th>Possessive Pronoun</th></tr>
<tr><td>I</td><td>me</td><td>my</td><td>mine</td><td>myself</td></tr>
<tr><td>you</td><td>you</td><td>your</td><td>yours</td><td>yourself</td></tr>
<tr><td>he</td><td>him</td><td>his</td><td>his</td><td>himself</td></tr>
<tr><td>she</td><td>her</td><td>her</td><td>hers</td><td>herself</td></tr>
<tr><td>it</td><td>it</td><td>its</td><td>its</td><td>itself</td></tr>
<tr><td>we</td><td>us</td><td>our</td><td>ours</td><td>ourselves</td></tr>
<tr><td>you</td><td>you</td><td>your</td><td>yours</td><td>yourselves</td></tr>
<tr><td>they</td><td>they</td><td>their</td><td>theirs</td><td>themselves</td></tr>
</table>

2. This is when to use them:

	When to Use Them	Examples
Personal Pronouns (subject form)	To carry out the action of the verb They usually precede the verb.	• *I live in Victoriaville.* • *She comes from Gaspé.* • *They are studying science.*
Personal Pronouns (object form)	To receive the action of the verb They follow the verb.	• *I gave **him** a surprise party.* • *He invited **you** to the beach.* • *We saw **them** on TV.*
Possessive Adjectives	To show ownership They agree with the "possessor," not the object.	• *Angela lost **his** cell phone. (John's)* • *Angela lost **her** cell phone. (Angela's)* • *Someone stole **our** car.*
Possessive Pronouns	To show ownership They replace a possessive adjective and the noun it modifies.	• *That cell phone is **hers**. (Angela's)* • *That paper belongs to me; it is **mine**.* • *The future is **yours**.*
Reflexive Pronouns	When the subject and the object are the same by + reflexive pronoun = without others; without help	• *You should give **yourselves** a pat on the back.* • *They are playing **by themselves**.* • *I did it all **by myself**.*

⚠ WARNING

Be careful not to confuse
it's (it is) and **its**
(possessive adjective)!

• *It's raining!*
• *The dog is chasing **its** tail.*

✪ The possessive adjective always refers to the person who is the owner: *Jane's book = her book.*

Demonstrative Pronouns

Demonstrative pronouns are used for a **person, place** or **thing** that **must be pointed to**. There are four demonstrative pronouns: *this, that, these* and *those.*

	When the object is near the speaker	When the object is at a distance from the speaker
Singular	this	that
Plural	these	those

IN CONTEXT

I'LL TAKE THESE SHOES. AND, I'LL TAKE THIS SCARF...

OH, AND HOW ABOUT THAT CUTE DRESS OVER THERE AND...

...THAT BEAUTIFUL SWEATER AND... RAYMOND?

There Is/There Are

There is/there are is a common structure used to indicate that something is present.

Use **there is** with **singular** nouns and **there are** with **plural** nouns.

	There is	**There are**
Form	Singular noun	Plural noun
Affirmative	• *There is a hotel on Main Street.*	• *There are posters on their walls.*
Contraction	• *There's a hotel on Main Street.*	
Negative	• *There is not a room available.* • *There is no room available.*	• *There are not any books there.* • *There are no books there.* • *There are zero books there.*
Contraction	• *There isn't a room available.*	• *There aren't any books on the shelf.*

WARNING

Watch out for the difference between **there** and **their** and **they're**.

Prepositions

A preposition is a word that is used to describe the relationship between other words in a sentence. Prepositions are generally used to show **where** (prepositions of location or direction), **how** (prepositions of maner) and **when** (prepositions of time).

Prepositions of Location

- The socks are **on** the floor.
- The papers are **in** the wastebasket.
- The basket is **under (underneath)** the desk.
- The light switch is **above (over)** the nightstand.
- The stereo is **between** the speakers.
- The dresser is **in front** of the window.
- The white pillows are **behind (in back of)** the blue pillow.

- The desk is **across from** the dresser.
- The guitar is **against** the wall.
- The alarm clock is **next to** the lamp.
- The hockey stick is **near (close to)** the guitar.
- The computer screen is **far from** the window.
- The pencils are **to the left of** the screen.
- The books are **to the right of** the telephone.

Zoom, Zoom...

In English, we ride:

- **in** a car and a taxi (and we get **out** of them)

- **on** a horse, bicycle, motorcycle

- **on** a bus, train, plane, boat, train

- **on** the subway (and we get **off** all of these)

Prepositions of Manner

Prepositions of manner help you describe how actions are completed. The most common prepositions of manner are:

by: *Fabrice comes to school **by** bus.*
in: *Please do not write **in** red ink.*
like: *Stop crying **like** a baby.*
with: *I eat my peas **with** honey...*

Prepositions to Show Direction

across: over to the other side: *I swam **across** the lake.*
into: entering a place or building: *He went **into** the store.*
onto: up to the top of something: *She threw it **onto** the pile of clothes.*
through: in one side and out the opposite: *He drove **through** the tunnel.*
toward: in the direction of: *We walked **toward** the crowd.*

Prepositions of Time

Three Very Common Prepositions of Time

	Used with:	Examples:
on	– days of the week – dates	• *School begins **on Monday**.* • *I was born **on May 25**.*
in	– months/seasons – time of day – years – after a specific length of time	• *His birthday is **in September**.* • *The concert is **in the afternoon**.* • *She was born **in 1991**.* • *I will call you back **in twenty minutes**.*
at	– a certain time	• *I will call you **at 9 a.m.***

Exception:
at night
• *The accident happened at night.*

For Telling Time...
*It's ten **to** seven. (6:50)*
*It's half **past** four. (4:30)*

Some Prepositions of Time in Context

before	*I will meet you **after** work. I finish at 5 p.m. so I should be there **between** 5:30 and 5:45, for sure **before** 6. We can have supper together, but I have to be home **by** 9, so I can stay **until** around 8:40.*
after	
by	
between	
until	

Something to *Watch* For
Have you ever noticed that almost all watches in advertisements are set between 10:07 and 10:10? It's true.

Still More Prepositions to Show Time

Preposition	When to Use It	Common Markers	Examples
since	To show when the action began	• Specific days, months or years • Dates	• *She has been in Rimouski **since 1989**.* • *They have been married **since May 12, 2004**.*
for	To show how long	• The number of minutes, hours, days, months, etc.	• *He lived in Boston **for five months**.* • *They have been married **for 12 years**.*
during	To show when (no specific time)	• *During* + a noun	• *Carla slept **during the film**.* • *I had an accident **during the storm**.*
ago	To show when in the past	• Period of time in the past	• *We saw that show **several years ago**.* • *That happened **two Saturdays ago**.*

Adjectives

Adjectives are words that are used to describe nouns.

In English, adjectives almost always go **before** the nouns they describe:

*Examples: A **big** problem, a **messy** room, a **private** place, a **yellow** bird...*

More Than One Adjective

Sometimes, we want to describe a noun with more than one adjective. The general rule for deciding which adjective to place first is:

Use commas to separate adjectives:
five, cute, little, white kittens

Opinion	Before	Fact
An opinion is what you THINK about the noun.		A fact is what is DEFINITELY TRUE about the noun.
*Example: A **pretty**, pink purse*		*Example: An old, **round** table*

You can also use the word **with** in your descriptions:

Examples:
- *A beautiful, new chair **with** large, red, vertical stripes*
- *A delicious chocolate sundae **with** whipped cream and a bright, red cherry*

In English, adjectives are **always** invariable. That means they do not have a plural form:
- *30 **big, red** balloons*
- *many **strange** events*

For a **long string of adjectives**, here is the usual order:

Determiner	Opinion	Appearance	Age	Colour	Origin	Material	Purpose	Noun
a, an, the, ten... *Two*	*beautiful,*	(size, shape, condition) *big,*	*old,*	*red,*	*Chinese,*	*brass,*	*reading*	lamps.
An	*itsy-bitsy,*	*teeny-weeny,*		*yellow,*		*polka dot*		bikini.
A	*fantastic,*	*shiny,*	*new,*	*black,*	*Canadian,*	*fiberglass,*	*hockey*	helmet.

(Note, however, that sometimes this order can be changed to show emphasis.)

Using Adjectives to Compare Things

Adjectives can be used to show comparisons:

	Equivalent	Comparative	Superlative
When to use:	Use this structure to "equate" **two** things, or show their "sameness":	Use the **comparative** form to compare **two** things:	Use the **superlative** form to compare **three or more** things:
One-syllable adjectives	as... as as *fast* as	adjective + **er** + than *faster than*	the + adjective + **est** *the fastest*
Two-syllable adjectives ending in: -er, -y, -le	as... as as *pretty* as as *simple* as	Change **y** to **i** adjective + **er** + than *prettier than* *simpler than*	Change **y** to **i** the + adjective + **est** *the prettiest* *the simplest*
Adjectives with two or more syllables	as ... as as *famous* as as *effective* as not as *interesting* as	more/less + adjective + than more *famous than* more *effective than* less *interesting than*	the most/least + adjective *the most famous* *the most effective* *the least interesting*
Irregular comparisons	as *near* as as *far* as as *many* as as *few* as as *little* as as *bad* as as *good* as	*nearer than* *farther than* *more than* *fewer than* *less than* *worse than* *better than*	*the nearest* *the farthest* *the most* *the fewest* *the least* *the worst* *the best*
		*Some adjectives use either form: *quieter, more quiet;* *simpler, more simple...*	*Some adjectives use either "-est" or "most": the *quietest*, the *most quiet...*

IN CONTEXT

*I'm definitely not **as superstitious as** my brother. He is **the most superstitious** child in our family. But I am **more superstitious than** my little sister. Mom is **less superstitious than** my father and my grandmother is **the most superstitious** of us all.*

WARNING

Be careful not to mix up **then** and **than**:
then = next
than = comparison

Adverbs

- Adverbs are words that modify a verb, an adjective or another adverb.
- They add description and detail to your writing and speaking.

Adjective Ending	Rule	Adjective	Adverb
1. For most adjectives	Add **-ly**.	*quiet* *careful* *dangerous* *strange*	*quiet**ly*** *careful**ly*** *dangerous**ly*** *strange**ly***
2. **-ble**	When the adjective ends in **-ble**, change it to **-bly**.	*incredible* *responsible* *probable* *possible*	*incredi**bly*** *responsi**bly*** *proba**bly*** *possi**bly***
3. **-y**	When the adjective ends in **-y**, change the **-y** to **-i** and add **-ly**.	*easy* *happy* *lucky*	*eas**ily*** *happ**ily*** *luck**ily***
4. **-y**	When the adjective ends with **-ic**, add **-ally**.	*ironic* *realistic* *scientific* *basic*	*iron**ically*** *realist**ically*** *scientif**ically*** *bas**ically***
Some adverbs are the same as the adjective.		*fast* *hard* *far* *first* *early*	*fast* *hard* *far* *first* *early*

Exceptions:
- *good → well*
- *bad → worse*

- There are **four** basic categories of adverbs:
  1. adverbs of frequency
  2. adverbs of time
  3. adverbs of manner
  4. adverbs of intensity and degree

1. Adverbs of Frequency

- Adverbs of frequency are used to indicate the **regularity** of actions.
- They are placed before the verb unless the verb is *to be*.

Examples:
- *We **often** go to the beach in the summer.*
- *He **never** misses my birthday.*
- *You are **seldom** late for class.*

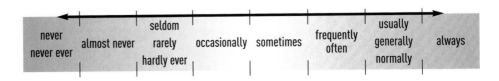

2. Adverbs of Time

- Adverbs of time are used to indicate **when actions take place**.
- They can refer to the past, the present or the future.

Past	Examples: • **Yesterday**, I went shopping with my friends. • That CD came out **last year**. • **This past week**, she was on vacation. • We left **on Sunday**.
Present	Examples: • They are going to the mall **this afternoon**. • There is a concert **tonight**. • I am **finally** done practising! • He's **still** in the car sleeping.
Future	Examples: • He will arrive **eventually**. • She's babysitting **tomorrow night**. • She will be back **soon**. • **Next week**, I'm going to Florida. • I will clean my room **later**. • **On Saturday**, we're having a party.

3. Adverbs of Manner

- Adverbs of manner are used to indicate **how actions are done**.
- Very often they end in –ly.

Examples: carefully, completely, marvellously, frantically, etc.

4. Adverbs of Intensity and Degree

- Adverbs of **intensity** and **degree** show the extent.
- Adverbs of **intensity** modify adjectives or other adverbs. They go **before** the adjective or the adverb.

*Examples: I'm **quite** happy. You work **very** hard.*

- Adverbs of **degree** modify verbs. They go **after** the verb.

*Examples: He worked **a lot**. We tried **a little bit**.*

Common Adverbs of Time

- *Once/Once upon a time*
- *Yesterday*
- *Last week, last month, etc.*
- *On Friday, Saturday evening*
- *Before class*
- *After the party*
- *Tonight*
- *Tomorrow*
- *Next week*
- *Later on*
- *In the future*
- *Some day*
- *One day*
- *Etc.*

Adverbs of Intensity

- *Very*
- *Really*
- *Extremely*
- *Quite*
- *Fairly*
- *Etc.*

Adverbs of Degree

- *A lot*
- *Enough*
- *A little bit*
- *Not at all*
- *Etc.*

Asking Questions

How to Form the Interrogative:

Verb Tense	Auxiliary	Verb Form	Examples
Simple present	do/does	base form	**Does** he live in the city?
Simple past	did	base form	**Did** he go to the store?
Future	will	base form	**Will** he study after school?
Present continuous	am/are/is	base form + ing	**Is** he going to the party?
Past continuous	was/were	base form + ing	**Was** he going home?
Present perfect	have/has	+ past participle	**Has** he left yet?
Past perfect	had	+ past participle	**Had** he received a gift?
Conditional	would	base form	**Would** he come with us?

There are three different types of questions in English:

1. Yes/No questions
2. Tag Questions (Yes/No questions with question tags)
3. Questions formed with question words.

1. Yes/No Questions

Yes/No questions are questions that can be answered with either "Yes" or "No."

How to form yes/no questions:

Auxiliary	Subject	Verb	Rest of the Question
Does	Rosie	go	skiing every day?
Has	Steve	decided	to buy a van?
Will	they	record	a new CD?

2. Tag Questions

- Tag questions are **a form of Yes/No questions.**
- Tag questions are used in a conversation **to solicit a reaction** from the person you are talking to.
- Most often, but not always, this reaction will be in the **affirmative form.**
- Tag questions are usually used **in spoken conversation** and very rarely in texts.
- **Contractions are always used** with question tags.

Tag Questions
If the statement is in the affirmative, put the tag in the negative. **Affirmative statement → Negative tag** *This is exciting, isn't it?* *Vanessa's father's a lawyer, isn't he?* *She's coming to get us after class, isn't she?*
If the statement is in the negative, put the tag in the affirmative. **Negative statement → Affirmative tag** *He's not from here, is he?* *You're not serious, are you?* *They didn't do their homework, did they?*

Use the same auxiliary for the statement and the tag.
- *I can come, can't I?*
- *They have been through a lot, haven't they?*
- *We would travel all over the world, wouldn't we?*

You saw that film, didn't you?

Get out! Johnny Depp is incredible, isn't he?

Yes! The acting was great, wasn't it?

Yes! He's so cool!

- Use **how many** for things you can count.
- Use **how much** for things you cannot count.

3. Questions Formed with Question Words

The main question words are:

Who	To know about a person	Where	To know the place
What	To know about a thing	Why	To know the reason
When	To know the time or moment	How	To know the manner

Asking Questions		
Who?	About people	**Q** *Who is this man?* **A** *He is a **police officer**.*
Whose?	About possession	**Q** *Whose laptop is this?* **A** *It's **Jonathan's**.*
Which?	About choices	**Q** *Which film do you want to rent?* **A** **The Day After Tomorrow**.
What?	About things, objects, animals, actions, etc.	**Q** *What are you doing?* **A** *I'm **reading a novel**.*
When?	About time	**Q** *When are we leaving?* **A** *We're leaving **in two hours**.*
Where?	About places	**Q** *Where is your car parked?* **A** *It's in the **parking ramp**.*
Why?	About reasons	**Q** *Why are you laughing?* **A** **Because it's funny!**
How?	About ways or manner	**Q** *How did she figure it out?* **A** *She **paid attention to details**.*
How + adjective?		**Q** *How far is Sherbrooke from here?* **A** *About **150 km**.*
How + adverb?		**Q** *How early did he go jogging?* **A** *Very early... **At 5:30 a.m.***

Asking Questions with Question Words

How to form a question with a question word:

Question Word	Auxiliary	Subject	Verb	Rest of the Question
Where	does	Rosie	go	*skiing?*
Why	has	he	decided	*to buy a pick up truck?*
When	will	they	record	*a new CD?*

Exceptions: Questions made with *who* and *what* as <u>subjects</u>.

Question Word	Auxiliary	Subject	Verb	Rest of the Question
		Who	goes	*skiing?*
		Who	decided	*to buy a pick up truck?*
		Who	will record	*a new CD?*
		What	is	*the title of the film?*

IN CONTEXT

Q — *Did you see what happened?*

A — *Partly.*

Q — *What time was it?*

A — *Around 3:45.*

Q — *Where were you?*

A — *I was coming out of the pharmacy.*

Q — *What colour was the car?*

A — *Black.*

Q — *Did you get the license number?*

A — *No, but it was a 2001 Honda Civic.*

Q — *How can you be so sure?*

A — *It's my brother's car.*

Modal Auxiliaries

Like other auxiliary verbs, modal auxiliaries "assist" main verbs in expressing an action. They are used to show **capability** and **obligation**, make **requests**, give **advice** and grant **permission**.

Modal	Negative Form	When to Use It	Examples
can	cannot can't	• To express capability • To indicate permission • To make a request	• *She **can** play the flute. (She knows how.)* • *We **can** leave early. (It's okay.)* • ***Can** you help me, please?*
could	could not couldn't	• To make a polite request • In the negative, to express incapacity (past action)	• ***Could** you sing for us, please?* • *When I won the award last night, I **couldn't** speak. I was too surprised.*
should	should not shouldn't	• To give advice	• *You **should** study more.*
ought to	— (rarely used)	• To give advice	• *You **ought to** study more.*
may	may not	• To make a polite request • To indicate permission • To express possibility	• ***May** I go to the washroom please?* • *You **may** sit anywhere you like.* • *It **may** rain this weekend.*
might	might not	• To express possibility	• *We **might** watch the game tonight. (It all depends…)*
must	must not mustn't	• To express an obligation	• *He **must** help his father after school.* • *We **must not** smoke in public buildings. (It is illegal.)*
will	will not won't	• To express intention	• *I **will** clean my room later, I promise.*
would	would not wouldn't	• To express something conditional	• *I **would** go with you <u>if</u> I had enough money. (But, I don't so I won't…)*

To Have To

To have to is also used to show **obligation in the affirmative**. It is used in all tenses.

Examples:
• *My marks are not good; I **have to** study more.*
• *I couldn't go to the game; I **had to** help my father.*
• *There is so much snow! We **have had to** shovel every day.*

To Not Have To

In the negative form, **to not have to** means that there is **no obligation** to do the action.

Examples:
• *They **have to** wear a uniform. (obligation)*
• *We **don't have to** wear a uniform. (not required; no obligation)*

Cannot is one word, not two.

Conjunctions and Connectors

A conjunction is a word that <u>connects</u> words, phrases or clauses.
Some of these you are already familiar with:

First Part of the Sentence	Conjunction (connecting word)	Last Part of the Sentence
You	**and**	Susan are so different.
I'm running late	**but**	I'll call you tonight.
I can come and meet you	**or**	you could come to my place first.
We aren't going to the game	**because**	my boyfriend has to work.
I left early	**so**	I could come and see you.
Michael will come	**if**	his brother can also.
I was getting on the bus	**when**	the storm really hit hard.
Adam watches the news	**while**	he eats supper.

Transition Words

Try using some of the following words to help your conversation
or writing flow from one idea to the next:

For a Shift in Time	To Summarize	To Conclude
• At first, Initially • Before, Previously • After, Later, Subsequently • Then, Next	• Briefly • In brief, In short • Overall • To sum up	• Therefore • In conclusion • Thus • So

Verb Tenses

- Verbs are words that are used to express **actions, emotions** and states of being.
- There are many different verb tenses in English.

Here is a table explaining the main ones:

Tense	How to Form It	When to Use It	Examples
Past perfect	**had** + past participle	• For an action in the past that happened before another one	• *They **had** already **left** when Marina arrived.* • *I **had left** before you called.*
Past continuous	Past of **to be** (was/were) + base form + **ing**	• For an action that was going on in the past when something interrupted it • For two simultaneous actions	• *She **was playing** the trumpet when the announcement came.* • *We **were eating** supper when he got the news.* • *She **was talking** on the phone while she **was eating**.*
Present perfect	**have (has)** + the past participle	• For an action that is finished but that has a direct link with the present. There is more action to come.	• *The family **has visited** France many times.* • *Romano **has learned** to speak French very well.*
Simple past	Add **–d, –ed** or **–ied** to the base form of regular verbs. *Irregular verbs must be memorized.* • *For the negative, use **didn't** + base form.*	• For an action that finished sometime in the past	• *I **lost** my cell phone this morning.* • *My brother **bought** a new car yesterday.* • *We **didn't see** the program.* • *She **didn't have** time to finish.*
Simple present	Base form *Third person singular always ends in "**s**."* • For the negative, use doesn't (don't) + the base form.	• For habits or usual activities • For facts • For likes and dislikes	• *I **take** piano lessons every week.* • *We **don't understand**.* • *Madrid **is** the capital of Spain.* • *He **likes** living in Toronto.*
Present continuous	Present of **to be** (am, is, are) + base form + **ing**	• For an action that is happening right now • For an action that will happen in the near future • For irritations (with *always*)	• *Mark **is planning** a surprise party.* • *We **are taking** a trip in June.* • *Telemarketers **are always calling** us at suppertime.*
Future	**will** + base form of the verb	• For an action in the future • To express a future intention • To make predictions	• *I **will travel** to Australia in two years.* • *I **won't forget** to call your mother.* • *The Black Hawks **will win**.*
Conditional	**would** + base form of the verb	• For a hypothetical action • For an action that will happen only under certain circumstances	• *I **would go**, too, but I am sick.* • *They **would like** to live in Mexico.* • *Jack **would love** to own a Porsche.*

The Negative Form of Verbs

How to form the negative:

Verb Tense	Auxiliary	Verb Form	Examples
Simple present	do not/does not don't/doesn't	+ base form	*I **don't know**.* *He **doesn't care**.*
Simple past	did not/didn't	+ base form	*They **didn't come**.*
Future	will not/won't	+ base form	*We **won't go** there.*
Present continuous	am not/is not/are not isn't/aren't	+ base form + ing	*I'm **not reading**.*
Past continuous	was not/were not wasn't/weren't	+ base form + ing	*They **were not talking**.* *Linda **wasn't chewing** gum.*
Present perfect	have not/has not haven't/hasn't	+ past participle	*She **has not seen** them.* *You **haven't been** there.*
Past perfect	had not/hadn't	+ past participle	*Barbra **hadn't seen** him.*
Conditional	would not/wouldn't	+ base form	*I **wouldn't go** there.*

Tense Markers

Markers are adverbs, prepositional phrases or other words that specify the time of an action. They help us determine the verb tense.

Common Markers

PAST PERFECT
- *Already*
- *Not yet*
- *Never*
- *Once*
- *Before*
- *Until then*

PAST CONTINUOUS
- *When*
- *While*

PRESENT PERFECT
- *Already*
- *Ever*
- *So far*
- *Not yet*
- *Since*
- *Until now*
- *Up to now*

SIMPLE PAST
- *Yesterday*
- *Two days ago*
- *Last (weekend, month, etc.)*
- *The day before yesterday*
- *When I was younger*

SIMPLE PRESENT
- *Usually*
- *Often*
- *Normally*
- *Before going to bed*
- *On Sundays (Mondays, Fridays, etc.)*
- *In general*
- *Every morning*
- *In the afternoon*

PRESENT CONTINUOUS
- *At the moment*
- *Right now*
- *Listen!*
- *Look!*

FUTURE
- *In five minutes*
- *Later*
- *Next month*
- *Tomorrow*
- *In three days*
- *When I'm old*

CONDITIONAL
- *I wish that...*
- *If...*

Sequence of Verb Tenses

Verbs are divided into three distinct time frames: *past*, *present* and *future*.

- The **simple past**, **present** and **future** are the usual time frames.
- The **present perfect** is a verb tense in the **past** that carries over to the **present**.
- The **present continuous** is a verb tense of the **present** that carries on into the **future**.

Past	Present	Future
Simple past *Example:* **I played** tennis **last night**.	**Simple present** *Example:* **I play** tennis **every day**.	**Simple future** *Example:* **I will play** tennis **next year**.

Past continuous

Example:
I **was playing** tennis **when he called**.

The action is finished. It was going on when something interrupted.

Present Perfect

Example:
I **have played** tennis **many times**.

The action is finished, but there is a link with the present. There is more action to come.

Present Continuous

Example:
I **am playing** tennis **tonight**.

The action is going on right now. Or, the action is going to happen in the near future.

Past Perfect

Example:
I **had** already **left** to play tennis **when he phoned**.

Use the past perfect to show that an action in the past happened before another one.

Conditional

Example:
I **would play** tennis everyday **if I could**. Unfortunately...

The verb : *to be going to* is often used for future actions:

We **are going to** Africa next summer.

Verbs in Context

So predictable...

My father always follows the same routine. He gets up at 6 a.m. every morning, puts on a pot of coffee and jumps in the shower. Then he shaves and gets dressed. He reads the paper while he eats breakfast. Then he brushes his teeth. At precisely 7:20, he kisses my mom goodbye and leaves. He catches the bus at 7:27. It's always the same routine. I wish that he would do something different just once!

Markers that indicate habits and repeated actions or activities

Hypothetical

Connections with the present

I have asked my father over and over to change his routine. Today, he finally did it, but not on purpose...

Usually, my father gets up at 6 a.m., but this morning he didn't get up until 7. He took a quick shower, but there was no time to shave or read the paper. He brushed his teeth, put the newspaper in his briefcase and his electric razor in his coat pocket. He blew my mom a kiss as he hurried out the door.

Events that happened in the past

When a past continuous action is interrupted, it is always by a simple past action.

When my father left the house, the bus was turning the corner. He had to run to catch it. He got on, sat down, opened his newspaper and took out his razor. He was busy shaving and reading the paper when, suddenly, he realized that he had missed his stop. What a morning! I'm sure he will be happy to return to his old routine tomorrow morning.

Marker for the future

The Passive Voice

The passive voice is used less frequently than the active voice, which is the "usual" voice.

How to form the passive voice:

Subject	Auxiliary (to be)	Verb (past participle)	Object
Many people	*are*	*influenced*	*by advertising.*
That ad	*was*	*made*	*with teenagers in mind.*
Some commercials	*have been*	*banned*	*from airing.*

When to use the passive voice:

1. When we want to emphasize the object or give it importance.

Active Voice	Passive Voice
• *Millions of people watch the Super Bowl commercials.*	• *The Super Bowl commercials are watched by millions of people.*
• *The campaign committee paid for the ad.*	• *The ad was paid for by the campaign committee.*

2. When we do not know the subject.

Active Voice	Passive Voice
• <u>*X*</u> *use publicity stunts to attract customers.*	• *Publicity stunts are used to attract customers.*
• <u>*X*</u> *will place the ad on a billboard.*	• *The ad will be placed on a billboard.*

Direct and Indirect Speech

Direct speech is reporting what someone says. If the exact words are used, we put them in quotation marks. Often, however, we report what someone says without using direct quotations.

Usually, we do not use the exact words to report what someone has said. This is called **indirect speech** (or **reported speech**).
In reported speech, no quotation marks are used and there is a shift in tenses.

Direct Speech
George says, "I am learning English."
George says that he is learning English.
Indirect Speech
George told me that he was learning English.

Simple present	→	Present perfect
Simple past	→	Past perfect
Present continuous	→	Past continuous
Future	→	Conditional

Often, there is also a shift in pronouns. For example, **I** becomes **he** or **she**.

Say and Tell

Say and tell have similar meanings. They are both used to report speech.
Here is a simple way to use them correctly:

- *You **say** something to someone.*
- *You **tell** someone something.*

Say
To say something
Say is followed immediately by a noun clause or a direct quote.
Example: The third pig **said** that he saw the wolf. The third pig **said**, "I saw the wolf."
To say something to someone
Say is followed by "to" and a person. This is known as reported speech.
Example: He **says to his brother** that he has seen the wolf.

Tell
To tell someone something
Tell can also be used for a direct quote, but you must mention the person who is being addressed.
Example: The third pig **told his brother**, "I saw the wolf."
To tell someone something
Tell is also used for reported speech, but there is no "to."
Example: He **tells his brother** that he has seen the wolf.
"Tell" is also used to give instructions.
Example: He **told** him how to build his house.

Capitalization

In English, capital letters are used for the following:

1.	**The first word in a sentence.** *The cat is on the table.*
2.	**The pronoun "I."** *I said that **I** would call him after school.*
3.	**The names of...** • **People:** *Terry Fox, Nelson Mandela, Meagan Winslow* • **Relatives when used with the person's name:** *Uncle Tom, Aunt Agatha* • **Titles when they are included with the person's name:** *Detective Brady, Major Lucie Madison, Ms. Jeannette Turner, Dr. Albert* • **Places:** *Nova Scotia, Lake Louise, Harvard, New York City, the Eiffel Tower* • **Planets, stars and constellations:** *Uranus, Earth, Venus, The Big Dipper* • **Events:** *the Miss Universe Contest, the Quebec Winter Carnival, the Stanley Cup* • **Days and months:** *Tuesday, Thursday, February* • **Holidays and holy days:** *Christmas, Kwanzaa, Valentine's Day, Yom Kippur* • **Languages, nationalities, races and religions:** *English, Chinese, Europeans, African-American, Jewish, Buddhism* • **Organizations:** *the United Nations, the Salvation Army* • **Organizations that use acronyms (all capitals):** *UN (United Nations), NHL (National Hockey League)* • **Brands or trademarks:** *Jell-O, Kleenex*
4.	**Lists when the elements are on separate lines:** like the above list
5.	**The first word in a direct quotation:** *He said, "**C**all me tomorrow."*
6.	**Only the first word in the closing of a letter:** ***Y**ours truly, **V**ery sincerely, **W**ith love, **Y**our friend*

In titles, capitalize:

- The first word
- The last word
- All nouns, adjectives, verbs and adverbs
- All words with five letters or more
  - *A **T**ale of **T**wo **C**ities*
  - ***L**ife with the **M**an in **B**lack*

Do not capitalize

- seasons:
  fall, winter, spring, summer
- directions (unless they are part of a name):
  north, south, east, west North Carolina, the West Island

Punctuation Marks

Punctuation marks are signals to the reader. They help make the message clear. Sometimes, the meaning of a sentence can change completely depending on the punctuation.

Punctuation Mark	When to Use It	Examples
Period (.)	• To indicate the end of a complete sentence	• *My passion is singing.* • *He is an excellent artist.*
Comma (,)	• To separate items in a list • To separate two phrases • After introductory words	• *Please buy cheese, eggs, milk and bread.* • *Before you leave, please turn off the lights.* • *Dear John, tomorrow, I will do it.*
Question mark (?)	• To indicate a question	• *Where are you going?*
Exclamation mark (!)	• To indicate surprise or strong emotion	• *Wow! I can't believe you won!* • *That's fantastic!*
Apostrophe (')	• In contractions • To show possession	• *They don't want to take a taxi before 7 o'clock.* • *Jane's phone number* • *the Smiths' address*
Colon (:)	• To introduce a list of items • In a business letter greeting • In time	• *This is what you need: a sleeping bag, a pillow, an extra blanket and warm clothes.* • *Dear Madam:* • *8:15 p.m.*
Semi-colon (;)	• To join related sentences into one sentence • For lists that already have commas in them	• *I told him not to go; it is too dangerous.* • *They toured: Toronto, ON; Montreal, QC; Halifax, NS and Moncton, NB.*
Hyphen (-)	• To make compound words • To write compound numbers • To join prefixes to words	• *Ghetto-blaster;* • *Seventy-seven;* • *Semi-colon; mini-mystery*
Parentheses ( )	• To give additional, non-essential information	• *She thinks that Gabriel (who sits in front of me in French) is really cute.*
Quotation Marks (" ")	• To indicate a person's words • For titles of poems, articles, stories and songs	• *"Make yourself at home," she said.* • *Who is the author of "The Last Dance"?*

There is no **comma** after the next to the last item.

There is no **hyphen** in *New York*, *New Brunswick*, etc.

• **Commas and periods** always go **inside** the quotation marks.
• **Semi-colons and colons** always go **outside**.
• **Question marks** go inside if the question is part of the quotation and outside if it is not:
  – *"What is the answer?", he asked.*
  – *Is the title "Celluloid Heroes"?*

Spelling

Spelling in English can be quite complicated. There are lots of rules — and lots of exceptions! Sometimes, it's just as easy to use a dictionary as it is to try to learn them all by heart.

Here is a list of 100 words that are often misspelled:

1. a lot	21. changeable	41. height	61. omission	81. scissors
2. absence	22. committee	42. heroes	62. parallel	82. sincerely
3. accommodate	23. conscientious	43. humorous	63. parliament	83. soldier
4. accordion	24. criticize	44. independent	64. particularly	84. strength
5. achieve	25. defendant	45. insurance	65. pastime	85. studying
6. across	26. definite	46. interfere	66. permanent	86. success
7. address	27. develop	47. judgment	67. pigeon	87. surely
8. advertise	28. embarrass	48. language	68. possess	88. surprise
9. aggression	29. enough	49. length	69. precede	89. tariff
10. agree	30. equipment	50. lightning	70. privilege	90. through
11. apology	31. especially	51. literature	71. pronunciation	91. tomorrow
12. argument	32. exaggerate	52. lose	72. raspberry	92. traffic
13. athlete	33. exercise	53. marriage	73. receipt	93. transfer
14. basically	34. extraordinary	54. medieval	74. recommend	94. truly
15. believe	35. foreign	55. millennium	75. referred	95. twelfth
16. broccoli	36. forty	56. millionaire	76. relevant	96. until
17. business	37. friend	57. necessary	77. rhyme	97. vehicle
18. calendar	38. genius	58. ninth	78. rhythm	98. weird
19. carburetor	39. government	59. no one	79. ridiculous	99. wholly
20. cemetery	40. guarantee	60. occurred	80. rough	100. writing

Does the word personal take one N or two in English?

I'm not sure. You'd better look it up in the dictionary.

Phrasal Verbs

A phrasal verb is composed of a verb and a preposition. Adding the preposition gives the verb a new meaning. Here are some examples.

Phrasal Verb (verb + particle)	Meaning
to **ask** *out*	to ask someone to go on a date
to **ask** *over*	to invite someone for a visit
to **break** *up*	to end a relationship
to **bring** *up*	to raise children; to mention a topic
to **call** *back*	to return a telephone call
to **call** *off*	to cancel
to **call** *up*	to make a telephone call
*to **catch** *up*	to reach the same position or level
to **check** *out*	to borrow a book from the library
to **cross** *out*	to draw a line through
to **do** *over*	to do again
*to **drop** *out*	to quit school or classes
to **figure** *out*	to find the solution to a problem
to **fill** *in*	to complete a sentence by writing in a blank
to **fill** *out*	to write information on a form
to **fill** *up*	to fill completely with gas, water, etc.
to **find** *out*	to discover information
to **get** *along*	to have a good relationship
to **get** *in*	to enter a vehicle
to **hand** *out*	to distribute something, usually to a group of people
to **hang** *up*	to end a telephone call
to **keep** *up*	to continue
*to **look** *after*	to take care of something/someone
to **look** *up*	to search for information
to **make** *up*	to invent; to patch up an argument
*to **pass** *away*	to die

Phrasal Verb (verb + particle)	Meaning
to **pick** *up*	to lift
to **put** *away*	to put something in its usual place
to **put** *back*	to return something to its original place
to **put** *down*	to stop holding or carrying something
to **put** *off*	to postpone or to delay
to **put** *on*	to put clothes on one's body
to **put** *out*	to extinguish a fire, a cigarette, etc.
*to **put** *up with*	to tolerate
*to **run** *into*	to meet someone by chance
to **shut** *off*	to stop a machine or turn off a light
to **start** *over*	to start again from the beginning
*to **take** *after*	to resemble
to **take** *off*	to remove something, especially clothes from one's body
to **take** *up*	to start a new activity
to **tear** *down*	to destroy a structure, like a building
to **tear** *off*	to detach something; to tear along a dotted or perforated line
to **tear** *up*	to tear into small pieces
to **throw** *away/out*	to put in the trash
to **try** *on*	to put on clothing to see if it fits
to **turn** *down*	to decrease the volume; to decline an offer
to **turn** *off*	to stop a machine or to shut off a light
to **turn** *on*	to start a machine or to flick on a light
to **turn** *up*	to increase the volume; to appear somewhere
to **write** *down*	to write a note on a piece of paper

* These phrasal verbs are non-separable; the object of verb must appear after the particle.
Example: *They are **looking** **after** their dogs.*
Incorrect: *They are **looking** ~~their dogs~~ **after**.*

List of Irregular Verbs

Colour Code	Examples:
A – A – A	bet – bet – bet
A – B – A	become – became – become
A – B – B	bend – bent – bent

Base Form	Simple Past	Past Participle
awake	awoken	awoken
be	was, were	been
beat	beat	beaten
become	became	become
begin	began	begun
bend	bent	bent
bet	bet	bet
bite	bit	bitten
bleed	bled	bled
blow	blew	blown
break	broke	broken
bring	brought	brought
build	built	built
burn	burnt/burned	burnt/burned
buy	bought	bought
catch	caught	caught
choose	chose	chosen
come	came	come
cost	cost	cost
creep	crept	crept
cut	cut	cut
deal	dealt	dealt

Base Form	Simple Past	Past Participle
dig	dug	dug
do	did	done
draw	drew	drawn
dream	dreamed/dreamt	dreamed/dreamt
drink	drank	drunk
drive	drove	driven
eat	ate	eaten
fall	fell	fallen
feed	fed	fed
feel	felt	felt
fight	fought	fought
find	found	found
fly	flew	flown
forbid	forbade	forbidden
forget	forgot	forgotten
forgive	forgave	forgiven
freeze	froze	frozen
get	got	gotten
give	gave	given
go	went	gone
grow	grew	grown
hang (suspend)	hung	hung

Base Form	Simple Past	Past Participle
hang (execute)	hanged	hanged
have	had	had
hear	heard	heard
hide	hid	hidden
hold	held	held
hurt	hurt	hurt
keep	kept	kept
know	knew	known
lead	led	led
leave	left	left
lend	lent	lent
let (allow)	let	let
light	lit	lit
lose	lost	lost
make	made	made
mean	meant	meant
meet	met	met
pay	paid	paid
put	put	put
quit	quit	quit
read	read	read
ride	rode	ridden
ring	rang	rung
rise (get up)	rose	risen
run	ran	run
say	said	said
see	saw	seen
sell	sold	sold
send	sent	sent
set	set	set
shake	shook	shaken
shine	shone	shone

Base Form	Simple Past	Past Participle
shoot	shot	shot
show	showed	shown
shrink	shrank	shrunk
shut	shut	shut
sing	sang	sung
sink	sank	sunk
sit	sat	sat
sleep	slept	slept
slide	slid	slid
speak	spoke	spoken
spend	spent	spent
stand	stood	stood
steal	stole	stolen
stick	stuck	stuck
sting	stung	stung
stink	stank	stunk
strike	struck	struck
swear	swore	sworn
sweep	swept	swept
swim	swam	swum
swing	swung	swung
take	took	taken
teach	taught	taught
tear	tore	torn
tell	told	told
think	thought	thought
throw	threw	thrown
understand	understood	understood
wake	woke	woken
wear	wore	worn
win	won	won
write	wrote	written

Iconographic references